William Carlos Williams

William Carlos Williams and Ezra Pound, photographed by Richard Avedon, Rutherford, N.J., July 1958

William Carlos Williams

The American Background

MIKE WEAVER

Lecturer in American Literature, University of Exeter

CAMBRIDGE

At the University Press

1971

Published by the Syndics of the Cambridge University Press
Bentley House, 200 Euston Road, London N.W.1
American Branch: 32 East 57th Street, New York, N.Y.10022

© Cambridge University Press 1971

Library of Congress Catalogue Card Number: 77–149431

ISBN: 0 521 08072 X

Composed in Great Britain by
W. & J. Mackay & Co. Ltd
Printed in the United States of America

LIZ

Contents

Plates

Preface

In 1923 William Carlos Williams wrote: 'It would be a relief to discover a critic who looked at American work from the American viewpoint.'[1] Forty years later it seemed to me that his plea had hardly been heard in his own country, and in Great Britain not at all. Challenged by Williams to hear his poems in the American language, I realised that as an Englishman there was much in his idiom which, for lack of his viewpoint, I could not 'hear', and so I came to understand that the question of idiom is more profound than a matter of adjusting the ear to a new music; the difference between the British and American idioms rests on important divergences in attitudes of mind.

I have tried to provide the prolegomena to a study of Williams, presenting his American viewpoint but not offering an evaluation of his work. In stressing the local side of his personal, literary, aesthetic, intellectual, and social background, I have taken for granted his debt to Ezra Pound,[2] and chosen to neglect the parodic element in *Paterson* relating to Homer, Goethe, Joyce, and Eliot, with whose work Williams was, of course, familiar. I have presented him in the company of those who supported him emotionally and intellectually throughout his long career.

It is to the unregarded carriers of art and literature, who with few exceptions will not survive in the public memory, that this book owes its largest debt, for they were the instigators of more than four hundred fugitive little magazines which I studied in libraries in England, France, and the United States in my effort to establish the American viewpoint. Yet reliance on published sources alone proved insufficient

---

[1] W. C. Williams, *The Great American Novel* (Paris, 1923), p. 61.
[2] Emily Mitchell Wallace, 'Pound and Williams at the University of Pennsylvania', *Pennsylvania Review* I, 2 (Spring 1967), 40–53.

to prove Williams' interest in his reading matter, even when, from the remnants of his library at Yale University and Fairleigh Dickinson University in Rutherford, it was possible to tell what had found its way into his home. For instance, the extent of his interest in American Indian music could only misleadingly be judged by the simple discovery of the printed source for a quotation from Frances Densmore used as foreword in *Pictures from Brueghel*.[1] It was reasonable to assume, one would have thought, that Williams knew the text in full and at first hand, and that he had perceived a relation between the structure of Indian music and his concept of an indigenous American measure in poetry. It was a salutary lesson to receive the following account from Tram Combs of how he came upon it:[2]

In his last few years I made a point of calling on the doctor on his birthday, and as his gift in 1961 I presented him with a 3 × 5 slip of paper on which I had written a quotation from an essay by Frances Densmore; when I had met the clause a few years before in my reading, I had immediately thought 'wouldn't Bill love that!', and I was delighted to see the joy of his response; he immediately said with great animation that he was going to put that in the front of the book of poems he had shipped off to Laughlin the day before; and there it sits as the foreword to *Pictures from Brueghel*.

I am especially grateful to the many people who provided me with documents and information by which I could corroborate my own judgement of what was important in the formation of Williams' thought: Ethel M. Albert, Boski Antheil, Richard Avedon, Mary Barnard, Charles G. Bell, Norma Berger, Charles Boultenhouse, Basil Bunting, Nicolas Calas, Tram Combs, Jack Conroy, Malcolm Cowley, Ellman Crasnow, Robert Creeley, Donald Davie, James J. Davis, Marcel Duchamp, Gladys Eckardt, Herbert A. Fisher, Martin L. Friedman, Donald C. Gallup, Edward J. Gorin, Edward M. Graf, Louis Grudin, Ben Hagglund, Jim Higgins, Kathleen Hoagland, Beckett Howorth, Grover Jacoby, Matthew Josephson, Horace M. Kallen, Standish D. Lawder, Howard A. Levin, Jane Lidderdale, David E. Lilienthal, Diana June Logie, Edward M. Longwell, David Joseph Lyle, Louis L. Martz, Jerome Mazzaro, Elizabeth K. Miller, the late Fred R. Miller, Robert Motherwell, the late Gorham B. Munson, Henry

[1] W. C. Williams, *Pictures from Brueghel* (Norfolk, Conn., 1962) [1].
[2] Letter to the author, 12 December 1965.

Niese, the late Donald J. Paquette, H. B. Parkes, Norman Holmes Pearson, Robert D. Pepper, Hayden Phillips, Stephen Prokopoff, Carl Rakosi, John Riordan, Emanuel Romano, Suzanne Rutter, Arthur Sale, Winfield Townley Scott, Eli Siegel, Mary Ellen Solt, Parker Tyler, Liz Weaver, Anne Whelpley, Florence H. Williams, Jonathan Williams, Robert N. Wilson, William Wolarsky, and George Zabriskie.

I was supported financially by the Department of Education and Science and the American Council of Learned Societies. Finally, I thank my wife and my father who both typed for me.

Key to Sources

—————

Where no source is given for an unpublished document the original may be assumed to remain in private hands. The library symbols of the Library of Congress are used to locate all other unpublished documents and collections of books and periodicals formerly in William Carlos Williams' possession:

CtMW	Wesleyan University, Middletown
CtY	Yale University, New Haven
ICN	Newberry Library, Chicago
InU	Indiana University, Bloomington
MdBE	Enoch Pratt Library, Baltimore
MH	Harvard University, Cambridge
NBu	Buffalo Public Library
NBuU	University of Buffalo
NjFD (Rutherford)	Fairleigh Dickinson University, Rutherford
RPB	Brown University, Providence

A Culture in Effigy

The Family Background

William Carlos Williams was born on Constitution Day, 1883, in the small country town of Rutherford, New Jersey, to parents of mixed extraction. His father was an Englishman, said to have been born in Birmingham; his mother in Mayagüez, Puerto Rico, to a Basque mother and a Jewish father. His middle name was taken from his mother's brother who practised medicine in Panama City. If his ancestry was in any way Spanish it was more by cultural adoption than by blood. He was half English, one-quarter Basque, and one-quarter Jewish.

Williams' religious background was equally mixed. His Jewish grandfather had married a Catholic, and his Anglican father had done the same. Once established in Rutherford, the family cast aside its former affiliations to become a founding family of the local Unitarian Society.[1]

The year of the poet's birth saw the reorganisation of the land company which had purchased the portion of Union Township known as Boiling Spring.[2] It had been named the Rutherfurd Park Association after the largest landowner in that part, John Rutherfurd. In the years following the arrival of the Williams family the name of the village changed interestingly; Boiling Spring first became the aristocratic Rutherfurd Park, then in 1883 this was replaced by the thoroughly unhistorical Rutherford. Possibly the inhabitants were unhappy with the association of the former lord of the manor, and preferred to think of the place where an imaginary river 'Ruther' could be easily crossed.

In *The Build-Up*, part three of the trilogy of novels following the

[1] Two letters from Williams to Louis Untermeyer, 5 March 1941 and 7 February 1942 (InU).

[2] Kathleen Hoagland, 'A Brief History of the Rutherford Area', in *Directory of Municipal Officials, Boards, and Services*, Borough of Rutherford, 10 February 1966.

progress of his wife's family, Williams conveys the ethos of this young town bent on self-improvement. He contrasts Rutherford ('Riverdale') with Carlstadt ('Kronstadt'), the little German town on the Hackensack road with its Sommergarten of folk-songs and beer-steins.[1] Unlike Rutherfurd Park it was called for its founder's first name. The tailors of Carlstadt formed a conservative community, not by means of churches but with ample beer. Psychologically, as Williams suggested, Rutherford was quite different, being composed of commuters, heterogeneous in their origins, who refused – and still refuse – to have a licensed bar in their town. The Union club was determined that it, too, would remain dry; 'a desirable resort for all the members and a place where their wives or parents can find no objection to their attendance'.[2] Williams' father was a member of its board of governors. There his two sons enjoyed their first stage entertainments, dances, and concerts.

Just as sobriety was a condition of enjoyment, so truth was a condition of religious belief. The Unitarian Society of Rutherford, of which Williams' father was a prominent member, expressed the members' point of view as follows:[3]

They agree that the individual's religious faith is a matter of serious concern, but that it is important, not so much that a person shall profess any given beliefs, as that he shall, in fact, believe that which he may be willing to profess. They think that the church, itself, should have but one imperative dogma which may be expressed in five words –

NOTHING THAT IS NOT TRUE

Such a constitution was as clear a declaration of ecclesiastical independence as the public referendum in favour of the creation of the borough of Rutherford had been some years before.

The values of the family that had helped to create Rutherford were still based on the past. The idealism of the mother was, as Williams himself explained it, that of the defeated romantic.[4] Her career in Paris as a painter had been thwarted not so much by lack of talent as by lack of money. If the prizes of Paris were without price, then her ideals were

---

[1] W. C. Williams, *The Build-Up* (N.Y., 1952), pp. 66–7.
[2] J. M. Van Valen, *History of Bergen County* (N.Y., 1900), p. 443.
[3] 'Unitarian Church', *Bergen County Historical Society*, Twentieth Annual Report, 15 (1921–2), 77–9;79.
[4] W. C. Williams, *Yes, Mrs. Williams* (N.Y., 1959), p. 33.

equally absolute; if her sons were her 'vicarious atonement'[1] for not having achieved artistic success, then she transferred to them her passionate desire for its attainment. In the early years of Williams' youth her idealism cost him nothing less than mental agony and physical deprivation. The sober ambition of the young family, as of the newly constituted town, ended by imposing arbitrary prices upon immeasurable commodities:[2]

Once her elder son, in a fit of despair and philosophic resolution stood her and her husband up against the sideboard in the dining room and bitterly told them: I don't love you because you are my parents. I love you if I love you at all because you are lovable and for no other reason! Could she not see that? Could she not have seen that that was his attempt to liberate her, to liberate them all, his father, his mother and himself – that they might fall into each others' arms and be melted together. But they were shocked and he crawled away defeated. The resistance was too hard, the barriers were too great and mounted rather than diminished as time went on.

This outburst, it may be supposed, followed several years of effort to please his mother. It was largely as a result of his mother's devotion to the memory of her brother, Carlos, who had sent her to Paris, that Williams was persuaded to enter the medical profession. He began at the University of Pennsylvania with dentistry, but soon gave it up for medicine. But if maternal influence was a factor in his choice, at least he was not averse to medicine; 'I do like it as well or better than anything else but my mind is a book of questions and until I find their answers I will never be settled.'[3]

In his first years at university Williams fulfilled his parents' wishes to the full. He attended the French Church, refused to drink in celebration of a football victory, was a member of the fencing team, and admired an oil painting by a certain H. M. Walcot at the Academy of Fine Arts exhibition.[4] But by the end of his time he would confess to his brother that his work bored him and he really wanted to do something else:[5]

I don't think I'll ever be a great success at anything, I sort of keep going out of an instinctive dread of failure but lord knows I don't feel that divine fire which

[1] *Ibid.* p. 5.   [2] Ms. of *The Autobiography* (CtY).
[3] Letter to his mother, 10 October 1904 (NBuU).
[4] Letters to his mother, 1902–4 (NBuU).
[5] Letter to his brother, 31 March 1907 (NBuU).

I long for and I know a man must have to succeed. I'm just a low down mediocre lazy mucker and I know it. I tell you honestly Bo if it wasn't for you people sort of restraining me I'd throw up the whole thing and go into some fool venture or another that would give me satisfaction or do me up for once and all.

Eighteen months later he spoke of success in terms of writing and not of medicine at all:[1]

I have been writing a great deal recently and somehow or other at some time or other I will succeed and if I ever do succeed Bo, I know it will be real, real, real. But oh how hard it is with the seriousness and vast importance of it all in my eyes to feel that in the eyes of all around I am wasting time, for it does take time and even I am not always sure I am not a fool. Bo, if I didn't have you it would be impossible.

Evidently he had discovered a new idea of success, and another approach to truth. The family's approach was essentially that of reason, of Darwinian science and Unitarian faith. Now, quite quickly, Williams saw a third approach offering itself, that of passion:[2]

It all happened very quickly. Somehow poetry and the female sex were allied in my mind. The beauty of girls seemed to me as the beauty of a poem. I knew nothing at all about the sexual approach but I had to do something about it. I did it in the only terms I knew, through poetry.

Early Literary Influences

In 1903 W. B. Yeats, passing through Philadelphia on a tour, paused briefly to read to the students at the university, but Williams did not hear him. His taste was, as he said himself, 'ripe for a fall, to the ground'.[3] To his brother, in a letter filled with his Unitarian philosophy of truth and beauty, he recommended James Whitcomb Riley's 'Knee Deep in June' and 'Don't Cry, Little Girl, Don't Cry'.[4] At home his father would read Kipling's 'Brushwood Boy',[5] then at the height of American fashion, and Paul Lawrence Dunbar.[6]

The predominant influence in American poetry was a Canadian

---

[1] Letter to his brother, 12 November 1908 (NBuU).

[2] W. C. Williams, *I Wanted to Write a Poem* (Boston, 1958), p. 14.

[3] Mss notes: miscellaneous and unidentified (CtY).

[4] Letter to his brother, 16 November 1904 (copy: CtY).

[5] Letter to his brother, 2 December 1907 (copy: CtY).

[6] W. C. Williams, 'Note on the Translation of *El Hombre Que Paresia Un Cavallo*', *New Directions* 8 (1944), 318–19;*319*.

poet, Bliss Carman. Pound later went so far as to say that, 'In America the poetic life was almost exclusively contained in the "Songs of Vagabondia" by Carman and Hovey'.[1] In May 1907 Edgar Williams gave his brother a copy of the ninth edition, and against Carman's 'The Joys of the Open Road' Williams put a marginal comment, 'Great', with special marks beside the couplet:[2]

> A lover of books, but a reader of man
> No cynic and no charlatan.

Williams' response to Carman and Hovey is all the more interesting in the light of his reaction to Pound's first book, *A Lume Spento*, which can be gauged from Pound's own letter in reply.[3] Evidently Williams considered the volume bitter and personal, even dissolute and decadent; Pound had taken no heed of the eyes of a 'too ruthless public'. But exactly why he thought Pound's work anarchic Pound could not guess; Williams contented himself with speaking portentously of 'ultimate attainments of poesy', and avoided detailed criticism saying that he felt powerless to deny another man's work. He concluded that Pound's vagabondism was simply unconstrained. Williams noted Pound's earlier recommendation[4] that he should read a story about a disguised baronet languishing from melancholia in a London slum, who regained his optimism when he met a street-urchin living among fallen women and thieves, whose 'mere animal joy in the temporary animal comfort of the moment stirred and uplifted them from their depths'.[5] But he did not follow its moral so closely as to provoke such an incident as the Wabash College affair, when Pound was dismissed for harbouring a stray girl in his room. *A Lume Spento* was neither unreflective of experience nor decorously forced. Williams, like Carman, still preferred a melancholic interpretation of life to a bitter appraisal of the facts of existence.

In mid-July 1909 Williams went to Leipzig to combine further medical studies with learning German; the following March he spent

---

[1] Ezra Pound, *Profile: An Anthology* . . . (Milan, 1932), p. 14.
[2] Copy inscribed to Williams by his brother (NjFDU[Rutherford]).
[3] *The Letters of Ezra Pound*, ed. D.D. Paige (N.Y., 1950), pp. 3–7.
[4] Letter from Williams to his mother, 1 March 1906 (NBuU).
[5] Frances Hodgson Burnett, 'The Dawn of a To-Morrow', *Scribner's Magazine* XXXVIII, 6 (December 1905), 643–57;657. The story continued in the following issue, XXIX, 1 (January 1906), 34–52.

a week in London with Pound. In correspondence Pound had gently told him he was 'out of touch', and had recommended that he read Yeats, Browning, Francis Thompson, and Swinburne, as well as poets of the 'second rank' like Margaret Sackville, Rosamund Watson, Ernest Rhys, and Jim G. Fairfax.[1] Now that Williams was briefly in London Pound doubtless pushed home his lessons. But if the Imagist doctrine was already presaged in Pound's first dictum, 'To paint the thing as I see it', his second, 'Beauty', was commonly held by the poets he had recommended, as well as by H. D. and Richard Aldington to whom beauty was religion. As Aldington wrote, 'you had to know the passwords – Omar, Vita Nuova, Aucassin'.[2] Williams knew enough to be identified as friend.

The visit to London produced the title for *Kora in Hell*, which Williams acknowledged as Pound's. For Pound the source of their discussion of the myth of Persephone was in a long-forgotten poem by E. W. Sutton Pickhardt, 'Ariadne Diainomene'.[3] For Williams, Botticelli's *Primavera*, which he had seen with the *Birth of Venus* at the Uffizi Gallery in Florence just prior to coming to London, provided a visual correlation. Pater's idealised and mysterious view of the Renaissance lay behind both their tastes.

The local representatives of American poetic life to whom Williams could turn on his return from England were *The Papyrus*, a magazine edited by Michael Monahan, and *The Bang*, edited by Alexander Harvey. Williams knew *The Papyrus*,[4] and it is probable that he would have heard of the New York literary club, The Vagabonds, for which *The Bang* was a bulletin, since Harvey lived in nearby Hackensack. There were other magazines like *The International*, and *Moods*, both edited by B. Russell Herts and Richard Le Gallienne. *The Papyrus* was subtitled 'A Magazine of Individuality'; Carman's *The Making of the Personality* and James Huneker's *Egoists* indicate the range of its interests – from Hellenist perfection to Nietzschean iconoclasm.

Whatever sympathy Williams might have had with the local egoists was soured by the presence of Ferdinand Earle, the 'Gregory Ives' of

---

[1] *Ibid.* p. 8.
[2] Richard Aldington, *Life for Life's Sake* (N.Y., 1941), p. 100.
[3] Pound, *Profile*, p. 14.
[4] Collection of his magazines (CtY).

The Build-Up.[1] Earle knew the Vagabonds group and was editor of *The Lyric Year*, an anthology of American poems published by Mitchell Kennerley.[2] In May 1912 it was announced in *The Papyrus* that a new poetry series would also be published by Kennerley, including Carman, John Davidson, Le Gallienne, Noguchi, Swinburne, Charles Hanson Towne, and Ferdinand Earle.[3] Earle, besides being the impressionist painter of *The Build-Up*, was a writer of sonnets who excluded Williams from *The Lyric Year*.[4] To add insult to injury, Earle then left his wife and eloped to Germany with Charlotte Herman whom Williams had once wanted so badly. Earle had seemed destined to be his enemy from the moment when, invited to the wedding of Williams and Florence Herman, Charlotte's sister, against their wishes he had the doors roped against their going-away.[5] Earle was a barrier not easily to be cut through. Williams' first critical publication was, accordingly, an attack on *The Lyric Year*.[6]

A Precedent for 'Paterson'

In March 1908 Ezra Pound, who was passing through Rutherford on his way to Europe, saw Williams' long Keatsian poem, 'Philip and Oradie', and pronounced it 'great'.[7] Its origin lay most probably in his association with Hilda Doolittle, to whom Pound was now temporarily engaged. H.D. introduced Williams to *Aucassin and Nicolette*, undoubtedly in Andrew Lang's translation, in which prose and verse were mixed.[8] It was she, furthermore, who so much impressed him at Bryn Mawr's May Day celebrations in 1906 when she appeared in Lincoln green as a member of Robin Hood's band.[9] His love of nature had first inclined him to the thought of forestry as a career,[10] and now

1 *The Build-Up*, pp. 277 ff.
2 *The Lyric Year*, ed. Ferdinand Earle (N.Y., 1912).
3 *The Papyrus* IV, I (May 1912) [43].
4 Ferdinand Earle, *Sonnets* (London, 1910). As Ferdinand Pinney Earle he later made a career as an art director in Hollywood, working for instance on sequences in *Ben-Hur* (1926).
5 *The Build-Up*, p. 306.
6 *Poetry* II, 3 (June 1913), 114–15.
7 Letter to his brother, 18 March 1908 (copy: CtY).
8 *The Autobiography of William Carlos Williams* (N.Y., 1951), p. 52.
9 Letter to his brother, 6 May 1906 (NBuU): 'Do you know Bo I'm dead in love with that girl. She isn't good looking and she isn't graceful; she isn't a beautiful dresser and she cannot play any music but by Gee! she is a fine girl and she can have me alright.'
10 Tape-recording of a C.B.S. broadcast, August 1951 (Free Public Library, Rutherford).

newly qualified as a doctor, he spent his weekends painting the Passaic river (Plate 1) even as Carman sat contemplating the St John. His technique inclined towards Impressionism, but he would surely have known the work of George Inness, the New Jersey landscape painter who painted the nearby Hackensack Meadows more than fifty years before in a personal but realistic vein.

Williams' essay 'Edgar Allan Poe' is a determined attempt to make of an apparent anti-Americanism on Poe's part the truly American response to a landscape for which there was no European precedent: 'His attack was *from the center out*. Either I exist or I do not exist and no amount of pap which I happen to be lapping can dull me to the loss. It was a doctrine, anti-American.'[1] In referring to 'pap' Williams endorses Poe's rejection of Bryant, Lowell, and Longfellow as genteel poets of the picturesque, and his critical attitude towards the too-ready acceptance by Hawthorne and Cooper of local material sentimentalised in a spirit of colonial imitation. To employ European conventions in coping with an uncultivated landscape was to surrender to the idea of a European sensibility being valid for the American scene. The scale of that scene, 'the GRAND scene', is not the same as in Europe. It is equivalent in terms of landscape to 'the great beast' that Hamilton called the people, or as Williams named it 'the UNFORMED LUMP'.[2]

Williams' fear of the lump, the unformed Passaic region which was his own natural locality and in which he could have easily lost himself copying the Jersey landscape, can be detected in his assiduous avoidance of any open reference to treatment of that scene by earlier writers. The number of poems written on Passaic Falls during the Early National Period was, of course, considerable. But none was better known to the members of the *Knickerbocker* circle than Washington Irving's 'On Passaic Falls', written in 1806 but not published until 1827:[3]

> In a wild, tranquil vale, fringed with forests of green,
> Where nature had fashion'd a soft silvan scene,
> The retreat of the ring-dove, the haunt of the deer,
> Passaic in silence roll'd gentle and clear.

[1] W. C. Williams, *In the American Grain* (N.Y., 1952), p. 219.
[2] *Ibid.* pp. 227–8.
[3] *The Atlantic Souvenir; A Christmas and New Year's Offering* (Philadelphia, 1827), pp. 146–8.

No grandeur of prospect astonish'd the sight,
No abruptness sublime mingled awe with delight;
There the wild flowret blossom'd, the elm proudly waved,
And pure was the current the green bank that laved.

But the spirit that ruled o'er the thick-tangled wood,
And had fixed in its gloomy recess his abode,
Loved best the rude scene that the whirlwinds deform,
And gloried in thunder, and lightning and storm.

All flush'd from the tumult of battle he came,
Where the red-men encounter'd the children of flame,
While the noise of the warhoop still rung in his ears,
And the fresh, bleeding scalp as a trophy he wears.

Oh! deep was the horror, and fierce was the fight,
When the eyes of the red-men were shrouded in night;
When by strangers invaded, by strangers destroy'd,
They ensanguined the fields which their fathers enjoy'd.

Lo! the sons of the forest in terror retire,
Pale savages chase them with thunder and fire;
In vain whirls the war-club, in vain twangs the bow,
By thunder and fire are the warriors laid low.

From defeat and from carnage the fierce spirit came,
His breast was a tumult, his passions were flame,
Despair swells his heart, fury maddens his ire,
And black scowls his brow o'er his eye-balls of fire.

With a glance of disgust he the landscape survey'd,
With its fragrant wild florets, its wide-waving shade,
Its river meand'ring through margins of green,
Transparent its waters – its surface serene.

He rived the green hills – the wild woods he laid low,
He turn'd the still stream in rough channels to flow,
He rent the rude rock, the steep precipice gave,
And hurl'd down the chasm the thundering wave.

A scene of strange ruin he scatter'd around,
Where cliffs piled on cliffs in wild majesty frown'd –
Where shadows of horror embrown the dark wood,
And the rain-bow and mist mark the turbulent flood.

9

Countless moons have since roll'd – in this long lapse of time,
Cultivation has soften'd those features sublime,
The axe of the white man enliven'd the shade,
And dispell'd the deep gloom of the thicketed glade.

Yet the stranger still gazes, with wondering eye,
On rocks rudely torn and groves mounted on high –
Still loves on the cliff's dizzy border to roam,
Where the torrent leaps headlong embosom'd in foam.

Here man's experience of the landscape is presented in terms of pastoral innocence and the corrupt taste of the picturesque. The 'stranger' is at first the colonist, who ravages the land and its native inhabitants. He is followed by the tourist who romanticises the earlier rape according to a Gothic imagination; the supernatural force of the sublime, by which the 'fierce spirit' of the place – and Irving – protests geologically, is assimilated by the tourist as the colonial sensibility substitutes for actual rape a literary taste for its imagined terrors. Irving's exploration of the psychological causes of the tumultuous strife of the passions embodied in the landscape is superior to any of the exercises on waterfalls in Kettell's *Specimens*, or *The New-York Book of Poetry*,[1] where the theme of the river of life is predictably treated without reference to an actual relation of man to his landscape.[2] John Brainard (1796–1828), the author of a poem 'The Falls of Niagara',[3] had never seen them, but

---

[1] *Specimens of American Poetry*, ed. Samuel Kettell (3 vols, Boston, 1829); *The New-York Book of Poetry* [ed. C.F. Hoffman], (N.Y., 1837).

[2] The four initial lines of a ms. exercise on Passaic Falls done by a Yale College student, John Hustis, in 1833 (Eberstadt Collection, Yale University Art Gallery) were transposed from 'The Waterfall' by Henry Pickering (1781–1831) to be found in Kettell's *Specimens*, vol. II, pp. 281–3:

> 'Impetuous Torrent! Nature piled
> Thy rocks amid the sylvan wild;
> With flower and shrub their crags she graced,
> And through them thy dark pathway traced.'
> Impetuous Fall! from thy rude scene
> Let Fancy some instruction glean.
> Like the stream of human life,
> Mid Passion's wild tumultuous strife
> In mad career with changing force,
> Rushes along its onward course.
> Till calmly sinking in the sea
> Of peaceful blest eternity.

[3] Kettell, *Specimens*, vol. III, p. 203.

the Passaic Falls, only nineteen miles from New York, were more accessible.[1]

Irving's second 'stranger', the tourist, was treated in an article which Williams knew in the American edition of *Meyer's Universum*.[2] The writer asserted that the ivy-covered castles and ruined monasteries towering over river-valleys from commanding heights in the Gothic romances of Europe were unfortunately absent in America:[3]

History and the romantic have no part in the composition of landscape paintings. The original red-skinned inhabitant has no history, his legends have disappeared, and the frail works of his hands vanished even more quickly than his footprints in the forest. European colonization at various points on the East Coast hardly extends as far as the fourth or fifth generation – that is, as far as our great-grandfathers' day.

Therefore America could only rival Europe in the sheer scale of its landscape, not in its associations. Even then, industry had robbed the Passaic Falls of half their volume. The wild beauty of nature was being replaced with commerce. The bear and the eagle had flown, the nocturnal calls of wild animals were being replaced with the songs of men, and the sound of the Falls vied with that of bands playing.[4] The romantic stories of the region he described as childish, compared with those of Europe's knights and saints, and concluded with a significantly erroneous version of the story of Sam Patch, in which he is not the foreman-weaver of history but a trapper who, falling on hard times when the bears and wolves were driven from the region, took to retrieving the fish swept over the Falls, and who became a formidable swimmer in the process. His decision to leap over the Falls is presented entirely as a commercial inspiration: 'A lucky leap into the abyss and the river in front of a few thousand spectators – that might make the last years of your life more tolerable.'[5] In this version frontier skills are capitalised as sensational entertainment in the circus tradition.[6]

[1] Peter Archdeacon, *A Sketch of the Passaic Falls* (N.Y., 1845), p. 96: 'There is ample time to inhale the pure mountain breeze, and refresh under the shady Oak, and return to the city the same day.'

[2] 'Passaic-Falls bei Patterson' [*sic*], *Meyer's Universum* (Americanische Ausgabe) V, 3 (1853), 42–4. Translated by the author from a copy in part of Williams' library (CtY).

[3] *Ibid.* p. 42.

[4] *Ibid.* p. 43.

[5] *Ibid.*

[6] George C. D. O'Dell, *Annals of the New York Stage* (15 vols, N.Y., 1927–49), has many references to two plays of the period 1837–65, *Sam Patch* and *Sam Patch in France*. The first

Nevertheless, there was an attempt to associate the spot with sentiment as well as with sensational daring. Some verses about Mrs Cumming, whose story like Sam Patch's was to be re-told in *Paterson*, were written for the 'Poetical Department' of a local newspaper just eight years after her demise.[1] Thus traditions were easily made when journalism and tourism required them. By the end of the nineteenth century the Gothic splendour of the scene which Paul Sandby depicted had vanished.[2] A view of the city from Garret Mountain showed the Falls in diminutive scale and crowned with a chimney stack at the edge of the panorama. The Morris canal and the railway, both of which have today fallen out of use, occupied the foreground (Plate 2). Paterson had become a bourgeois seat of industry. The only poem of this later period took no more account of the transformation that the river had undergone in more than fifty years of industrial use than did Williams' painting.[3]

In the last two pages of his *Autobiography* Williams claimed that he had once considered Newark as a suitable city-subject for his poem on the region. He also spoke of the story of Sam Patch as being too good not to be taken up, somehow suggesting that he had discovered it for himself.[4] What Williams nowhere acknowledged was that his poem belonged to a tradition of poems on the Passaic region. His early resolution not to be contaminated by an unformed lump of landscape susceptible to the tradition of the picturesque, a resolution derived from his reading of Poe, made him unusually reticent about his sources. He presented Poe's work as he might have presented his own: 'It seems to fall back continuously to a bare surface exhausted by having

---

play made the name of the actor Danforth Marble: 'Mr. Marble will leap from the extreme height of the theatre, a feat never attempted by anyone but himself, and prove that cold water don't drown love' (programme cited by O'Dell, IV, 321). Theatrically, the Yankee Jumper's story was associated with courtship but a newspaper advertisement such as one in the *Morning Signal* (28 May 1840) suggests that a circus-performer was jumping under his name for nothing but money.

[1] Ms. poem by Jacob F. Van Winkle headed '– Poetical Department – Passaic Falls, Patterson [*sic*], N.J., August 10th 1820' (Eberstadt Collection, Yale University Art Gallery):

> I sought the rock from which they tell
> A bride young fair and blooming fell
> And sunk beneath the waves...

[2] See Plate 9.
[3] John Alleyne Macnab, *The Song of the Passaic* (N.Y., 1890).
[4] *Autobiography*, pp. 393–4.

reached no perch in tradition.'[1] Yet an examination of the sources of Williams' quotations from Poe shows Williams to have been aware at a very early stage in his career of the existence of a traditional perch for his long poem. In an aside from his main theme – resistance to the temptations of local colour in favour of a method by which the writer was established at the centre of his landscape – Williams seemed as if compelled to inoculate himself against the colonial tradition of the picturesque by reference to an essay by Poe on one of his contemporaries.[2] He offered the quotation as an example of resoluteness when faced with minor work,[3] without revealing that the object of Poe's criticism was *Passaic, a Group of Poems Touching that River*, by 'Flaccus'.[4] The pseudonym was that of a Newark doctor-poet, Thomas Ward (1807–73).[5]

The table of contents of Ward's *Passaic*, a poem of one hundred and fifty octavo pages, forms an interesting comparison with the general organisation of Williams' *Paterson*:[6]

Sonnet to Passaic,
Introductory Musings on Rivers,
Passaic – Tale I.
   The Great Descender – Canto I.
   The Great Descender – Canto II.
Passaic – Tale II.
   The Worth of Beauty: or, a Lover's Journal. Canto I. First Love,
   Canto II. – Second Love,
Passaic – Tale III.
   The Last Look,
Passaic – Tale IV.

[1] *In the American Grain*, p. 223.

[2] 'Flaccus – Thomas Ward', *Graham's Magazine* XXII, 3 (March 1843), 195–8; reprinted in the edition of Poe's *Works* by E.C.Stedman and G.E.Woodberry, (10 vols, Chicago, 1895), vol. VIII, pp. 179–92.

[3] *In the American Grain*, p. 220 (final paragraph).

[4] Flaccus, *Passaic, a Group of Poems Touching that River: with other Musings* (N.Y., 1842). See Appendix A for a selection from this work.

[5] See *The Dictionary of American Biography*, ed. Dumas Malone (N.Y., 1936), vol. XIX, pp. 440–1. On the occasion of the ninety-fifth anniversary of the poet's birth in 1902, a local newspaper noted that his fame rested mainly on Poe's excoriation of his work, which led the curious to take out his little volume from the Newark Public Library on average only once every two years (*Call*, Newark, N.J., 8 June 1902: a clipping in the collection of the New Jersey Historical Society).

[6] *Passaic*, [v].

The Martyr: a Revolutionary Ballad,
Passaic – Tale v.
The Retreat of the Seventy-six,
Conclusion – To Passaic.

Williams' books ('parts' as they are called in his author's note)[1] bear an obvious relation to Ward's tales; his parts are Ward's cantos. Both poems have a preface of introductory musings. Both poems were originally published in sections in magazines and later re-arranged; Ward's second tale was originally his third, the fourth originally the fifth, the introduction appearing last of all.[2] Both poems share certain conventionalities. Ward's 'Introductory Musings on Rivers' and Williams' description of 'the elemental character of the place', and the two poets' use of blazons and invocations offer ready points of comparison. Ward's mottoes are drawn consistently from models of the English literary tradition – from Denham, Dryden, Byron, and Spenser – whereas Williams' are taken from J. A. Symonds on the Greeks, Santayana, and the example of Toulouse-Lautrec.

As a member of the *Knickerbocker* school,[3] Ward naturally modelled his style on poets in the picturesque tradition of Denham's *Cooper's Hill* and Pope's *Windsor Forest*, as a narrator of tales he followed Byron, and as a lyricist Thomas Moore. But Poe showed no sympathy with Ward's attempt to write a Gothic romance in verse. Somewhat surprisingly, in the light of Williams' view of him, Poe applauded the conventional success of the final seven lines of the introductory musings but objected, as Meyer had done, to the suitability of Sam Patch as a fit hero for romance. The burlesque quality of the story produced the fluctuating tone of the romantic ironist; the lowness of the subject conflicted with the neo-classical conception of form and diction. Here

---

[1] W. C. Williams, *Paterson* (N.Y., 1963) [7].

[2] *Passaic* was first printed in *The Knickerbocker* as follows: 'The Great Descender (Canto I)', xv, 1 (January 1840), 61–4; 'The Great Descender (Canto II)', xv, 2 (February 1840), 119–24; 'The Last Look', xv, 3 (March 1840), 195–200; 'The Worth of Beauty (Canto I)', xv, 4 (April 1840), 298–302, xv, 6 (June 1840), 472–7; 'The Worth of Beauty (Canto II)', xvi, 1 (July 1840), 10–17, xvi, 2 (August 1840), 139–43; 'The Martyr', xviii, 3 (September 1841), 205–6; 'Introductory Musings', xviii, 5 (November 1841), 384–7.

[3] See Thomas Ward, 'The Sessions of Parnassus; or, The Bards of Gotham', in *The Knickerbocker Gallery* (N.Y., 1854), pp. 219–34. He was, not surprisingly, a friend of Evert Augustus Duyckinck, the anthologist (letter from Ward to Fitz-Greene Halleck, October 1865 [NBu]).

Williams would have agreed only in part. His own use of the Patch story shows that the lowness of the subject could not be a valid point of criticism for a democratic humanist. Furthermore, the intractable hero as buffoon, in the tradition of the popular American performing art of the circus, was not without appeal. But Williams would, indeed, have agreed with Poe that European neo-classical ideas of decorum were unsuitable for the treatment of popular American subjects. Ward's attempt to make Sam a martyr of science by the use of meteorological conceits he would have found an intolerably elevated aim. Again, in handling the story of Mrs Cumming, Ward attempted a public mode by taking as his motto some lines from Dryden's 'Ode to Mrs. Anne Killigrew', which the provincial milieu scarcely merited. His actual mode was the sentimental romance. Williams' handling is a psychological interpretation of the barest newspaper account, whereas Ward puts a high-flown Christian construction on the event.

The second of Ward's tales, 'The Worth of Beauty: or, a Lover's Journal', Poe approved in principle, but not in practice. In his notes to the poem Ward told how he had 'transplanted' the authentic prose journal 'in the richer soil of verse'.[1] Poe replied:[2]

The narrative of the friend of Mr Flaccus must, originally, have been a very good thing. By 'originally', we mean before it had the misfortune to be 'transplanted in the richer soil of verse' – which has by no means agreed with its constitution. But, even through the dense fog of our author's rhythm, we can get an occasional glimpse of its merit. It must have been the work of a heart on fire with passion, and the utter abandon of the details reminds us even of Jean Jacques. But alas for this 'richer soil'!

Study of the manuscripts of *Paterson* shows Williams turning prose into verse, and verse back again into prose and varying the form of his verse to include short lyrics in Ward's Byronic fashion. Thus there was a local, if colonially imitative, parallel for the method of *Aucassin and Nicolette*. Despite the conventional metres of Ward's verse there was, as Poe had noted, an occasional flash of fire from the authentic document of the lover. Williams was to rely heavily upon such material. His first motto in *Paterson*, also on the worth of beauty, was appropriately, a 'quotation' from his own preliminary drafts. The authentic

[1] *Passaic*, p. 284.
[2] *Works*, vol. VIII, p. 184.

fragment, dismounted from its former place in the fabric and replaced according to new exigencies, constituted an American method. The vulgarity of the Patch story, and the sentimentality of the Mrs Cumming story were 'starved and broken things',[1] but Williams took it as an act of faith that they could be transfigured in beauty if the method could only be found; 'a method springing so freshly from the local conditions which determine it, by their emphasis of firm crudity and lack of coordinated structure...'[2] A theme of Indians, of river scenery, and of women could only be permitted when such a method had been evolved, otherwise poetry fell into the lap of 'literature' instead of rising into the realm of the soul. Ward was impelled to copy; Williams was compelled to allude to his poem. In time Williams found a method by which he could use the local colour which Ward had also exploited. Writing later of the bridge over the Falls Williams noted: 'Capt. John Post did not burn the bridge at Aquackanonk but being a (can't think of the term) American took the boards up carefully and stored them for future use'.[3] The materials of *Paterson* were already to hand, the perch in the tradition of the regional poem established; it remained Williams' life-long task to evolve an indigenous method by which he could build a new bridge over the Passaic. To succeed would be to replace the effigy of Europe with the living image of a local culture.

[1] See Appendix B (*Paterson* [11]).
[2] *In the American Grain*, p. 231.
[3] Letter to Robert D. Pepper, 21 August 1951.

2

The Animate Touch

The Sexual Approach

When Williams was twenty-nine years old he wrote to a friend:[1] 'My father tells me, being asked directly whether or not in his estimation I was a simple jassack, that I am tardy in development, that is all.' His life until his secret engagement with Florence Herman just prior to his first visit to Europe in 1909 was, as we have seen, extremely conventional. The engagement itself was his first act of daring and resolution. The story of it is told in *The Build-Up* in the personages of 'Charlie Bishop' and 'Flossie'. 'Charlie's' brother 'Fred' (Williams' brother Edgar) has proposed to 'Lottie' (Florence's sister Charlotte) and, much to Charlie's chagrin, has been accepted. On the rebound, Charlie goes to Flossie, tells her he does not love her – but that he does not *love* anyone – and that he believes they could be happy together:[2]

It would be a marriage that would be founded on human understanding that would be difficult but passionate, passionate as one says of a saint – those saints that were womanly, or, like St.Francis, full of compassion. It would be like no other love that had been conceived between a man and a woman.

It was more than rebound, of course. Charlie was prepared to act boldly on a concept of marriage in which an uncompromising confrontation between a man and a woman relied upon the chemical process of sexual affinity to grow slowly into love. The proposition is for a self-arranged marriage, founded on despair but also on a science of spiritual closeness through physical proximity.

Williams' daring decision was influenced by a celebrated book by Otto Weininger, published during Williams' last year at medical

[1] Letter to Viola Baxter Jordan, 19 March 1912 (CtY).
[2] *The Build-Up*, pp. 262–3.

school.[1] His swift appraisal of the practical, economical Florence, which replaced his long devotion to the mooning, musical Charlotte, was not so much a spontaneous gesture as a deliberate act of will. Weininger's book provided a rationale for his development by crisis. The correlation in ideas, and very occasionally in verbal expression, between the book and Williams' early letters may be seen essentially in his endorsement of its main tenet – that man is genial and woman material.

He gave special attention to that part of Weininger's thesis which maintained that woman was essentially substance, subject to man's genial capacity for forming her according to his own power of impressing her. Woman was passive, man active; woman wholly sexual in her nature, man only partly so. But if man was genial, the quality of genius was not hereditary like talent but strictly individual; any man with sufficient nerve and strength could develop it.[2] The moral determination to do so is clearly reflected in Williams' letters. The only conflict of interests for him lay in his passionate attraction towards girls which he first vowed to resist:[3]

To do what I mean to do and be what I must be in order to satisfy my own self I must discipline my affections, and until a fit opportunity affords, like no one in particular except you, Ed, and my nearest family. From nature, Ed, I have a weakness wherever passion is concerned.

The genius, as Weininger defined him, was a person whose ego could comprehend the universe; he saw nature whole. Williams also believed in the clarifying power of genius through a love of all things, which could not be permitted to localise itself in particular affections:[4]

At home the people are in general small; they see their little neighbourhood. I have seen that, I have seen the world and love to contemplate and, in all humbleness of mind, wonder at even greater things. For that reason I have little interest in the people I have known.

Thus, this burgeoning consciousness of the comprehensive range of genius made Williams repudiate what was to be the very foundation of his later work. Writing of the narrowness of college life, analogous to that of the small town, he told his brother:[5]

[1] Otto Weininger, *Sex and Character* (London and N.Y., 1906).
[2] *Ibid.* p. 183.
[3] *The Selected Letters of William Carlos Williams*, ed. John C. Thirlwall (N.Y., 1957), p. 14.
[4] *Ibid.*
[5] Letter to his brother, 18 March 1908 (copy: CtY).

You have that in you which never can fail except in one way and that is through a confusion of values, that is *true* values, and I maintain you cannot appreciate true values till you eliminate special conditions. That is you have certain absolute qualities in you which are good all by themselves simply as good qualities without reference to anybody else in the whole universe. When you appreciate these qualities your sole object in life becomes to develop them not to change them. I say that college life dims the perception and appreciation of these qualities & tends to belittle the very motive of genius which is individuality. Special conditions can only bring special results.

His attitude towards college remained unchanged throughout his life, but special conditions – the local – later came to mean the only way by which he believed he could achieve universal values. Immediately before *Poems* (1909), however, his supreme hope of attaining universalism lay in individualism without respect of milieu.

Williams' attitude to science also found a parallel in Weininger; indeed, the elimination of local conditions was attendant upon it. Weininger argued that scientific experiment was always undertaken in direct relation to the condition of contemporary knowledge:[1]

The scientific man takes possession of a definite store of experimental or observed knowledge, increases it or alters it more or less, and then hands it on. And much will be taken away from his achievements, much will silently disappear; his treatises may make a brave show in the libraries, but they cease to be actively alive. On the other hand, we can ascribe to the work of the great philosopher, as to that of the great artist, an imperishable, unchangeable presentation of the world, not disappearing with time, and which because it was the expression of a great mind, will always find a school of men to adhere to it. There still exist disciples of Plato and Aristotle, of Spinoza and Berkeley and Bruno, but there are now none who denote themselves as followers of Galileo or Helmholtz, or Ptolemy or Copernicus.

Thus immortality, the power of the 'classic' to survive, could not be achieved by science. It worried Williams at first:[2]

It always depressed me and took the nerve out of me to think that here I slam away for a lifetime and build a big bridge or discover a great principle and then go the good Lord knows where never to return and that's about all the real good it does me. Then somebody does something better and rips down my work and I am forgotten as everything must be forgotten as men grow for never was there a plainer truth than this: That men keep and respect only that which is above

[1] Weininger, *Sex and Character*, p. 141.
[2] Letter to his brother, 22 March 1906 (copy: CtY).

them and better than them. Yesterday's idol is today's footstool. This depressed me I say but it does no longer.

The longing for immortality could only be assuaged in someone who had been brought up as a Unitarian by the idea of the perdurability of good works. But in Williams' religion those works included art:[1]

Now comes what to me is the greatest fault we have. We separate our work and our philosophy or religion, they are one to me, into two separate units when they are one and inseparable. How ridiculous it is for us to sit down on Sunday with folded hands and loaf, yes loaf and lose one day in which we might be working at some beautiful secret of nature. Our work is the man himself in a tangible form so that our sense can grasp him. The man is himself truth so his work must be the truth. I hate this mystic medieval conception of a divine power with frowning brows who swats us one when we get in a dark corner. If our works are not divine, if they are not truth in stone, wood or iron, they are nothing.

The desire for immortality was accompanied by a sense of destiny, which repeatedly found expression in Williams' letters in these early years. Weininger's view that all great men were convinced, as a matter of faith, that they possessed souls, carried Williams to the limits of his credulity. He would not use the word 'soul' again until the final years of his life, when his desire for immortality in art became great as death began to threaten its accomplishment. In 1906 his faith in truth and love, which he insisted was a practical attitude to life, was not a 'Sunday morning idea', but 'as indefinite as infinity and as real';[2] 'Remember you are going to live for ever and that's no darned fool poetic figure, it's got to be true for you to be happy and we must therefore do things that will last for ever.' The impulse towards genius was evidently as ascetic as that towards girls was passionate. He had, he believed, changed much and quickly:[3]

One thing that has helped me immeasurably is that idea I have had that someday I can show the world something more beautiful than it has ever seen before. This is constantly in my mind and how constantly you perhaps would hardly believe although you know me better than anyone else does. Everything I see immediately suggests some detail to be thought out in the ultimate plan and I cannot tell you how real all things appear in that light and how wonderfully happy it makes me.

[1] Letter to his brother, 22 March 1906 (copy: CtY).
[2] Letter to his brother, 18 March 1906 (copy: CtY).
[3] Letter to his brother, 21 October 1908 (NBuU).

He wrote that he was visiting the Metropolitan Museum, the Museum of Natural History, and the Botanical Garden in Bronx Park. He was reading a book on harmony, attending a course of lectures on the great masters of music, and making notes on architecture, besides running a little drama club with the Daniels sisters in Rutherford.[1] This he undertook in addition to his work first at French Hospital, and then at the New York Infant Asylum on West Sixty-first Street.

On his return from Europe Williams took up a correspondence with Viola Baxter, a friend whom he had met through Pound in 1907. His letters to her – gay, tortured, flirtatious and serious – continued into the first year or two of his marriage, and until she married Virgil Jordan, later a writer on business and economic affairs. He informed her that he had 'ceased approaching "earthly semblances" and gone on to wooing heavenly realities of soul and not of face':[2]

there shall be of my own creating a face beyond all others beautiful because of the soul which lives purely behind it.

I am not a virtuoso, I am not a good-fellow, I am never happy in any possession. I only wish to see myself creating those around me and within me into a beautiful reality.

Reality would be created in terms of actual experience – local, personal, and special. But now in courtship, despite his resolve, he was at least partly un-philosophised by passion:[3]

Men know it as babies know the mother – as a place (I mean men and women.) It is a force which can be felt, it is multiform – I have felt it to command me in opposite ways now and then, that its purpose be accomplished. It has large purposes and small purposes, it has favorite purposes – all mysterious. One counteracts upon the other. Then love is a repellant flame which can only be denied at the expense of all satisfying accomplishment – or else results barrenness. Love will have His way. Be wilful in spight of Him and you are met as by a hawk, swiftly!

Weininger's attitude to passion was that woman's valuation of man for his 'manliness' had resulted in a monstrous 'coitus-cult', a trap for man's enslavement, into which he had fallen with animal cries. He

[1] *Ibid.*
[2] Letter to Viola Baxter Jordan, 30 October 1911 (CtY).
[3] Letter to Viola Baxter Jordan, 1 December 1911 (CtY).

protested: 'But God forbid that it should be so; that would mean that there are no longer any *men*'.[1]

Weininger had also explored the nature of bisexuality, and Williams showed himself aware of the possibilities of inversion:[2]

You are quite right, Viola, quite right, men are not strong enough to 'bat air' with women. That forever proves to me I am not a man; they, men, disgust me and if I must say it fill me with awe and admiration. I am too much a woman.

and again:[3] 'What am I? I am to a man what you are to a woman – one might say an auto glove inverted; the inside, skin-side, outside. From inside of me comes what most wear lightly – namely hair and perspiration.' In the light of Williams' remark about disciplining his affections until a fit opportunity arose, Weininger had made a very interesting observation:[4]

Womanish men are usually extremely anxious to marry, at least (I mention this to prevent misconception) if a sufficiently brilliant opportunity offers itself. When it is possible, they nearly always marry while they are still quite young. It is especially gratifying to them to get as wives famous women, artists or poets, or singers and actresses.

One fit opportunity for Williams had been passed when in 1908 Pound became engaged to H.D., the poetess; and a second when in 1909 Edgar became engaged to Charlotte, the pianist; and the high-spirited and egotistical Viola Baxter was too much like Williams for him to marry her. Writing to Miss Baxter about one who would seem to have been his future wife, Williams declared that he admired her 'for her intense pursuit of the impalpable to do which she labors with the actual & strives to be efficient – economical'.[5] In later life he described her as 'hard and useful as the handle of a spade'.[6]

The full story of Williams' courtship of Florence Herman may not yet be told.[7] It was a passionate affair, as destructive as his proposal had been constructive. If Florence had eloped with him, as the romantic

[1] Weininger, *Sex and Character*, p. 333.
[2] Letter to Viola Baxter Jordan, 6 January 1911 (CtY).
[3] Letter to Viola Baxter Jordan, 21 January 1911 (CtY).
[4] Weininger, *Sex and Character*, p. 56.
[5] Letter to Viola Baxter Jordan, 20 October 1911 (CtY).
[6] Letter to Charles Keppel, 20 January 1940 (NBuU).
[7] Williams' letters to his widow (NBuU) may not be seen until fifteen years after her death.

Charlotte did later not with his brother but with Ferdinand Earle, love could have quietly begun to have its way. As it was Williams sailed alone for Europe in mid-July of 1909, and was away for the traditional year and a day. When he came back he had to earn the living that would support a wife. There were two more tortured years ahead: 'They were both drawn, pale and hollow-eyed as the engagement drew at last to a close.'[1] On 12 December 1912 they were married.

Dora Marsden and 'The Egoist'

In 1913 Pound recommended to Williams as the very best way to keep in touch with what was going on in London a paper called *The New Freewoman*. He had reviewed Williams' little volume *The Tempers* in it, and told him that if copies of the paper had not already come he should send for the issues since 15 May 1913.[2] Shortly afterwards, the paper changed its name to *The Egoist*. By July 1914 Williams was able to inform Viola Baxter that he was both an Imagist and an Egoist.[3]

No other poet had evidenced much interest in egoism as a contributory force in the Imagist movement in poetry. In fact the view then, as later, was that egoism was an irrelevance introduced as the name of the Imagist paper by the two 'philosophical feminists', Harriet Weaver and Dora Marsden; and since they were responsible for its financial existence the poets merely acquiesced. Glenn Hughes, the historian of the Imagist movement, doubtless taking his emphasis from Pound, wrote of Miss Marsden: 'What she wrote had not the slightest connection with the other contents of the paper, and was studiously overlooked by most readers.'[4] As far as Williams was concerned nothing could have been further from the truth. He read Miss Marsden assiduously, and addressed long letters to the paper. He began with her writings on egoism as an alternative to feminism, continued with her nominalist aesthetics, and finally took up her so-called 'Lingual Psychology'.

Miss Marsden, before the first issue of *The New Freewoman* appeared

---

[1] *The Build-Up*, p. 306.
[2] *Letters of Ezra Pound*, pp. 27–8.
[3] Letter to Viola Baxter Jordan, undated (CtY). Working from a reference to 'the baby's sixmonthiversary', and Williams' son's birthday as recorded in *The Build-Up*, p. 316, as 7 January 1914, the date would be 7 July 1914.
[4] Glenn Hughes, *Imagism and the Imagists* (Stanford and London, 1931), p. 32.

in November 1911, had been a militant suffragette in the Women's Social and Political Union until she fell out with that organisation and went over to the less militant Women's Freedom League.[1] A primary intellectual source-book for her was Max Stirner's *The Ego and his Own*; Weininger's *Sex and Character* was another. Weininger contended that woman could be respected by man only when she ceased to be merely an object or substance for man to work upon. He proposed, first of all, that the education of woman be taken out of the hands of her mother. With this Miss Marsden agreed. The shameless way in which daughters were schooled by their mothers to attract maintenance for life in a style to which they were accustomed, and to avoid 'cheapening themselves', which was to say lowering their value in the marriage-market, created a married prostitution rather than emancipated the individual for personal freedom. *The New Freewoman* was not concerned with reforms which would lead to the establishment of mere voices in the political structure, but with personal freedom achieved by economic means. In the course of the human struggle to obtain control over man's – and now woman's – own person it had become clear that ownership of self depended directly upon material property or wealth. Woman's position in society remained low simply because she chose to sell her legs rather than her brains.[2]

Williams wrote to Viola Baxter proposing the solution of egoism: 'An egoist is simply a person who owns himself to bestow himself perfectly.'[3] But he had long lost patience with the concept of virginity:[4]

To be alive means you are committed against virginity either by yielding to passion or by holding passion off. It begins at about the age of three and every blush proves there is no virginity. A few know their lack and good it is for all of us. Others mistake simple natural economy for the true principle which, as all abstract truths are, is a myth to us.

Weininger maintained that virginity was a man-made commodity, which woman trained herself artificially to conserve in order to raise her price, which man was willing to meet whatever the cost.[5]

[1] I am indebted for this information to Miss Jane Lidderdale, Harriet Weaver's biographer.
[2] [Dora Marsden] 'The Heart of the Question', *The New Freewoman* I, 4 (1 August 1913), 61–4.
[3] Letter to Viola Baxter Jordan, [7 July 1914] (CtY).
[4] Letter to Viola Baxter Jordan, 5 December 1911 (CtY).
[5] Weininger, *Sex and Character*, p. 333.

Williams' approach to Miss Marsden's philosophy began specifically with Weininger but he rapidly showed his divergence from the sexual philosopher's conclusions. For Williams, Weininger's great work lay in his division of the field of psychology into male and female halves, which he would have clearly recognised as reciprocal had he not been possessed by the idea of a third sex through which the duality of male and female could be resolved. Furthermore, Weininger, faced with woman's indestructible relation to the earth, could in Williams' estimation, only save man from a secondary role in nature by claiming a 'soul' for him. His error lay in that he credited man with the ability to clarify details, while allowing woman only the power to receive 'henids', a term coined to suggest undifferentiated thought and feeling received in inarticulate form. Williams denied this: 'Man is the vague generalizer, woman the concrete thinker, and not the reverse as he imagined. Man is the indulger in *henids*, and woman the enemy of *henids*.'[1]

However, Miss Marsden had committed an analogous error in trying to blend what Williams called, after Weininger, the male and female psychologies. Her problem, as Williams understood it, was to discover how to re-vitalise philosophy. In his first letter he had noted that his own interest in philosophy was principally drawn by the 'covert attack on the "creative artist"' implicit in Miss Marsden's treatment.[2] So when Williams re-stated the problem, we may imagine that he was doing so on behalf of poetry as well as philosophy:[3]

I think it is fairly safe to say that male psychology is characterized by an inability to concede reality to fact. This has arisen no doubt from the universal lack of attachment between the male and an objective world – to the earth under feet – since the male, aside from his extremely simple sex function, is wholly unnecessary to objective life: the only life which his sense perceives. He can never be even certain that his child is his own. From this may arise some of the feeling a man has for his mother, for in her at least is a connexion with the earth, if only a passive one, though even here he cannot be certain that his mother is his own, for being without the use of mind or senses at his own birth he can have no direct knowledge of it.

[1] W. C. Williams, 'Correspondence: The Great Sex Spiral', *The Egoist* IV, 7 (August 1917), 110–11;*111*.
[2] W. C. Williams, 'Correspondence: The Great Sex Spiral', *The Egoist* IV, 3 (April 1917), 46.
[3] *The Egoist* IV, 7 (August 1917), 111.

Thus man's only positive connexion with the earth is in the fleeting sex function. When not in pursuit of the female man has absolutely no necessity to exist. But this chase can never lead to satisfaction in the catch, since as soon as the catch is made the objective is removed and nothing remains but to make another catch of the same kind. Among the highly specialized bees we know that the drone performs his function once and is destroyed, as would certainly be the case with man if strict physical economy pertained.

Thus the male pursuit leads only to further pursuit, that is, not toward the earth, but away from it – not to concreteness, but to further hunting, to stargazing, to idleness. On this fundamental basis rests male psychology; it cannot but remain agnostic in a concrete world; it is extremely simple.

It is well established that primitive man – that is the tribesman – when not busied with women and when free to perform his own will is either hunting, fighting, loafing, or drunk. Man will only work when forced to do so, or when inveigled into it by a woman, or at least by a predominant female psychology. Whatever he does do is not for results, but for the drunkenness there is in it. *Soyez ivre*! If he find no drunkenness in his work it is empty for him.

Female psychology, on the other hand, is characterized by a trend not away from, but toward the earth, toward concreteness, since by her experience the reality of fact is firmly established for her. Her pursuit of the male results not in further chase, at least not in the immediate necessity for further chase, but to definite physical results that connect her indisputably and firmly with the earth at her feet by an unalterable chain, every link of which is concrete. Woman is physically essential to the maintenance of a physical life by a complicated and long-drawn-out process.

Thus reality – depending on sense-experience – is very different for the male and female. In neither case can one sex concede the reality of the experience that underlies the psychology of the other, since the completely opposed sense-experience of the male on the one hand and the female on the other cannot enter the other's consciousness. Either sex must hold to its own psychology or relinquish its sense of reality. For either sex the other's psychology must always be taken a priori. To the female mind male psychology (philosophy), which is agnostic, due to his experience, has no reality in her experience. To the female mind such a psychology (philosophy) will always remain a meaningless symbol – a negative attracting her attack.

In describing Miss Marsden's aim as '(1) The rekindling of life in a sterile philosophy by (2) the engendering action of analysis on a (3) redefined subject-matter',[1] Williams, as we have noted, was also thinking of the implications of her nominalist position for a sterile poetry, also the victim of male dominance. The naming of 'things', including

[1] *The Egoist* IV, 7 (August 1917), 110.

experienced emotion, was a militant reaction to aesthetic, as well as philosophical and political, authority.

Almost contemporaneously with the appearance of the Imagist manifestoes in *Poetry*, Miss Marsden began to relate the doctrines of the new movement to her own philosophical preoccupations. In an editorial, 'Thinking and Thought', she first attacked paradox as the refuge of the 'literary' and the 'cultured' who knew their powers of comprehension to be failing. Instead of thinking, they were content to manufacture thought. Ideas and concepts were, in her view, the unnecessary by-products of thinking, and not the process itself, which alone could develop man's intellect; 'The process of thinking is meant to co-ordinate two things which are real: the person who thinks and the rest of the phenomenal world, the world of sense.'[1] But thinking itself, Miss Marsden argued, only occurred intermittently, during man's temporary releases from stupidity and passion. The basis of knowledge lay in being, not thinking. Therefore, it followed, knowledge was experienced emotion not spurious thought.

In a subsequent article, 'The Art of the Future', in which she made specific reference to Pound, Miss Marsden defined art as the complement of science:[2] 'If science is the knowledge gained by applying to non-vital phenomena, the method of accurate description as opposed to that of imaginative interpretation, art is the product of the same method applied to vital (and mainly human vital) phenomena.' The experimental method would make the interpretative guess redundant in art as well as science. Poetry, as Miss Marsden defined it, would be 'the highest manifestation of self-consciousness, *re*-presented in terms of self-recognised emotion'.[3]

Beauty she approached by rejecting its categories as conceived, but not perceived, by so-called 'cultured' persons; the Sublime removed limitations (what Williams had once called 'special conditions') and therefore destroyed sharpness of focus, the Picturesque she named 'the natural, interpreted in terms of the made-up'. Then she introduced a new category, the Seductive, by which she was concerned to represent masculine interest in sex, whether in the virgin or in the whore.[4] To her,

[1] *The New Freewoman* I, 5 (15 August 1913), 81.
[2] *The New Freewoman* I, 10 (1 November 1913), 181.
[3] *Ibid.* p. 183.
[4] 'Concerning the Beautiful', *The New Freewoman* I, 6 (1 September 1913), 101–4.

as to Weininger, the choice offered was between a higher and a lower eroticism. Neither the idealisation nor the desecration of earth was to be confused with spirit. Beauty had nothing to do with these surrogates.

To Viola Baxter Jordan (as she was now) Williams proposed beauty as the place where men and women could meet in understanding, and sex as the obstacle preventing them from experiencing the world in the same way.[1] The Seductive and the Beautiful were not, indeed, the same:[2]

Love and beauty are eternally separate. I live to proclaim that. They are horribly confused. It is confusion that torments us all not dissatisfaction over some vague ideal. This world will be saved by a man with a reason. Then it will be lost again at once of course – yet there is a great saving chance for a man. I disdain nothing. I expect to reach heaven over a bridge of cobble stones. My whole life is a cleaving to the very nearest thing I can lay hand to with a re-enforcing determination to give up nothing without a completely convincing reason from any person who comes along...

I am here for one clear reason and that is that I cannot see how I can be anywhere else and do what I have determined to do. Daring? It's a myth. Daring is only another form of drunkenness, of forgetting but I chose to remember everything, always and to sit down for ten life-times if necessary and make my experience fit into its reason, if you can understand what I mean by that.

I continually work and plan to be the greatest man on earth as I will be it, or rather will to be it. Love to me is a law as sure as gravity (which I understand now is not at all sure). Of course I do not intend to picture love in such a way but – ideals and visions interfere very little with my love for any person.

The confusion lay in his first sentence. It was one of terms; here he had interchanged 'love' for sex. Later he realised that love has as little to do with sex as beauty, but already he understood that the Beautiful did not command or seduce man's love. Finally, the only sound approach to the Beautiful lay in trying to love someone. This was not a romantic conception of love; on the contrary, it was eminently practical. In *The Build-Up*, Charlie Bishop offered Flossie this kind of love:[3] 'There is a sort of love, not romantic love, but a love that with daring can be made difficultly to blossom. It is founded on passion, a passion of despair, as all life is despair.' There was another sort of poetry which

[1] Letter [7 July 1914] (CtY).
[2] Letter to Viola Baxter Jordan, 24 June 1914 (CtY).
[3] *The Build-Up*, p. 262.

could with difficulty be made to flower, founded also on the determination to cleave to what lay under the animate touch. The confusion lay in the way the objective world withdrew at the hand's approach.

Williams viewed Imagism as an aesthetic based not on male psychology, or conceptual philosophy, but on female psychology, or tangible philosophy. In *The Egoist* May Sinclair, the philosopher, made a sectarian analogy in an interesting comparison between Imagism and Symbolism:[1]

The Victorian poets are Protestant. For them the bread and wine are symbols of Reality, the body and the blood. They are given 'in remembrance'. The sacrament is incomplete. The Imagists are Catholic; they believe in Transsubstantiation. For them the bread and wine are the body and the blood.

Imagism did not consist in the separation of pure form from substance, but in the engendering force of the one acting upon the other. As an approach it was profoundly sexual, sacramental, or even liturgical. The object was not considered a symbol of reality, but as reality itself. It made all the difference between what Pound, in 'An Object' called 'acquaintance' and 'affections':[2]

> This thing, that hath a code and not a core,
> Hath set acquaintance where might be
> affections

From affections could grow the new kind of love, and its accompanying new sense of beauty, which Williams had decided to cultivate.

The 'Contact' Idea

In *In the American Grain*, Williams wrote, 'One is forced on the conception of the New World as a woman.'[3] If Poe was a new De Soto, then he would be a new Poe. In his last year of medical school, faced with his first delivery of a child he appeared to be as callow as many another medical student.[4] But, a year or two later in New York, he found him-

---

1 'Two Notes: I. On H.D. II. On Imagism', *The Egoist* II, 6 (1 June 1915), 88–9;89.

2 Ezra Pound, *Personae* (N.Y., 1926), p. 63.

3 p. 220.

4 Letter to his brother, 12 January 1905 (copy: CtY): 'I have to fool around an old bum's belly, a woman of course and see which way the kid is coming. Then in about two weeks I will have to yank the thing out. It will be my first experience in this line of work so I guess I will have lots of fun.'

self becoming acquainted with a new kind of reality. If he spent an evening going to see Alla Nazimova in grand opera,[1] he was by no means unfeeling towards the area in which he worked. He was conscious of the heterogeneity of American life, both in the emergency ward on Election Day,[2] and in the street:[3]

> Eyes that can see,
> Oh, what a rarity!
> For many a year gone by
> I've looked and nothing seen
> But ever been
> Blind to a patent wide reality.

On 21 August 1908 he went to see Isadora Duncan dance, and the following day wrote some lines which, crude and unfinished as they were, expressed a new sentiment:[4]

> I saw, dear countrymaid, how soon shall spring
> From this our native land great loveliness.

He began to write short plays on American historical subjects. *Betty Putnam*, a Puritan story, was praised by Charlotte Herman as 'so American'.[5] He urged his brother to read a review of Nicholas Murray Butler's *The American As He Is* which proposed an American variety of Calvinism consisting in 'Devotion to duty for its own sake, and a resolute determination to persevere to the end in any undertaking'.[6] Butler's estimate of the American arts was considered by the reviewer to be over-modest; the superiority of American architecture over French and English was claimed in terms of 'a finer adaptation to environment and background'.[7] It was as if Williams was saying to his brother, the young architect, that it was possible after all to be an American as well as an artist.

[1] Letter to his brother, postmarked 7 February 1906 (copy: CtY).
[2] Letter to his brother, 6 November 1906 (copy: CtY): 'Already I've had three cases. One a woman more than half "piffed" who had been stabbed in the hand by her husband. Another a coon for whom a mob had been laying for a long time. They hit him on the head with a bottle. He was a good sport. The last was a kid with one hand pretty well burnt up from being pushed into a fire. Oh I tell you there's nothing like it.'
[3] W. C. Williams, *Poems* (Rutherford, N.J., 1909), p. 16.
[4] Letter to his brother, 22 August 1908 (NBuU).
[5] Letter to his brother, 18 March 1909 (copy: CtY).
[6] [Unsigned] 'The Real American', *The Outlook* XCI (20 March 1909), 623–6;*624*.
[7] *Ibid.* p. 625.

When Williams returned to the American theme with a conscious programme of attack it was in alliance with Robert McAlmon with whom he edited *Contact*. In New York harbour, on board the barge *Connecticut*, McAlmon pursued a life on the water. He had formerly been a flyer on the West Coast, and it is not too much to say that his fierce belief in contact with the soil was at least partly derived from the sense of disembodiment which the media of air and water gave him. At the simplest level, contact meant coming in to land or stepping ashore. Neither the air nor the sea, as Williams often said, was man's home.

McAlmon's earliest recorded resolution to come down to earth was presented in a fable he wrote for *The Ace*, a magazine of aviation. In August 1919, before he had met Williams, the Air Poet of America offered his readers a poem entitled 'Air Visional'.[1] Its subject, and that of the 'Air Fragments' which appeared in the following issue,[2] was the aggressive softness and colourless beauty of space. In the fable he provided a prose gloss to his poems:[3]

After every flight into the sky my return to earth was with increased reluctance, yet I always felt a feverish anxiety to return to earth when I was in the sky. I needed, it seemed, repeated assurance that the earth was there. After my contact with nothing the earth was restful; even days when I landed recklessly, jarring my plane, it was restful – an assurance that here was matter, something that had been and would continue to be.

Probably through his friendship with Marsden Hartley, the painter, whom he had known since 1917, McAlmon was acquainted with Stanton MacDonald-Wright, the Synchromist painter. *The Ace* now presented an essay–manifesto on the influence of aviation on art.[4] The 'air-centaur' would scorn the earth-bound thinkers who carefully built reputations upon 'the little ripples of character accentuation, native to all men, but with them displayed in the spot-light of self-adoration'.[5] Against this, the flyer would evolve through his experience of space an

[1] *The Ace* I, I (August 1919), 6.
[2] *The Ace* I, 2 (September 1919), 6: '. . . Yet space remains. / Adamant, hard, / With the hardness / of unresistance . . .'
[3] 'No-Colored Encounters: Hallucinations of an Aerial Wanderer', *The Ace* I, I (August 1919), 27–8, 36;*28*.
[4] S. MacDonald-Wright, 'The Influence of Aviation on Art', *The Ace* I, 2 (September 1919), 11–12.
[5] *Ibid.* p. 12.

independence, and an 'accentuation of individuality'. McAlmon's contempt for the talkative and sychophantic groups of artists in New York, whom he attacked in a *roman à clef*,[1] agreed with such an attitude. His poems in *The Ace* were imbued with that 'cosmic consciousness' which MacDonald-Wright celebrated. But in glorifying the majestic vision of the aeronaut, freed from the superficial, realistic details of nature, by which he justified the pure mind of his own kind of abstract painting, MacDonald-Wright went too far. McAlmon, newly convinced of the meaning of contact with the earth, would not have agreed 'we must forget the specific in our contemplation of the general'.[2]

As well as concerning himself with art and aviation McAlmon was following John Dewey's essays and reviews in *The New Republic*, which he reflected in an essay on 'Schools and the Science of Aviation',[3] when he scoffed at the attitudes of teachers and advertisers who, in an industrial age, put literary education before everything else. But the main point of his essay was to support progressive education, by which the mere preservation of past knowledge would be replaced with the creation of ability. He set off against each other two typical boys; one the product of the English literary education, expected to be supercilious to people less learned than himself, and the other the product of an American functional education, who tinkers with machinery and tries to build an aeroplane, or who begins in business on his own.

A month after the appearance of the first issue of *Contact* McAlmon was still pursuing the theme of education and creative industry in *The Ace*, of which he was now officially named associate editor.[4] He now asked whether there was not such a thing as commercial genius, whose chief attribute was not the gift of money-making but the development of the industrial system in accordance with human needs. The inventor and the 'social discoverer', as McAlmon called the possessor of the genuine commercial mind, should work with artists to free the masses for a life worth living. To Europe's attacks on America as a commercial country McAlmon replied that Europe had made of the arts a mercenary asset, by which 'traditional, scholastic, and pretentious culture' had replaced any functional ability on the part of French

[1] R. McAlmon, *Post-Adolescence* (1920) [Paris, 1923].
[2] MacDonald-Wright, 'Influence of Aviation', p. 11.
[3] *The Ace* I, 6 (January 1920), 21.
[4] *The Ace* II, 6 (January 1921), 14–15.

writers, for example, to base their work on thought and discovery other than that borrowed from the past. Industrial life in America had so oppressed the people that few knew how to regard the arts except with a Europeanised false respect: '...condemning the "revolutionary" moderns who insist upon getting back to the source of all finest discovery, namely: contact with experience, and with life'.[1]

In July 1920 McAlmon wrote to Williams about the mimeographed sheets which would be the first *Contact*.[2] But he was in a very destructive mood over *The Little Review*'s respect for art and Richard Aldington. Joyce, Hudson, and Hardy he praised as prose-writers without a theory; of the poets contributing to the magazine *Others* only Williams was without a 'method'. He was looking about for allies who would favour direct experience of life before intellectualism of any kind. In response to a previous letter in which Williams informed McAlmon that he had written to Dewey about an article in *The Dial*, McAlmon proposed Mary Austin as another person who might join them.

In an article to which McAlmon now drew Williams' attention, Mary Austin attacked the centralisation of literary influence in New York. Reviewing in passing Waldo Frank's *Our America*, she protested at the large part given to the Americanisation of literature by Frank's Jewish friends, Stieglitz, Stein, Ornstein, Rosenfeld, and Oppenheim. Their mystical talk of the spiritual voice of America was based on an experience of the country bounded by Broadway and Fifty-ninth Street.[3] McAlmon reacted violently against Frank,[4] and filled his contributions to *Contact* with attacks on what he called 'Semiticism'.[5] From France, later, he continued to jibe at 'Jew-York'.[6]

Dewey's essay in *The Dial*, 'Americanism and Localism',[7] was published in the context of an essay by James Oppenheim earlier in the year.[8] Oppenheim had argued that the standardisation of American

---

[1] *Ibid.* p. 14.
[2] Letter to Williams, 31 July [1920] (CtY).
[3] Mary Austin, 'New York: Dictator of American Criticism', *The Nation* CIX, 2874 (31 July 1920), 129–30.
[4] Letter to Williams [*c.* 1920] (NBuU).
[5] See *Contact* 3 [Spring 1921], 17; 4 [Summer 1921], 16.
[6] 'La Peinture en Amérique', *La Revue Européenne* II, 11 (January 1924), 67–70;68.
[7] *The Dial* LXVIII, 6 (June 1920), 684–8.
[8] 'Poetry – Our First National Art', *The Dial* LXVIII, 2 (February 1920), 238–42.

surroundings belied the great diversity of the racial backgrounds of the people who lived in them. The American novel had failed to reveal character because, 'a people united only by conscious bonds, have, for the sake of unity, denied their unconscious and alien character; and behind the striking sameness gapes a void'.[1] Dewey neatly inverted this argument. His reason for the failure of the American novel was its lack of manners: 'For lack of manners is a product of the interaction of characters and social environment, a social environment of which the background, the tradition, the descent of forces, is a part.'[2] Local colour failed simply because the sense of background necessary for the expression of locality was missing: 'We have been too anxious to get away from home. Naturally that took us to Europe even though we fancied we were going around America.'[3] The national periodicals, whose readership was essentially composed of passengers, that is to say people in physical or mental transit, could not afford to be local. They could refer to no home town except in the perspective of the national news, and thus eliminated all expression of locality.[4] The local news-papers, on the other hand, Dewey described as 'the only genuinely popular form of literature we have achieved'.[5]

As the twenties progressed a new commentator appeared on the American scene from whose assertion of the need for localism Williams could draw sustenance – Count Hermann Keyserling.[6] He attributed the lack of soul in America to the colonial isolation of the several waves of settlers. They came with their bodies and their religious laws intact, but their souls died swiftly within them once they were cut off from the localities which produced them, and as soon as the urge towards Americanisation became conscious: 'And this can only lead, as time goes on, to complete soullessness, just as long as a new soul has not been born from a new communion with Mother Earth.'[7]

[1] *Ibid.* p. 239. [2] 'Americanism and Localism', p. 687.
[3] *Ibid.* p. 688.
[4] Cf. Williams, 'Sample Critical Statement: Comment', *Contact* 4 [Summer 1921], 19: 'American periodic literature, magazines which represent no position taken but which offer at best certain snippets in juxtaposition, implying that when one piece is like the other both are good, this is the worst in the local environment carried to the logical conclusion.'
[5] 'Americanism and Localism', p. 687.
[6] The index of Williams' *Autobiography* wrongly identifies this reference with Leon H. Keyserling instead of with the travelling philosopher, Count Hermann Keyserling.
[7] Count Hermann Keyserling, *America Set Free* (N.Y. and London, 1929), p. 17.

As a friend of Jung, Keyserling understood the role of the racial unconscious but, as a friend of Dewey, he was also aware of the tremendous pressure on the immigrant to standardise his conscious mind for the purpose of Americanisation. It tended to turn nomads into localists in a very short while. This was absolutely necessary for the development of an indigenous culture: 'Every autochthonous culture in the world began as a local culture. Culture is always a daughter of spirit, married to earth. A man who is not yet the native son of a soil can conquer matter spiritually only on a small scale.'[1] Or in another formulation of the theme:[2]

Localism alone can produce in America a thoroughly authentic type of man; this type alone can be the germ-cell of an authentic American nation. Again, localism alone can lead to culture, for culture, too, must start as a singular and, therefore, small thing. It will grow and spread as time proceeds.

'A Democratic Party Poem', written for the campaign of 1928–9, and which Williams was still attempting to have printed by the publishers of the second series of *Contact* in 1931, has a preface which accords perfectly with Keyserling's ideas:[3]

> The strongest feature of the Russian Soviets is their
> local character
>
> The first characteristic of the United States is that
> of so many decayed Soviets
>
> The old strength of Europe is its traditional localism
> fixed by a variety of languages
>
> The loss of China has been that of the conglomerate
>
> States' rights precede all other political virtues
>
> The Renaissance was the flowering of rival cities
>
> It is inevitable that in all things one must always
> know more than the rest of the world
>
> And what he knows is bred of some place

[1] *Ibid.* p. 48.
[2] *Ibid.* p. 51.
[3] Unpublished ms. (NBuU).

Williams' family was a good example of Keyserling's nomads turned localists. His brother Edgar designed the war memorial as well as the post office and public library. But for a first generation American Rutherford held no special attraction; a score of similar towns would have suited a country doctor just as well. It was simply the place from which Williams served six townships and four boroughs. He had deliberately planned his life in every respect; most importantly in his proposal to his wife, then in his determination to remain in Rutherford. He did not despair, as he would later, of the possibilities of communal life, and consciously began to engage himself in the affairs of his locality. In 1916 he was appointed a member of the Bergen County Mosquito Extermination Commission; in 1920 he was made medical inspector of schools, and campaigned for the building of a new high school.

McAlmon, however, was already uprooted from his native North Dakota. He would have set off for Mexico, South America, or Australia on the first boat had not H.D.'s friend, Bryher, offered him the marriage of convenience which carried him away to Europe. Williams' own marriage was self-arranged. But whereas Williams was strict in his carelessness, McAlmon was simply careless. As time went on the marriage of earth lodged, while that of spirit quickly dissipated. The *Contact* idea was McAlmon's, as Williams readily admitted.[1] When McAlmon gave it up in all but name and left for Europe Williams was broken-hearted,[2] but he held his ground.

[1] W.C.Williams, 'The Contact Story', *Contact* (San Francisco) 1 (1958), 75–7;75.
[2] *Selected Letters*, p. 51.

3
The Beginnings of Art

―――

Painting and Poetry

Late in 1915 Williams made his first effort to aestheticise his sexual approach to life; which is to say, to extend his sense of woman and locality as material to the materials of the poem. He did this in the immediate context of the London *Blast*. The phallicism implicit in the Vorticist attitude towards carving in sculpture was interpretable from Pound's statement in which he posed the alternatives of man as a receiver of impressions, or as a conceiver of actions.[1] Williams noted in the second *Blast* a manifesto by Henri Gaudier-Brzeska in which the sculptor spoke of deriving his emotions solely from the arrangement of surfaces; in sculptural terms this meant the planes and lines by which the surfaces were defined.[2] Williams directly applied these aesthetic ideas to his own situation:[3]

By taking whatever character my environment has presented and turning it to my purpose I have expressed my independence of it.

Thus in using words instead of stone I accept "plane" to be the affirmation of existence, the meeting of substances, whether it be stone meeting air or a sound of a certain quality against one of another or against silence.

Will and consciousness – egoism extended to aesthetics – removed the artist thus from both necessity and accident. The necessity of place and the accident of time, two constants in the life of the artist, were resolved in art by what Wassily Kandinsky called its 'inner necessity'.

In the prologue to *Kora in Hell* Williams makes a brief reference to Kandinsky's famous little treatise *On the Spiritual in Art*, paraphrasing the three fundamental principles every artist would accept if he

[1] Ezra Pound, 'Vortex', *Blast* 1 (20 June 1914), 153–4; *153*.
[2] H. Gaudier-Brzeska, 'Vortex from the Trenches', *Blast* 2 (July 1915), 34.
[3] 'Vortex – William Carlos Williams' (NBuU).

expected to create a work possessed of this 'inner necessity'.[1] Here they are given in full from *Blast*, where Williams undoubtedly read them first:[2]

1. Every artist, as a creator, has to express himself (Element of Personality).

2. Every artist, as the child of his epoch, has to express what is particular to this epoch (Element of Style – in an inner sense, composed of the speech of the epoch, and the speech of the nation, as long as the nation exists as such).

3. Every artist, as the servant of art, has to express what is particular to all art (Element of the pure and eternal qualities of the art of all men, of all peoples and of all times, which are to be seen in the works of all artists of every nation and of every epoch, and which, as the principal elements of art, know neither time nor space).

From these principles Kandinsky developed a fourth; that the first two elements only needed to be practised for the third to follow of itself. What was particular to all art was that it inhabited the world of spirit, which Williams chose to render in the prologue as the world of imagination. If the third element, however, existed noticeably in a modern work it could only do so at the cost of losing the first two elements and thus access to a contemporary public. It was with this theorem that Williams chose to browbeat Eliot and Pound. It was this that confirmed for Williams the necessary relation between the local and the spiritual, or between place and the imagination.

Kandinsky's little work was, of course, well-known. It was quoted in the *Little Review* in 1914.[3] But it is not often recognised that it was Marsden Hartley who was the first person to introduce it to the English-speaking world. In Germany in 1912 and 1913 Hartley met the Blaue Reiter group of painters, notably Kandinsky and Marc, and writing to Alfred Stieglitz in America about his visits to them, said that he knew that what he did himself coincided with Kandinsky's theories.[4] In April 1912 the first extracts in English appeared in Stieglitz's review, *Camera Work*.[5] In Paris in August 1913 Hartley met

---

[1] *Selected Essays of William Carlos Williams* (N.Y., 1954), p. 23.
[2] *Blast* I (20 June 1914), 119.
[3] *Little Review* I, 8 (November 1914), 53.
[4] Several letters from Marsden Hartley to Alfred Stieglitz, September 1912–September 1913 (CtY).
[5] 'Extracts from "The Spiritual in Art"', *Camera Work* 38 (April 1912), 34.

Charles Demuth, the painter, and told him to call on Stieglitz as soon as he got back to New York in September.[1] Some important links were being fashioned; Williams had known Demuth from his days in Philadelphia; before long he would meet Hartley.

Kandinsky was especially useful to the American artists because of the varied approaches that he offered them. He gave names to three modes of expression which he presented in an ascending order of importance:[2]

1. A direct impression of nature, expressed in purely pictorial form. This I call an 'Impression'.

2. A largely unconscious, spontaneous expression of inner character, non-material in nature. This I call an 'Improvisation'.

3. An expression of slowly formed inner feeling, tested and worked over repeatedly and almost pedantically. This I call 'Composition'. Reason, consciousness, purpose, play an overwhelming part. But of calculation nothing appears: only feeling.

Williams, like his friends, worked in all three modes, singly, successively, and at times combining them. Out of Kandinsky's careful distinction the American artist evolved a broadly-based composite structure, able to bear the 'total availability of materials, and freest association in the measure' of which Williams spoke as the distinctively American spirit in art.[3]

Having abandoned the borrowed nineteenth-century 'Composition' of his youth, Williams began with the 'Impression'. From 1913 to 1916 the portrait and the pastoral were his best media. If one were to turn for an analogy in painting for the poems in the collection *Al Que Quiere*, it would be to the Ashcan school of realism, in which the dignity of human life was rendered by impressionistic means. Williams' 'townspeople', although not products of the East Side slums, were similarly treated; for example, the old man who collects dog-lime from the gutter but whose walk is more majestic than that of the Episcopal minister.[4]

The new 'Composition' Williams did not become familiar with

---

[1] Letter from Hartley to Stieglitz [August 1913] (CtY).
[2] W. Kandinsky, *Concerning the Spiritual in Art*, ed. Robert Motherwell (N.Y., 1947), p. 77.
[3] Cited below, p. 114.
[4] *The Collected Earlier Poems of William Carlos Williams* (Norfolk, Conn., 1951), p. 124.

until Demuth returned from France in 1915. In an early draft of the *Autobiography* Williams said he learnt to understand Cézanne through Demuth,[1] and Demuth's experience in Paris was now supplemented by the arrival of the co-author of a book on Cubism, Albert Gleizes.[2] What aesthetic discussion took place at Grantwood, the little artists' colony near the Palisades, was mainly in painterly terms. The poet Alfred Kreymborg started a magazine, *The Glebe*, with Man Ray and Samuel Halpert, both artists, and Alanson Hartpence, who worked at the Daniel Gallery in New York. Pound urged Kreymborg to seek Williams' collaboration. In Walter Arensberg's studio on West Sixty-seventh Street the French contributors to a clutch of short-lived art magazines were assembling. Stieglitz's magazine *291*, which was a potent force in Grantwood,[3] would be supplemented by *The Blindman* and *The Soil*. When Arensberg provided money for a successor to *The Glebe* called *Others* the group was decidedly Franco–American, and as much painterly as literary in its interests (see Plate 3).

Williams' poem 'To a Solitary Disciple',[4] published in *Others* in February 1916, is a lesson in appreciation given by a Frenchman ('Rather notice, mon cher') on a Cubist-realist painting, which has for its subject a church with a hexagonal spire such as Demuth painted in his home town of Lancaster, Pennsylvania. Thus Gleizes explains Demuth to Williams. Since Cubism represented historically a reaction against Impressionism the stylistic element stressed was design or composition at the structural level of line rather than at the formal level of colour. The disciple is asked to notice rather

> that the moon is
> tilted above
> the point of the steeple
> than that its color
> is shell-pink.

Shell-pink, and turquoise, are tints perfectly married to the particular lines in question, and have nothing to do with time of day. Gleizes divided realism thus into two kinds, which he called 'superficial' and

---

[1] Ms. 'Autobiography', p. 40 (CtY).
[2] Albert Gleizes and Jean Metzinger, *Cubism* (London, 1913).
[3] Letter from Kreymborg to Stieglitz, 17 July 1915 (CtY).
[4] *Collected Earlier Poems*, p. 167.

'profound': 'The former claims the Impressionists – Monet, Sisley, etc. – and the latter Cézanne'.[1] Imagism, as Amy Lowell and John Gould Fletcher understood it, was impressionistic. In 1913 Williams had not disagreed with this view of Imagism; in fact, he had warmly approved of Ford Madox Ford's work in *Poetry*.[2] Imagism, as Pound named it, had in terms of painterly analogies begun with Whistler; Demuth tried to write in a Whistlerian vein.[3] But it was left to Williams to pursue the immediately contemporary American painters rather than the recently successful ones for a poetic analogy. In this sense he was genuinely 'solitary'. Demuth, despite his Steinian poem in *The Blindman*,[4] and Hartley with his taste for Ernest Dowson, Lionel Johnson, and Francis Thompson, were writers to one side of the local effort which Williams was making. Their sensibilities were more decadent than dynamic.

In the twenties Williams' favourite painter was the Cubist, Juan Gris:[5]

Here is a shutter, a bunch of grapes, a sheet of music, a picture of sea and mountains (particularly fine) which the onlooker is not for a moment permitted to witness as an 'illusion'. One thing laps over on the other, the cloud laps over on the shutter, the bunch of grapes is part of the handle of the guitar, the mountain and sea are obviously not 'the mountain and sea', but a picture of the mountain and sea.

The painting by Gris to which Williams refers is one he saw in black-and-white reproduction in *Broom*.[6] Gris contrasted his method with Cézanne's by saying that Cézanne turned a bottle into a cylinder, whereas he, Gris, made a bottle out of a cylinder.[7] Williams' sense of Gris' idea of imaginative reality came from his reading of a text published in two parts in *the transatlantic review*, in which Gris explained that the architectural abstraction of the elements in a picture must be explored by the painter as if he were his own spectator:[8]

---

[1] *Cubism*, p. 13.
[2] Letter to Viola Baxter Jordan, 11 June 1914 (CtY).
[3] See Charles Demuth, 'The Azure Adder', *The Glebe* 3 (December 1913).
[4] 'For Richard Mutt', *The Blindman* 2 (May 1917).
[5] William Carlos Williams, *Spring and All* (Dijon, 1923), pp. 34–5.
[6] *Broom* II, 3 (January 1922), 264.
[7] D. H. Kahnweiler, *Juan Gris*, trans. D. Cooper (London, 1947), p. 138.
[8] Juan Gris, 'Des Possibilités de la Peinture', *the transatlantic review* I, 6 (June 1924), 482–6; II, 1 (July 1924), 75–9. Translation from Kahnweiler, *Juan Gris*, pp. 142–3.

Until the work is completed, he must remain ignorant of its appearance as a whole. To copy a preconceived appearance is like copying the appearance of a model.

From this it is clear that the subject does not materialize in the appearance of the picture, but that the subject, in materializing, gives the picture its appearance.

As Williams understood him, 'Singly he says that the actual is the drawing of the face – and so the face borrowing of the drawing – by lack of copying and lack of a burden to the story – is real.'[1]

But if 'Composition' as plastic poetry began for Williams with the *Others* group, and increased as he became aware of Gris' work in reproduction in *Broom* and in *The Little Review*, Kandinsky's second possibility, 'Improvisation', must have also attracted him. The improvisation was what Williams, as he confessed much later, liked to do most of all.[2] Valéry Larbaud attributed his interest in it to Rimbaud, whose *Illuminations* Helen Rootham had translated,[3] but as Williams informed René Taupin, his knowledge of French culture was visual and not literary.[4] Hartley could just as well have provided the subtitle to *Kora in Hell: Improvisations* through Kandinsky. He told Alfred Stieglitz that in both his writing and his painting he tried to seize 'the mysticity of the moment'.[5] A little later, in the context of Amy Lowell's anthology *Six French Poets*, he spoke of making what he called ' "portrait" intimations, being abstract treatments of persons or maybe places, all of which is leading up to some real abstraction later'.[6] For Williams, the improvisations led up to *The Great American Novel*, *January: A Novelette in Prose*, and the unpublished manuscripts 'Rome' and 'Man Orchid', the latter written in 1946.[7] Throughout his career he worked at impressions, improvisations, and compositions. In *Paterson* they became as one – the 'Composition' of a man's whole life.

---

[1] W. C. Williams, *A Novelette and Other Prose* (Toulon, 1932), p. 22.
[2] Letter to Jim Higgins, undated.
[3] Valéry Larbaud, 'Lettres Américaines' [review of *The Great American Novel*], *La Revue Européenne* II, 9 (1 November 1923), 65–70;66.
[4] René Taupin, *L'Influence du Symbolisme Français sur la Poésie Américaine de 1910 à 1920* (Paris, 1920), p. 280.
[5] Letter from Hartley to Stieglitz [June 1915] (CtY).
[6] Letter from Hartley to Stieglitz, 2 August 1917 (CtY).
[7] 'Rome' [c. 1926] (NBuU); 'Man Orchid' [1946] (CtY).

Science and Poetry

In 1919, Albert Gleizes, discussing the growth of American culture, suggested that the processes of development were in no way analogous to those in European countries. He maintained that the transplanted immigrants could not be expected to forget their traditions and become as simple as the aborigines of a lost continent, newly discovered; they naturally reproduced the outward forms of their native countries without allowing for the conditions which determined them. Because America borrowed so widely from the various art-movements in Europe without regard for the special reasons which provoked them in individual countries a generalised idea of modern art had developed. America suffered under the illusion that Europe was a homogeneous unity; 'A generalized ideal is nourished on illusion, and American art is generalization.'[1] This generalisation of the European situation had, according to Gleizes, produced an 'impersonal' quality in American art.

The nature of this impersonality Gleizes did not satisfactorily define. He could have, if he had wished, detected a specifically individual or local quality in the watercolours of John Marin or Charles Demuth, or in the work of Stuart Davis and Marsden Hartley, but he did not. Nevertheless, his basic impression that European art-movements were unrelated to the American scene, and therefore likely to be compounded, or confused more likely, in an aesthetic amalgam of European tendencies in art, was apt. Kandinsky in Europe was exceptional in offering his three possibilities; perhaps because he was a Russian rather than a European and was therefore possessed pedagogically of an intellectual urge towards federation even in art. The background of general revolt in art inspired, in any case, a sense of fellow-feeling in which Expressionist and Constructivist painters, the Blaue Reiter group and the Cubists, thought of themselves as of one movement – the 'modern' movement. Williams, as it happened, was acquainted with a mixed group; mystical Cubists like Gleizes, Dadaists like Marcel Duchamp and Jean Crotti, and Expressionists like Hartley and Marin. In a period when he was producing improvisations on American history and daily occurrences, he was nevertheless

[1] A. Gleizes, 'The Impersonality of American Art', *Playboy* 4–5 (1919), 25–6.

sedulously studying such a profoundly constructive, or 'synthetic', Cubist as Gris. Furthermore, in presenting his grasp of Gris' aesthetic the style of *Spring and All* proceeded in an improvisatory manner which employed Dadaist typographical jokes. In this sense Gleizes was right. Williams' work was a composite plagiarism or generalised imitation of European innovations. While not being a painter himself he had joined the ranks of the painters who were poets 'on the side'; *Abseitigen* like Kurt Schwitters, Raoul Hausmann, Hans Arp, and Lajos Kassák.[1]

The advantages in taking as an aesthetic point of reference the European modern movement in art rather than the English tradition in poetry were very great for an American bent on releasing the native ground to the imagination. Williams' well-known aversion for T.S. Eliot was not merely personal envy of the success of *The Waste Land*, but a rejection of the philosophy, including the philosophy of art, of a literary tradition in which he felt he could play no part. He was persuaded, furthermore, that no American faced with his local conditions and his own temperament could find a use for Eliot. A comparison between *The Waste Land* and Williams' lyric, 'By the road to the contagious hospital', published within months of each other,[2] suggests how far apart in their sense of the ground Eliot and Williams really were. Eliot in London was abstracting spiritual values, or an absence of them, from the air; Williams, in the physical waste-land of his own part of New Jersey, detected an irrepressible force in the soil.

In the chapter 'To Rome' of *A Voyage to Pagany*, Williams' character Evans tells how he made a furious attempt to penetrate the problem of reality by approaching the medium of writing sexually: 'It was in Rome, in fact, during these days, that he most made a wife of his writing, his writing – that desire to free himself from his besetting reactions by transcending them – thus driving off his torments and going often quietly to sleep thereafter.'[3] The manuscript which resulted from those days was the climax to his improvisatory period, although Williams did add to it in the years between 1924, when it was begun in Rome, and 1926. Its basic theme was a definition of clarity of

---

[1] In March 1924 when Williams was staying at 20 Rathaustrasse, Vienna, Kassák sent him Arp's address (postcard from Kassák to Williams, 29 March 1924 [NBuU]).

[2] *Collected Earlier Poems*, p. 241; first published in *The Dial* LXXIV, 6 (June 1923), 562. *The Waste Land* also appeared first in *The Dial* LXXIII, 5 (November 1922), [473]–85.

[3] W.C.Williams, *A Voyage to Pagany* (N.Y., 1928), pp. 145–6.

understanding as motion. Weininger, with his will towards clarifica-
tion, was described by Williams as possessing the lucid mind of 'a good
bird-dog'. The overall image of the theme was again the sensual
approach to material: clarity was 'motion under way'; sex was of no
significance 'except as pure motion'; knowledge was nothing but 'the
pleasure of motion of relief'. Writing, of which Williams had made a
wife, was orgasmic; 'there is no writing but a moment that is and dies
and is again wearing the body to nothing'.[1]

He was in revolt against confusion of all kinds; in education, in
morality, and in literature. The endless renewal of force which Eliot
regarded as blind, Williams saw as the only road out of confusion. For
Williams the image of reality was a river of pleasure running through
a man's body. Yet, in another formulation, the image included a sense
of detachment: 'There is escape only by moments in walking out from
a self and in saying it was.'

The problem of reality, as of writing, seemed to lie in the relation
of motion to space and time. Williams' concept of motion was a day
spent rushing from one house to another in pursuit of his work. Space–
time was psychologically simplified as place, that small area identified
by the name of Rutherford, consisting of the groups of material objects,
including persons, with whom he came in contact according to the
minutes of a clock.

Writing to a new friend Williams showed he felt the need to distance
himself from the incessant motion, or to take advantage of the moments
of relief to lead himself consciously along a new path in writing. He
needed to introduce an element of self-observation, in short. But Eliot
could not provide the indication he needed:[2]

I must say Eliot inspires me with dread – since I see him finished and I do not find
myself stepping beyond him. Since I cannot compete with him in knowledge of
philosophy, nor even in technical knowledge of the conned examples of English
poetry which he seems to know well – what is left for me but to fall back upon
words? There they are just as they always were and the art of using them is no
more dependant upon philosophic catastrophes or past examples of writing than
are the words themselves...
  The words are there quite apart from any theory of arranging them...
  I imagine Eliot feels as frustrated as I do, at times or more often than I do ever.

[1] 'Rome' (NBuU).
[2] Letter to John Riordan, 23 December 1925.

45

Through words he has at least formalized his 'escape', but I'll be damned if I see why we need all of us fall into his trap, reversing his process and by swilling his words into us arrive in the end at his brand of despair.

It is no use going in bull-headed either, blindly hoping by slopping about in vers libre to write 'poetry'. It's been tried. Nor do we have to wait for new discoveries in philosophy to be at least adept. This is where McAlmon comes in. This is what fascinates me about him. I find something actually of writing in his stuff. It is not just setting it down and letting it go at that. He actually stands outside of Eliot as a writer, weak as he is. So does Gertie. She stands outside of Eliot by strength of knowledge outside of philosophy.

There is no satisfactory philosophy of art, no more than there is a satisfactory philosophy of a stone. Science, at least, as you say stays on the fact. So does Bob. Eliot is a romantic philosotaster. You cannot end art so. But he is a master of his kind of work. He is a definite obstacle which it is not easy to surmount...

For myself I don't know what to do. I must write poetry. That's where the opportunity lies. The answer to Eliot, as to Pound, is careful, thoroughly organized work, that discovers beyond them...

The person to whom Williams addressed these remarks, John Riordan, was a young engineer who was a member of the A. R. Orage writing class in New York. Williams was immediately attracted to him by his capacity for abstract thought. It was a quality of mind quite different from Williams' own ('...is my satisfaction merely that being a pole distant from me you confirm my fixities?').[1]

In an essay on Marianne Moore which owed a great deal to Juan Gris Williams made an allusion to mathematics: 'A course in mathematics would not be wasted on a poet, or a reader of poetry, if he remember no more from it than the geometric principle of the intersection of loci: from all angles lines converging and crossing established points.'[2] In the essay on Poe, which would appear within a few weeks of opening the correspondence with Riordan, Williams had spoken of the 'trigonometric measurements of literary form'.[3]

Poe's view that the highest order of the imaginative mind was mathematical coincided exactly with Gris' interest in the Golden Section. Yet John Riordan's approach was not initially as a mathematician, although he eventually wrote several books on mathematics, but as a member of Orage's writing class. He was interested in

---

[1] Letter to John Riordan, 16 November 1925.
[2] *Selected Essays*, p. 122. The essay, which appeared in *The Dial* (May 1925), is misdated 1931.
[3] Letter from Riordan to Williams, 25 June 1926 (NBuU).

Williams' work because it seemed to him that, 'The difficulties in writing a poem are as immense as those of writing a philosophy, and when anyone begins to know anything about what we call "emotions" and "nerve adjustments" it will be found that the structure of your poems (written intuitively) is as rigid as any mathematical solution.'[1] Behind this idea were both the Gurdjieffian discipline of observation without analysis or intellectuality in which Orage had trained his students, and the mathematician's interest in the theory of relativity. In the very letter to Riordan in which Williams confessed he did not know how to proceed further he asked him to send him a book by C. P. Steinmetz on relativity. In the spring of 1926 they discussed this subject thoroughly. In August Riordan sent Williams an essay he had written on his work, 'The Theory and Practice of Precision Poetry'.[2]

In this essay Riordan suggested that an attitude of objective participation between writer and reader would sharpen emotional focus and activate the imagination. Instead of the reader remaining simply an attentive recipient of the writer's conveyed intentions, or a mere spectator of his incomprehensible afflatus, a new relation could be achieved. He referred specifically to A. N. Whitehead's analysis of perception, identifying three relationships in the act of perception; the observer, position in space, and point in time. Riordan noted that mechanistic science had done its best to eliminate the human observer by means of invariable measuring instruments, attempting the maximum reduction of accidental or casual experience by abstraction:

Aesthetics to enjoy a similar clarity in taking its place beside science toward a comprehensive signification of man in his relation to the universe must assume the field science is unable to enter, functioning *to reduce the contingent relationships within a percipient observer's bodily life.*

In this way he stated as the function of art, and of poetry in particular, a new kind of precision, equivalent to scientific method but directed towards objectivising experience. To do this the writer had to become his own reader, a functioning perceiver observing himself in action. Riordan suggested that in *Kora in Hell* Williams had worked, 'without and outside of "scientific accuracy" – he made no attempt within the texture of any poem to relate his perceptions to the body of existing

[1] Letter from Riordan to Williams, 25 June 1926 (NBuU).
[2] I am grateful to Mr Riordan for giving me his manuscript.

knowledge or to codify or classify – but he did employ a rigorous emotional precision, i.e., he defined emotions emotionally'. In other words, Williams wrote with the aid of that impersonal part of himself, the reader; he observed himself in his daily activity in collaboration with another accurate observer.

Earlier Williams had told Riordan, '...you tend to run off into matters concerning measurement of your own adjustment rather than to absorption in the representation of your state of being. Of course both are the same – but one must DO it'.[1] Now he began to be interested in the measurement of adjustment as a way of consciously controlling his representation of being. In March 1926 he proposed to Riordan that they should write a 'Modern Prosody' together. Measurement at one level involved the practical concern of a new metre, and at the level of a general aesthetic implied a philosophy of the percipient act. In the former, Steinmetz on relativity was applied to the poetic foot; in the latter, Whitehead's *Science and the Modern World*, with which Riordan presented Williams in December, offered the new discoveries in philosophy for which Williams had been unwilling to wait.[2]

Steinmetz's book offered a general idea of the theory of relativity by means of an analogy such as the following one to illustrate the relativity of length and duration:[3]

The train stands on the track. I measure it from the outside, you measure it from the inside, and we find the same length. We compare our watches and find them to go alike. Now the train starts and runs at high speed. While it is passing me I measure its length again and find it shorter than before, while at the same time, you, traveling with the train, measure it again from the inside and find the same length we both found when the train was standing still. But while passing over it you measure a piece of the track and find it shorter than I find it when measuring it from the outside. While you pass me on the train I compare your watch with mine and find your watch slower than mine. But, at the same time, you, comparing your watch with mine, while passing me, find MY watch slower. Then the train stops, and both our measurements agree again. What then is the

[1] Letter to John Riordan, 26 January 1926.
[2] In the inscribed copy Williams wrote: 'Finished reading it at sea, Sept. 26., 1927 – A milestone surely in my career, should I have the force & imagination to go on with my work' (NjFDU).
[3] Charles Proteus Steinmetz, *Four Lectures on Relativity and Space* (N.Y. and London, 1923), pp. 6–7.

'true' length of the train and the 'true' time – that which I get when measuring the train while it passes me at high speed or that which you get while moving with the train? Both, and neither. It means that length is not a fixed and invariable property of a body, but depends on the condition under which it is observed.

From such an illustration Williams derived his concept of the relative length of a line of verse, 'the variable foot'. If the poet was analogous to the person riding the train and the reader analogous to the observer beside the track, it was clear that according to the theory of relativity the length of track (the line of verse) and the elapsement of time (the measure) were relative to the conditions of their observation. There could, in fact, be no 'true' length of line, nor a 'true' duration of time. These depended upon the relative speed of the moving body, in this case the projected voice of the poet. The length and duration, therefore, of a line was variable and not constant.

In describing the characteristics of space Steinmetz approached the problem again in terms which Williams thereafter applied to the poem:[1]

From what we have discussed, therefore, it follows that the metric axioms do not rigidly hold in physical space, and figures cannot be moved in space without stretching or contracting when passing from a point of space to a point of different curvature. Measurements and dimensional relations, therefore, are not rigidly possible in physical space, and strictly, we cannot speak of the length or the size of a body, as we cannot measure it by bringing the measure to it, because the length and shape of the measure change when it is moved through space.

The relative measure, with its unit the variable foot, were thus derived as a new poetic concept of measurement rivalling the fixed metric axioms or metres of traditional verse. *Vers libre* as Williams resolved to pursue it was only relatively free, and yet could only be relatively fixed. Thus Steinmetz made it clear to Williams that space, time and motion were relative phenomena, and that the laws of nature were universal whether applied to the speeding train or the moving poem.

In his chapter 'The Romantic Reaction', in *Science and the Modern World*, Whitehead explained Wordsworth's moral rejection of science and Tennyson's attempts to come to terms with it as the result of a dichotomy between the mechanism of the old scientific realism based on invariable instruments, and the view of man as a self-adjusting organism. Whitehead proposed a theory of 'organic mechanism' in

[1] *Ibid.* p. 121.

which the general laws of mechanistic science were modified according to the organic situation in which they were objectivised. This view, the basis of his objectivist philosophy, was of course derived from his understanding of the theory of relativity. The organic situation consisted in the meaning of the general laws relative to a particular location in space and point in time. The purpose of objectivist philosophy was to bridge 'the gap between science and that fundamental intuition of mankind which finds its expression in poetry and its practical exemplification in the presuppositions of daily life'.[1] The choice of poetry as the expression of that intuition confirmed Williams' sense of having discovered an analogue in philosophy by which he could pursue his lust for poetry with a degree of control.

Whitehead presented the objectivist – or the precisionist, as Riordan called him – in contrast to the subjectivist. Subjectivism consisted in 'the expression of the individual peculiarities of the cognitive act', whereas objectivism began from quite a different standpoint:[2]

that the actual elements perceived by our senses are *in themselves* the elements of a common world; and that this world is a complex of things, including indeed our acts of cognition, but transcending them.

According to this point of view the things experienced are to be distinguished from our knowledge of them. So far as there is dependence, the *things* pave the way for the *cognition*, rather than *vice versa*. But the point is that the actual things experienced enter a common world which transcends knowledge, though it includes knowledge. The intermediate subjectivists would hold that the things experienced only indirectly enter into the common world by reason of their dependence on the subject who is cognising. The objectivist holds that the things experienced and the cognisant subject enter into the common world on equal terms.

The common world of which Whitehead speaks is, of course, only uncommonly apprehended, and in his terms only by the objectivist. He conceived man as an object functioning within an arena filled with objects of similar orders such as other higher animals, and of widely different orders such as rocks, stones, and trees. Thus Riordan's original introduction to the theme of precisionism, or objectivism taken from Whitehead's view of the percipient act, presented itself to Williams as a valid approach to the poem:[3]

[1] A. N. Whitehead, *Science and the Modern World* (N.Y., 1948), p. 139.
[2] *Ibid*. pp. 128–9.   [3] Letter to Louis Grudin, 26 January 1930.

I see no reason why a scientist or philosopher should be ignorant of the simple fundamentals of the artist's dilemmas, in fact they may sometimes, quite accidentally even, serve very nicely the artist's purpose. So may an artist and so should an artist regard the other human interests of a major sort.

However, his attitude towards science was far less instinctive than his feeling for painting. The feeling he had for Riordan as a person was largely responsible for the attention he paid to the younger man's scientific interests. Riordan had offered him a scientific analogy leading to the philosophic attitude of an objectivist like Whitehead, which suggested that art had a function which science could not fulfil; the precise definitions of the emotions in their relation to experience, by means of observing oneself in the act of experiencing the world. There was no question, however, of becoming a scientist:[1]

Certainly the idea that there was a man named Williams currently absorbed in the role of poet was repugnant to Williams; he had no other role. The doctor had been foregone, and everything rode on the poet. A recasting would have been disastrous; indeed there are echoes of this in the distrust I earned from him from what he regarded as my 'devotion to science'.

In fact in the next three years Williams launched a series of attacks on science, as well as philosophy and religion. He accumulated a lengthy manuscript entitled 'The Embodiment of Knowledge',[2] which only found an outlet in talks and in private letters, and publication in the first of his essays on Gertrude Stein. The essay on Stein concluded with a proposition which clearly reflected Whitehead and Riordan, but widened the attack on the insufficiencies of science to include the humanities: 'To be most useful to humanity, or to anything else for that matter, an art, writing, must stay art, not seeking to be science, history, the humanities, or anything else it has been made to carry in the past'.[3] Writing, in short, had its own logic and its own contribution to make to knowledge. 'The Logic of Modern Literature', a title Williams took for a talk on Joyce and Stein in 1931, began 'toward that point not to be predetermined where movement is blocked (by the end of logic perhaps)'.[4] Williams' objection to science, philosophy, and

---

[1] Letter from John Riordan to the author, 9 June 1966.
[2] 'The Embodiment of Knowledge: (first writing)', [1928–9] (CtY).
[3] *Selected Essays*, p. 120.
[4] *Ibid.* p. 118.

religion was expressed in terms of two images, 'lumber' and 'burden'.[1] Life at any moment was movement unencumbered for the man who would take advantage of it:[2]

And to him, unless he is a fool, his life is a thing at any moment absolute and perfect as a tree or a stone. And the sooner he regards it objectively as such with composure and assurance (not with blind conceit) the sooner he will be of use to himself and his world.

[1] *Ibid.* pp. 115–16.
[2] Letter to Louis Grudin, 26 January 1930.

1 [*The Passaic River*] by William Carlos Williams: oil on board, *c.* 1912, 14″ × 10″

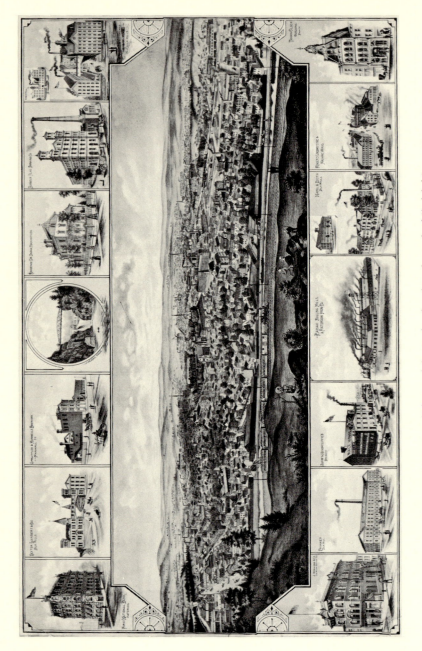

2　*Paterson, N.J. 1880*: lithograph by Packard and Butler Ltd, Philadelphia; $33\frac{1}{4}'' \times 20\frac{1}{4}''$

4

Precisionist Poetry

—

The Objectivist Co-operative

In the spring of 1930 there appeared in New York *The Last Imagist Anthology*, edited by Richard Aldington. Williams was a contributor; Pound, who was alienated from Aldington and resented the resurrection of a movement he considered his very own, was not. In the autumn of that year, however, Louis Zukofsky, who was Pound's *Exile* representative in America, and whom Williams had first met in March 1928 at Pound's instigation, was invited by Harriet Monroe to edit an anthology of contemporary work for *Poetry*. Miss Monroe doubtless felt that the publicity that an aspect of poetic solidarity would occasion could do her magazine no harm.[1] Reluctantly Zukofsky agreed to present such an aspect. The previous January he had written an essay on Charles Reznikoff using two terms 'sincerity' and 'objectification', and now he gave his issue of Miss Monroe's little magazine the title '*Objectivists*' *1931*.[2] When the anthology re-appeared later as a separate publication Zukofsky made it clear that, 'The quotes around "objectivists" distinguish between its particular meaning in the Program of Feb. *Poetry*, and the philosophical etiquette associated with objectivist'.[3] According to one of the contributors to the anthology, Basil Bunting, 'the true construction of Louis' title for the volume is "The anthology collected by an objectivist." He was describing himself, and not the rest of us. Williams wasn't fond of manifestoes, and I detested them.'[4] But as Zukofsky's disclaimer showed he did not consider himself an objectivist in anything but a lexical sense. He now states that

---

[1] Letter from Louis Zukofsky to Mary Ellen Solt, 24 February 1961.
[2] *Poetry* XXXVII, 5 (February 1931).
[3] *An 'Objectivists' Anthology*, ed. Louis Zukofsky (Le Beausset, Var, 1932), p. 9.
[4] Letter from Basil Bunting to the author, 28 February 1965.

he had not read Whitehead at that time,[1] although he omits to mention that Williams, with whom he was then corresponding on poetic matters, had. It is interesting to note that of all the poets represented in the anthology, including the editor himself, so far as we can now tell only Williams had a first-hand knowledge of Whitehead's term.

Nevertheless, there was some degree of acquiescence among the poets of the anthology in *Poetry*. Carl Rakosi says that the title was approved by him before it was used,[2] and it may be assumed that in the short time available before the deadline of publication Zukofsky cleared it with some others. For most of the poets concerned it was an embarrassment to be associated with an aesthetic programme at all, although Zukofsky had clearly offered one; they tended to regard the anthology exactly as Miss Monroe had wished, as a sign of collaboration.

Before long objectivism became associated with this spirit of collaboration in the practical form of a press. When George Oppen returned from France, where he had had experience of private presses publishing among other things Williams' *A Novelette in Prose* and *An 'Objectivists' Anthology*, he agreed with Reznikoff that if they were to launch a new series of books from New York it would be wasteful not to take advantage of whatever momentum the name had gathered. Thus the various suggestions made during the summer of 1933, 'The Writers-Publishers Inc.', 'Writers Extant', 'Cooperative Publishers', were rejected in favour of The Objectivist Press.

The first book to be issued under its imprint was, fittingly, Williams' *Collected Poems* in 1934. The author advanced 250 dollars towards the cost of production and was later repaid in full; Rakosi, Oppen, René Taupin, Tibor Serly, and a Frank Heineman, one of Zukofsky's students at the University of Wisconsin, contributed between them a comparable sum. Reznikoff contributed the heavy postage, and Zukofsky the heavy labour. Thereafter, the poets paid individually for their own books.[3]

The Objectivist Press was therefore a co-operative publishing venture rather than an aesthetic movement. But still the question remains

[1] A remark volunteered at a talk given at Yale University, 8 March 1967.
[2] Letter from Carl Rakosi to the author, 3 December 1966.
[3] Letter from Louis Zukofsky to Mary Ellen Solt, 24 February 1961.

as to what degree of aesthetic agreement there was among the share-holders. George Oppen summarised it as follows:[1]

We were all very much concerned with poetic form, and form not merely as texture, but as the shape that makes a poem possible to grasp. (Would we all have thought that a satisfactory way to put it?) 'Objectivist' meant, not an objective viewpoint, but to objectify the poem, to make the poem an object. Meant form.

Zukofsky's Program offered 'sincerity' or clarity of detail on the one hand, and 'objectification' or the making of the poetic object on the other. The first was related to Imagism's unblurred image; objectivism also stressed the visual apperception of reality. The second was related to the geniunely new concern with aural movement as the configuration of a poem.

Photographic Imagism

In the Objectivist Program the first lexical definition of 'objective' was taken from optics: 'The lens brings the rays from an object to a focus.'[2] The process by which images are produced on specially prepared surfaces, by means of an *objectif* through which light passes, provided an underlying analogy for the new poetry. Photography as an art, as well as a mechanical process, played an extremely important part in the revived emphasis on the image.

Williams' relations with the 'straight' photographers of the Stieglitz school had always been close. In 1923 he had met Charles Sheeler, the photographer and painter, for the first time, at Matthew Josephson's house,[3] in Grantwood days, when the influence of Stieglitz at the famous Photo-Secession Gallery at 291 Fifth Avenue was at its height. But in 1929 there was a new, and special opportunity for Williams to review the work of Stieglitz and Paul Strand in the very gallery which Stieglitz had told Williams he had named for *In The American Grain*. In the spring of 1932 a Stieglitz retrospective show and a show by Strand were presented at An American Place, which was opened in 1929. In July 1932 Williams recommended to Zukofsky the Stieglitz show and one of the European photographers at the Julien Levy Gallery.[4]

[1] Letter from George Oppen to Mary Ellen Solt, post-marked 18 February 1961.
[2] *Poetry* XXXVII, 5 (February 1931), 268.
[3] Letter from Matthew Josephson to the author, 29 January 1964.
[4] Letter to Louis Zukofsky, 17 February 1932 (CtY).

Photography meant much more for the American artist than for his European counterpart.

Photography's acceptance as a fine art in America was undoubtedly due to Stieglitz. Strand, writing in terms of the moral determination to accept both the industrialised soil and mechanical invention, provided a broad, theoretical American base for the medium. In *Seven Arts* he offered photography as the medium in which Stieglitz rendered New York, and Clarence White presented the American small town – 'by an intense interest in the life of which they were really a part, they reached through a national to a universal expression'.[1] The national was, in Williams' terms, too large a unit but the concept of contact with the soil was central to Strand's thought. As Williams himself noted: 'The photographic camera and what it could do were peculiarly well suited to a place where the immediate and the actual were under official neglect'.[2]

In *Broom* Strand, very much in accordance with the magazine's preoccupation with the machine in art and industry, asked whether science and artistic expression were at last coming together. Futurist hysteria was not the American attitude; 'We in America are not fighting, as it may be natural to do in Italy, away from the tentacles of a medieval tradition towards a neurasthenic embrace of the new God. We have it with us and upon us with a vengeance, and we will have to do something about it eventually.'[3] The photographer was playing a particular role in the artistic control of the new God, the Machine. By means of a science of optics, a chemistry of light acting upon sensitive papers and plates, and a rigorous concept of craftsmanship in the medium, the photographer could indeed link science with qualitative expression; 'He has evolved through the conscious creative control of this particular phase of the machine a new method of perceiving the life of objectivity and of recording it'.[4] It is in the practical results of such a broad base for photography as an American art that its influence upon the other arts may be best gauged.

There was a Stieglitz story which Williams often repeated, about two doors in a wall. One had 'This Way to See God' over it, and over the

[1] P. Strand, 'Photography', *Seven Arts* II (August 1917), 524–6;525.
[2] *Selected Essays*, p. 160.
[3] P. Strand, 'Photography and the New God', *Broom* III, 4 (November 1922), 252–8;257.
[4] *Ibid.* p. 258.

the other was the legend 'This Way to Hear a Lecture about God'. The crowd, in Stieglitz's estimation, would always take the less challenging alternative. The implication was that a courageous artist – a straight photographer in particular – would reject the lecture in favour of the confrontation.

The word 'straight' as used by the photographers of Stieglitz's day, was described as an absence of manipulation in the printing process. The print was a straight one in that it was taken direct, without enlargement, local shading, or retouching, from a negative which was equally free from human interference.[1] The intention was to rid the photographic medium of painterly techniques. But the moral fervour, which accompanied this devotion to the inherent capacities of the machine camera to render precisely what has been visualised by the operator, later invested 'straight' with a meaning which suggested a complete aesthetic; moral vision and technical honesty were inseparable in Stieglitz's view. The reality of life, as well as of God, implied an unswerving confrontation with the facts. Thus the weight of straight lay not only on the printing process, the post-visualised phase, but also on the pre-visualising phase before the negative was made. Permitting only a mechanical process as intermediary, the straight print was a direct transcription of the image perceived by the photographer.

The dead eye of the camera is passionless. Its mechanism admits a minimum of light under the strictest control; the aperture set, at the hands of the straight photographers, as small as possible to achieve the sharpest images. The accumulation of details by means of this mechanism was one response to the soil; a desert as much industrial as agrarian but as inescapable as the 'squallid, horrid American Desart' of which Cotton Mather wrote.[2] The Puritans, as Williams presents them, were also makers of detailed images, unequalled in their uncompromising vision of the facts. What Williams praised them for was, 'their tough littleness and weight of many to carry through the cold...if they were pure it was more since they had nothing in them of fulfilment than because of positive virtues'.[3]

Like the camera-eye they were empty; released only by the dictates

---

[1] See Beaumont Newhall, *The History of Photography* (N.Y., 1964), pp. 111–33.
[2] Cited in *In the American Grain*, p. 82.
[3] *Ibid.* pp. 65, 63.

of a soul which was merely a 'pale negative'. They 'looked black at the world and damning its perfections praised a zero in themselves'.[1] Yet, if their emphasis had fallen on the positive of their own toughness, and the weight of the accumulated commonwealth, their souls might, even then, have grown as seeds planted in new soil, rather than have been disembodied as spirit. In Keyserling's terms, they had denied the locality in their imaginations, even while working it hard with their hands. The consequences, according to Williams, were violence and despair, perversion and murder:[2]

Today it is a generation of gross knownothingism, of blackened churches where hymns groan like chants from stupefied jungles, a generation universally eager to barter permanent values (the hope of an aristocracy) in return for opportunist material advantages, a generation hating those whom it obeys.

It required an eye as coldly efficient as a Puritan's – or a camera's – properly to register the American scene in the thirties. The inhuman clarity of the lens, the objective, in the controlling hands of the human observer pre-visualising and composing the image on his ground-glass, could render even the ugly beautiful. In referring to Know-Nothingism Williams carried his attack on religious perversion into the field of social and political murder. The Know-Nothings were the Ku Klux Klan of the 1840s, obsessed with offences against morality, which as 100% Americans they attributed to the influence of Irish and German Catholic immigrants.[3] In a state like New Jersey, first in the Union in concentration of immigrants where less than 40% of the people had parents who had been born in the United States,[4] Williams, himself a first-generation United-Stateser, sided with the contemporary victims of the Know-Nothings. A new Puritan, capable of a clear vision of the social facts, was needed. Walker Evans responded, as did other photographers employed by the Farm Security Administration.

Charles Sheeler and the Shakers

In the early thirties the Downtown Gallery in New York, run by Edith

[1] *Ibid.* p. 65.
[2] *Ibid.* p. 68.
[3] Morris Schonbach, *Radicals and Visionaries: A History of Dissent in New Jersey* (Princeton, N.J., 1964), pp. 27–33.
[4] John T. Cunningham, *New Jersey: America's Main Road* (Garden City, N.Y., 1966), p. 233.

Halpert, was a place where Williams would meet Zukofsky and Sheeler. It was the home of the so-called Precisionist view in painting. The craftsmanship valued so highly there extended in a tradition back to a folk-collection of the people known as Shakers. Edward and Faith Andrews, the great Shaker collectors and historians, had just begun to publish articles. Constance Rourke, Sheeler's first biographer, also wrote on them.[1] Williams was not the first American writer to interest himelf in the Shakers; Artemus Ward, Horace Greeley, Melville, Hawthorne, Whitman, and Howells were all attracted to their communities. But if it was curiosity as to the nature of their communal and educational Utopianism which drew the earlier writers, Sheeler and Williams, like Constance Rourke, were more in search of an indigenous artistic tradition. Their approach was not literary but visual.

The difference between the spirit of the original Puritans and that of the Shakers is neatly illustrated in the accounts of their respective voyages upon which Williams and Constance Rourke commented. Of the man on the *Mayflower* who was washed overboard in a storm and caught hold of a chance halyard Williams writes: 'the one man of it, at sea, in the merciful guardianship of God, (washed away, howbeit), relying on his own hands and feet saves himself by force of himself, is hauled back by others like himself'.[2] The Shaker voyage is apocalyptic as well as reliant upon self-help: 'Angels appeared over the masts of the damaged and leaky ship on which the small band travelled to America in 1774. It was typical that its members should see them in the midst of a storm and also man the pumps'.[3] Mother Ann charged her followers to be joyful, entertaining visions of the millennium of the Second Coming, and of a Blakean America. The band was more important than the one man; men and women were equal. They began with an enthusiastic acceptance of the mystery of psychic elevation, which did not end with its Puritan perversion. They affirmed 'the generous soil of North America' in song and dance.[4] The revulsion against the visible world and terror of the invisible by which Williams characterised the first Puritans were conspicuously absent in the Shakers. The married

---

[1] Constance Rourke, *The Roots of American Culture, and other Essays* (N.Y., 1942), pp. 195–237.
[2] *In the American Grain*, p. 67.
[3] Constance Rourke, *Roots of American Culture*, p. 203.
[4] Cited from a Shaker source, *ibid.* p. 214.

pruriency of the Puritans gave way to a kind of celibate salacity; the Shakers were neither afraid of sexual passion nor of the supernatural.

Their artistic strength was expressed in architecture and furniture which embodied the principles of functionalism. They avoided all talk of beauty, emphasising plainness and economy and repudiating ornament and embellishment. Miss Rourke wrote of their abstract turn of mind, and their fondness for the use of the word 'type'.[1] Their draughtsmanship was a drawing of archetypal designs, which Sheeler interestingly rendered in the modern idiom as a set of 'standards'. He spoke of a painting by Stuart Davis: 'I think that all things should have that similar title appropriate with the variations of the subject. "Standard Still Life", well, that exists now, "Standard Lansdcape"…Then you have an anchor post from which to deviate – "Substandard" or "Superstandard" and so forth.'[2] Sheeler himself chose to use the word 'classic', which, applied to American industrial scenes, falsely arouses a sense of irony in the spectator. Unlike Demuth, who consciously gave his industrial works ironic titles, Sheeler possessed a Shaker-like vision of another world both abstractly and literally rendered in the scene before him. As a historian of Precisionist art wrote: "Classic Landscape", austere in its ordered cubes and cylinders, is for Sheeler the modern Arcadia.'[3]

The Precisionists never issued a manifesto, and at no time expressed an involvement with the social crises of industrial life. Hilaire Hiler, an old friend of Williams', wrote in a letter that one of the Precisionist painters, Niles Spencer, was interested 'in structure and relations rather than in symbols, propaganda, esoteric theories, drama or melodrama'.[4] Williams, writing of another, Louis Lozowick, admired his paintings of American cities, adding that they also refuted 'the stupid dicta of the bellyaching end-of-the-worlders'.[5]

Sheeler, like any Imagist, strenuously rejected the symbol – what was seen in his pictures was intended to be seen without overtones; or

[1] *Ibid.* p. 236.
[2] Tape-recorded interview with Martin L. Friedman, 18 June 1959 (Walker Art Center, Minneapolis).
[3] *The Precisionist View in American Art,* catalogue of an exhibition, 13 November – 25 December 1960, Walker Art Center, Minneapolis, with an introductory essay by Martin L. Friedman (Minneapolis, 1960), p. 34.
[4] *Ibid.* p. 43.
[5] Letter to John Riordan, 26 January 1926.

as Williams put it in one of his essays on Sheeler, 'that well seen becomes sight and song itself. It is in things that for the artist the power lies, not beyond them'.[1] A clear confrontation of the land in all its details destroyed the Puritans' mysteries: 'picturesque smallness: children, dwarfs, elves; the diminutive desires of the lowly for – they scarcely know what'.[2] No mystery at all was best: 'I think Sheeler is particularly valuable because of the bewildering directness of his vision, without blur, through the fantastic overlay with which our lives so vastly are concerned, "the real", as we say, contrasted with the artist's "fabrications".'[3] The Precisionist was against imagination if by that was meant fabrication of the real. He wished to paint the real itself. As Zukofsky wrote of a Primitive painter: 'He does not trust his memory and always paints with people, objects and landscapes before him'.[4]

An Arcadian in Babylonia – a primitive in a complex world – was how Williams regarded the situation of the American Primitive. The Primitives held back a wilderness by the sheer demarcation of one object from another:[5]

It was the intensity of their vision coupled with their isolation in the wilderness, that caused them one and all to place and have placed on the canvas veritable capsules, surrounded by a line of color, to hold them off from a world which was most about them. They were eminently objective, their paintings always remained things.

The Precisionists, modern Primitives, were equally objective; their hard-edged paintings were also things. Taking for their subject the machine-made world, they successfully avoided anecdotal painting while keeping within the objective tradition of George Bingham, and the literal tradition of William Harnett. If the Precisionists developed those traditions they did so through the mechanical mediation of photography. The perfection of detail obtainable in a straight photograph relieved the painter of the task of remaining in Harnett's magic realist or literalist tradition. He could afford to cultivate what Sheeler called a 'selective realism'.[6] The traditional painter's sketch was re-

---

[1] *Selected Essays*, p. 234.
[2] *In the American Grain*, p. 64.
[3] *Selected Essays*, p. 231.
[4] Louis Zukofsky, 'Dometer Guczul', *View* III, 3 (October 1943), 87–8,95;88.
[5] *Selected Essays*, pp. 333–4.
[6] Tape-recording cited above.

placed by the photograph, from which a permanent definition of structures and forms could be obtained. The immediate contact with actuality was not lost while the painting was in the making. For at least a decade from about 1929, Sheeler practised a direct, selective realism based upon the evidence of his photographs. Thereafter, by means of a technique in which he transferred his photographic 'sketches' on to plexiglas, he would superimpose sequential views of a subject to form a composite blueprint for the final picture. His own special development from Cubism to stereoscopic realism was thus achieved principally by means of the camera.

Williams was not, however, happy about the relation between Sheeler's photographs and his paintings. He voiced his misgivings in a letter to Constance Rourke:[1]

My feeling about Sheeler is mixed. His great strength, to me, is his ability to see the subjects of his canvasses in the life about him. He has not been daunted by 'ugliness'. At the same time I begin rather to fear the influence of the photograph upon him. He works too constantly from the photograph which I am sure takes away the predominance of color and *paint* from his pictures. I say I fear this influence. I don't say that Charles has gone too far. I'd like to see Charles sit in front of a tree and paint it as *he* sees it, not as the camera saw it. Maybe I'm crazy but I still believe his Bucks County barns have a painty quality that his later works lack.

This feeling was brought to a head the other day by something John Marin said. Marin objected to Chas. Demuth's paintings in the recent Demuth show. He said, How can a painter follow a *line*, or allow his paint to be controlled by it. The painter should follow his *paint*.

I know about Vermeer, Holbein and some others – but for myself I like to see the paint more imaginatively used – as paint. I hate to see Charles working so minutely. I want to see him loosen himself up again. I think to work as he does is doing something to him.

This is all for you from a perhaps prejudiced and certainly unskilled viewpoint, it is not to be spoken of, please, before anyone. I may change my viewpoint in a year but I have been vaguely disturbed – Maybe it's a sign of Charles' genius to disturb me. But I don't see enough of Charles in these paintings which tend to become impersonal. Perhaps that too is what he wants. There is too much withdrawal from life in them. I want more of a comment, a cry of some sort – a criticism of life from Charles. He isn't scared. But he does tend to pull away. He needs to be warmed up, infused – someone should smash his camera and open his brain.

[1] Letter to Constance Rourke, 10 January 1938 (copy: CtY).

Two days later Williams sent a postscript:[1]

What I fear is the too facile copying by the camera. It tends toward an empty realism. I don't say Charles isn't aware of this. I know he is. I write this letter because I feared I may have over emphasized my point in the last.

The tendency today in some quarters is toward realistic drawing untouched by the imagination. We all fall into that error at times. I know I do.

But yesterday I was looking at the well known print of Charles' American Interior. The color was the thing that showed me wherein I was mistaken in speaking as I did in the last letter. Not mistaken exactly, an overemphasis rather.

Without referring directly to Williams' letter Miss Rourke defended Sheeler point by point in her book on him: Marin's criticism was the manifestation of an expressionist temperament; emphasis on colour assumed that shades of white could not be sensuous in their effect.[2] She felt that such critics were reacting against what they took to be an extension of the Puritan tradition, whereas they were really failing to see that impersonal art was simply an especially reticent form of subjectivism.[3] As a mark of faith she reproduced a photograph of a stairwell which Williams had pronounced 'uninteresting'.[4] Finally, she challenged Williams' view that the photograph eliminated the need for design; the straight photographers had come to an impasse, in her opinion, in refusing to crop their prints. Sheeler did crop, specifically to enhance design.[5] She might have added that the Precisionist constantly 'cropped' or edited the subject to enhance design; it was the real proof of Sheeler's deeply painterly preoccupation. Of all the photographers of the straight school he remains the only important painter. His willingness to crop can be directly correlated with the second clause of his famous definition: 'Photography is nature seen from the eyes outward, painting from the eyes inward'.[6] Williams made a not dissimilar formulation: 'To be a poem a writing must have two movements, from outside inward and from inside out. The movement must be generated from the nature of the material and the material must take its structure from the emotion, the quality of the driving person behind

[1] Postscript to Constance Rourke, 12 January 1938 (copy: CtY).
[2] Constance Rourke, *Charles Sheeler: Artist in the American Tradition* (N.Y., 1938), pp. 176–7.
[3] *Ibid.* p. 188.
[4] *Ibid.* p. 192.
[5] *Ibid.* p. 122.
[6] *Ibid.* p. 119.

it'.[1] But Sheeler was not as dynamic as the forceful members of the Stieglitz circle in general. He was by temperament diametrically opposed to Williams. But, as we have seen, so was John Riordan. Williams, a driving person of confused passions, valued them all the more for the ways in which they differed from himself.

[1] W. C. Williams, Review of Parker Tyler's *The Granite Butterfly*, *Accent* VI, 3 (Spring 1946) 203–6;*203*.

5

An American Measure

Musico-mechanico

We have seen that Williams' analogies for invention in poetry in the late twenties were drawn from physics rather than from linguistics. While superficially sharing with the New Critics the principle of the autonomy of the poetic object, he did not share the preoccupations of Allen Tate and John Crowe Ransom with literary precedent. In *avant-garde* circles the applications of popularised versions of the theory of relativity to theories of the work of art were proliferating. Robert McAlmon told how conversation raged on relativity during Williams' second visit to Paris in 1926;[1] George Antheil, the American composer, produced several manifestoes on the relation between relativity and music;[2] and in 1930 Mary Butts announced an essay on relativity and the artist in general.[3] If Zukofsky had not read Whitehead he had, nevertheless, translated Anton Reiser's biography of Einstein which contained a twenty-four page chapter on the concept of space–time,[4] while Williams continued his interest in the abstract design of mathematics, quoting Scott Buchanan to make an unusual manifesto for the first issue of a magazine, *Pagany*.[5] Pound, who had already moved on

[1] Robert McAlmon, *Being Geniuses Together* (London, 1938), pp. 197–9.
[2] George Antheil, 'Abstraction and Time in Music', in *The Little Review Anthology*, ed. Margaret Anderson (N.Y., 1953), pp. 336–8.
[3] 'Notes on Contributors', *Hound and Horn* III, 2 (January–March 1930) [144].
[4] Anton Reiser, *Albert Einstein* (N.Y., 1930). Zukofsky's name does not appear on the title-page; a typed bibliography provided by Mr Zukofsky for Mary Ellen Solt identifies him as the translator.
[5] 'Manifesto', *Pagany* I, I (January–March 1930), I: ' "The ghosts so confidently laid by Francis Bacon and his followers are again walking in the laboratory as well as beside the man in the street," the scientific age is drawing to a close. Bizarre derivations multiply about us, mystifying and untrue as – an automatic revolver. To what shall the mind turn for that with which to rehabilitate our thought and our lives? To the word, a meaning hardly distinguishable from that of place, in whose great virtuous and at present little realized potency we hereby manifest our belief.' The first sentence is

with Antheil to endocrinology, felt it incumbent upon himself to reprove his infatuated friends: 'A whole school or shoal of young American writers seems to me to have lost contact with language as language...One of my colleagues says he "likes the mathematical use". I think the good poem ought probably to include that dimension without destroying the feel of actual speech.'[1] It was a warning Williams undoubtedly appreciated but for the moment his search for a measure of control while retaining motion in writing was obsessive.

It was Zukofsky who made Williams fully conscious of the steps he had taken in the sequence of poems, 'Della Primavera Trasportata Al Morale', towards a mode deriving its force from gesture and intonation. The driving person had made a special advance in the use of image, as Zukofsky said, 'from a word structure paralleling French painting (Cézanne) to the same structure in movement'.[2] The retention of the term 'image' in the context of movement was as confusing as the term 'objective', but Williams' term 'measure' was not yet in use.[3] Zukofsky continued to refer to 'musical shapes', and to 'objectification' as 'the complete satisfaction derived from melody in a poem'.[4] In the preface to An 'Objectivists' Anthology, which Zukofsky read to Williams in Grey's Restaurant on East Eighteenth Street a year before the book appeared,[5] he tried to modify the visual emphasis originally suggested by 'objective'. As lens, 'objective' had wholly photographic connotations, while the military usage of something to be aimed at only reinforced the photographic shooting of a still. Now Zukofsky attempted to associate the term with musical form:[6]

The melody, the rest are accessory –
....my one voice; my other...
An objective – nature as a creator – desire for what is objectively perfect,
Inextricably the direction of historic and contemporary particulars.

---

acknowledged by Williams as coming from Scott Buchanan, *Poetry and Mathematics* (N.Y., 1929), p. 18.

[1] *Active Anthology*, ed. Ezra Pound (London, 1933), pp. 253–4.
[2] Louis Zukofsky, 'American Poetry 1920–1930', *The Symposium* II, 1 (January 1931), 73.
[3] The earliest use of the term by Williams, so far as the author can determine, is in a letter from him to Yvor Winters, 11 January 1928 (copy: NBuU).
[4] *Poetry* XXXVII, 5 (February 1931), 276, 282.
[5] Postcard from Williams to Zukofsky, post-marked 1 October 1931 (CtY).
[6] An 'Objectivists' Anthology, p. 10.

The accessories to the melody were what Pound and Antheil described as the vertical or chordal elements of harmony. The one voice against the other was the inter-medial counterpoint of sound and vision.[1] In the sixth section of his long poem *A*, in which the formulation above first appeared, Zukofsky equated his temporary passion for physics with his life-long love of music:[2]

> Asked Albert who introduced relativity –
> 'And what is the formula for success?'
> 'X = work, Y = play, Z = keep your mouth shut.'
> 'And what about Johann Sebastian?'
> 'What about Johann Sebastian? The same formula.'

The theme of this section of the poem is 'Can / The design / Of the fugue / Be transferred / To poetry?'[3] Bach was apparently playing an important part in the theory of the poem; Zukofsky and Williams shared an admiration for his *St Matthew Passion*.[4] Williams commented at this time:[5]

In Bach, not as with the music of some other later composers, it seems not to be the purpose to seduce the sense by leading it away from the value of the notes (words) as musical particulars. On the contrary, though a sequence of sounds is attained it is never a 'burden' of necessity less than themselves.

Rhetoric was a seducer, rapacious and predaceous ('that seductively takes us up – as a man might carry a child').[6] It was what Pound called 'the romantic bait'.[7] Ideally, a lexicon of pristine words unsullied by use would offer its virgin self willingly to the poet, but since no language save mathematics – an iron maiden – has evolved from the

[1] *Ibid.* p. 139: To the version of the statement in *A – 6* were added two lines to make a cinematic analogy:
> The thought in the melody moves,
> Lines, flash of photoplay.

[2] *Ibid.* p. 134.

[3] *Ibid.* p. 151.

[4] Zukofsky's *A* was related in theme and form to the *St Matthew Passion* (*Poetry* XXXVII, 5 [February 1931], 294). Williams' *Voyage to Pagany* devoted chapter XXVI to an account of a performance of the same work.

[5] W. C. Williams, Review of *An 'Objectivists' Anthology*, *The Symposium* IV, I (January 1933), 117. Cf. 'Bach might be an illustration of movement not suborned by a freight of purposed design, loaded upon it as in almost all later musical works; statement unmusical and unnecessary' (*Selected Essays*, p. 117).

[6] *Ibid.* p. 115–16.

[7] *Active Anthology*, p. 254.

drawing-board Williams accepted ready rather than exact words as his material provided he felt they were capable of retaining some specific meaning.[1] The emphasis on the etymological meaning of a word, which is a discernible characteristic in American poetry from Pound through Zukofsky and Olson to the younger followers, pares the accrued meaning down to an irreducible minimum. As Zukofsky stated the principle, 'One is brought back to the entirety of the single word which in itself is a relation, an implied metaphor, an arrangement and a harmony'.[2] Clearly, Pound and Fenollosa on the Chinese written character are behind such a view. But Williams also speaks of 'word-characters' which unite to form the 'aggregate tonality' of Zukofsky's nonpictorial images.[3] Zukofsky was careful to indicate that 'musical shape' was not an exact term since the poem was made 'not of notes as music, but of words more variable than variables'.[4] Nevertheless, he later attempted translations of Catallus in which, by rendering the vowel and consonant values of Latin as nearly as possible in American, he attempted a melodic equivalence. Williams was opposed to such attempts at syllabic exactitude. Translation based on any more than a temporal equivalence, such as he understood Pound's translations from the Provençal to be, would in his view be robbed of the possibility it offered for fresh melodic excellence in the new language. He took a more rudimentary view of Pound's sense of melopoeia than Zukofsky: 'The music measure is not the syllabic measure of so many sounds to a line – but many notes (syllabic) almost infinitely variable to a given time measure'.[5]

Behind the Objectivists' concern to renew the structure of verse there lay another common source in Pound's book *Antheil and the Treatise on Harmony*. Williams first encountered a use of the word 'measure' in a wholly musical context, in an excerpt of the book in a little magazine:[6]

[1] *The Symposium, ibid.* p. 117.
[2] *Poetry* XXXVII, 5 (February 1931), 279.
[3] *The Symposium, ibid.* p. 116.
[4] *An 'Objectivists' Anthology*, p. 17.
[5] 'The Poem as a Field of Action' [1948] (NBuU).
[6] *Antheil and the Treatise on Harmony, with Supplementary Notes by Ezra Pound* (Chicago, 1927), p. 133. What Williams initially read was the section 'Varia' (pp. 129–36), in 1924 4 (December 1924), 132–5. He wrote and congratulated Pound on the new sense of form he had derived from these notes (Letter to Pound, 23 December 1924 [CtY]).

Musical training or learning consists in refining or making accurate the sense of pitch; and of developing the inner metronome; that is about all that can be done by rote; but the pupil should be told of the existence of shape, line, form, etc...

He should be told to observe WHAT he is measuring with his MEASURE.

He must not cut off the nose of subjects because they don't coincide with the marks on his foot-rule.

Pound, distinguishing between trained and natural musicians, continued by distinguishing between the art of writing music and improvising on an instrument. Notation was unable to capture the movement which Williams was then beginning to refer to as the characteristic of a poem in action. According to Pound, the trained musician was not necessarily the best interpeter of such movement because 'millimetric training' did not guarantee a full perception of melody; he might be sensitive to 'size', by which Pound meant quantity but not to 'shape', or what Williams came to call 'quality'.[1] Thus it was that Pound, taking as his example Antheil, suggested the possibility of a musical precisionism which while being mechanistic in its structure was organic in its form.

Antheil was to music what Gris was to painting. He was the only native-born American who was physically a part of the Constructivist scene in Europe. He was a member of the *De Stijl* group, and was associated like Jane Heap of *The Little Review* with the Bauhaus.[2] In him, it might be said, Mina Loy's Futurist manifesto in *Camera Work*, the mechanical animism of *The Soil* and *Broom*, and Sheeler and Strand's heroic machine-age film *Manhatta* found a refined culmination. *The Little Review's* Machine-Age Exposition, Louis Lozowick's paintings, and Fernand Léger's film *Ballet Mécanique* represented the principal plastic-mechanical analogies with which Williams was familiar.[3] Now Antheil produced his *Ballet Mécanique*.

Pound stated that had there been a Vorticist music in 1914 the equal of Gaudier's sculpture he would have embraced it, but he was wrong to claim that there had been little structural revaluaton of the melodic

[1] *Ibid.* pp. 130–2.

[2] He was to have contributed a book 'Musico-mechanico', she one entitled 'Die neue Welt', to the series of Bauhausbücher (Hans M. Wingler, *Das Bauhaus* (Bramsche, 1962), p. 141).

[3] He saw Léger's film in New York on 12 May 1926, commenting that it was 'too uniform in its resources but thrilling by moments' (letter to John Riordan, 13 May 1926).

line. In a series of articles in *The Egoist*, which Pound almost certainly would not have missed, a writer on contemporary music told how he had discussed 'modern "horizontal" free counterpoint as opposed to "vertical" or harmonic chordal writing' as early as 1909.[1] Now, in 1924, Pound laid emphasis on the solidity and precision of the mechanical musical shapes, which Antheil called 'mechanisms'.[2] He likened their 'monolinear', 'lateral', and 'horizontal' action to 'a projectile carrying a wire and cutting, defining the three dimensions of space'.[3] Antheil called this 'the spacing-off and draughtmanship of TIME-SPACE by the means of various points of sound'.[4] The projective element he defined as the fourth dimension, characterising it as locomotive.

This was one context of Williams' 'Author's Introduction to *The Wedge*', in which he wrote:[5]

Prose may carry a load of ill-defined matter like a ship. But poetry is the machine which drives it, pruned to a perfect economy. As in all machines its movement is intrinsic, undulant, a physical more than a literary character. In a poem this movement is distinguished in each case by the character of the speech from which it arises.

Therefore, each speech having its own character, the poetry it engenders will be peculiar to that speech also in its own intrinsic form. The effect is beauty, what in a single object resolves our complex feelings of propriety.

The general laws by which the poem is organised are presented as plastic and not grammatical, the parts of the poem differ in their intrinsic values according to the situation in which they find themselves as speech. It was Williams' poetic application of Whitehead's theory of organic mechanism.[6] The mechanical-plastic analogy of the Objectivist phase resulted in a conception of the poem as an abstract design of inter-connected working parts, where the projective power of the verse was derived entirely from the organisation of those parts. But this analogy represented only one possibility to Williams. By 1944, when the passage above with its images of engendering and pruning was

[1] Leigh Henry, 'Liberations: Studies in Contemporary Music. II Ballila Pratella and Futurist Music', *The Egoist* I, 8 (15 April 1914), 147–9;*148*.
[2] *Antheil* ... p. 41.
[3] *Ibid.* p. 50.
[4] George Antheil, 'Abstraction and Time in Music', in *The Little Review Anthology*, ed. Margaret Anderson (N.Y., 1953), p. 338.
[5] *Selected Essays*, p. 256.
[6] Whitehead, *Science and the Modern World*, p. 116.

written, another analogy less consonant with the scientific age and more closely related to human capacity for projective power had presented itself again. It came from jazz.

' *Man Orchid* '

For more than a decade Williams' closest friend and ally was Fred R. Miller, an unknown young writer who edited the American radical story-magazine *Blast* till the late thirties when his commitment to proletarian life gave way to a musical and social concern for the Negro. He had taught himself to play the piano and at the same time had amassed one of the best collections of early jazz records of his day. He was in the vanguard of the white man's interest in classic jazz which was to enjoy a popular revival in the forties.

The revival of classic jazz found its centre in Bunk Johnson. Encouraged by collectors Bunk had re-emerged from the obscurity of a small Louisiana town and, with a new set of teeth provided by his benefactors, began to play again in 1942. In the spring of 1945 the New York public heard him at a Sunday afternoon session at which it is likely Miller was present.[1] Williams ordered some of his records.[2] Miller's plan to educate 'Joe Square', among whom he would have surely numbered his friend Williams, was to offer him something good but modern, and work back to New Orleans jazz by stages; 'The longest way "round to Basin Street is the shortest way home" – from New York, 1945'.[3] His task was soon to be made easier; Bunk Johnson was coming to town for a season and Williams responded enthusiastically.[4] Then a handbill advertising Bunk's opening in New York came through the post and Williams, not sure that it had come from Miller and not wishing to be slow, quickly informed him that he was going to the opening on Friday, 28 September 1945.

[1] Morroe Berger, 'Jazz Pre-History and Bunk Johnson', in *Frontiers of Jazz*, ed. Ralph De Toledano (N.Y., 1947), pp. 91–103;*92–4*.
[2] Letter to Fred R. Miller, 20 April 1945.
[3] Fred R. Miller, 'Breaking In a New Pair of Shoes', *The Jazz Record* 35 (August 1945), 9,17;*17*.
[4] Letter to Miller, 7 August 1945: 'I'd be wild to hear old Bunk Johnson in the flesh and hear him play. Let me know when and how. But I'm not much interested (lack of time more than anything else) to get any more jazz discs. No chance to play them, not even my own machine, had to borrow Jinny's and the stuff jams Flossie's ears.'

On 23 November Williams re-visited the Stuyvesant Casino with his daughter-in-law, Virginia. That second evening there was some discussion of an inter-racial literary magazine. They spoke of buying the established but failing *South Today*, but also of what it would mean if with the best of intentions inferior black writers should find themselves beside better white ones. For Miller it was a disappointing evening as tutor; Williams had waited in vain for Bunk to 'get hot':[1]

He did, after you left! Towards the end of the evening he and the band kicked off with the *St. Louis Blues* and it was so good the customers wouldn't let them quit; dancers stopped dancing to crowd in front of the stand for a better listen, and Moon and Dorais and I grabbed up our beer mugs and joined them. The St. Louis went on and for about 20 minutes and it was too bad you weren't there to hear it.

Nevertheless, Bucklin Moon and Bill Dorais would blossom as characters in two stories based on jazz themes; Moon as the hero of 'Man Orchid', an unpublished and unfinished collaborative novel by Williams and Miller,[2] and Dorais as one of the two protagonists in Miller's short story, *Gutbucket and Gossamer*, eventually published in 1950.[3]

Williams was always keen to collaborate on joint projects, as we have seen in the case of John Riordan. Now Miller proposed the idea of a novel written without a plot; they would write alternate chapters.[4] Within a week Williams sent him a draft of the first chapter:[5]

In his person he was the contract (one might almost say the expanse!) between classic & New Orleans music.

To resolve such a person would be to create a new world, to resolve him in the mind lucidly, dramatically, or as he is – in the flesh – to make the flesh mindful – or the mind fleshful. His flesh – the suburbs of his mind – informed.

[1] Letter from Miller to Williams, 25 November 1945 (CtY). Williams, who later celebrated 'Ol' Bunk's Band' (*The Collected Later Poems*, rev. edn, Norfolk, Conn., [1963], p. 236) had nevertheless heard a rare combination: Bunk Johnson (trumpet), Jim Robinson (trombone), George Lewis (clarinet), Lawrence Marrero (banjo), Baby Dodds (drums), and Alcide Pavergeau (bass).

[2] Mss hitherto unidentified among Williams' uncatalogued correspondence (CtY). Mr Moon was writing or compiling several important volumes on inter-racial themes at this time: *The Darker Brother* (Garden City, N.Y., 1943); *Primer for White Folks* (Garden City, N.Y., 1945); *The High Cost of Prejudice* (N.Y. [1947]); *Without Magnolias* (Garden City, N.Y., 1949).

[3] Fred Miller, *Gutbucket and Gossamer*, The Outcast Chapbooks 18 (Yonkers, N.Y., 1950).

[4] Letter from Miller to Williams, 4 December 1945 (CtY).

[5] Draft not in typed mss (CtY).

Why should a novel *not* wear its skeleton on the outside – our bones open to the air – like a crab. An intelligent crab – a fat intelligent crab – what an advantage it would be.

Next Williams invited a third person to participate in the novel. Lydia Carlin had been brought up in Florida, and was 'told to imagine herself as a fat, light yellow nigger boy and tell us some factual stuff about her childhood background',[1] which she did. But by now Miller was in a quandary. He could not go on with the hero; he felt he did not know enough about him: 'And I can't fake what I don't know. That last is bad. In jazz "faking" is a name for playing by ear or improvising. If I can't fake, what'm I doing trying to help out on a verbal improvisation?'[2] Williams had only met Moon once and therefore felt free to improvise, since he was only superficially committed to his hero's real identity. He suggested Miller should leave Moon to him and that he should develop a separate novel not to touch the Moon novel just yet but to be merely aligned with it: Miller would develop a novel about a woman, 'She, the white, impossible queen'.[3]

In June 1946 Williams inter-cut all the available material and sent it to the typist. Miller went on to develop his romance in a jazz setting, *Gutbucket and Gossamer*. Nearly a year later Williams was still thinking of their collaborative effort: '...the "novel", for that might easily be a magnificent thing if we can ever get to the writing – the composition; the beauty of the form we are inventing would be its adaptability, something to make the ordinary "story" just a piece of stodge'.[4] Nine years later he was still speaking of reaching a novel-length script: 'It excites my imagination.'[5]

The hero of 'Man Orchid' is Cholly Oldham, publisher's reader and trumpet-player. As Williams conceived him he was an extremely light-coloured Negro, born of a Greek father and Negro mother. During the day he reads and writes the pseudo-scholastic jargon of the day, and in the evenings he tries to write a novel. But as the 'contract' – or expanse – between classical music and Negro jazz he is profoundly

---

1 Letter from Williams to Miller, 28 May [1946]. Mrs Carlin knew nothing of Miller, nor did she see the other contributions to the novel (letter from Mrs Carlin to the author, 27 April 1966).
2 Letter from Miller to Williams, 26 May 1946 (CtY).
3 Letter to Miller, post-marked 29 May 1946.
4 Letter to Miller, 28 March 1947.
5 Letter to Miller, 28 February 1956.

frustrated. The mixing of the blood has resulted in an impediment in his speech. Cholly stutters. As Williams rendered the theme much earlier: '"White blood and colored blood don't mix", said he nursing his injury. "Doc, I got a hemorrhage of the FLUTE", he said'.[1] Similarly, Cholly's problem is one of inarticulateness in the face of literary ambitions. The instrument of his language is inadequate; Bunk Johnson is a pure antelope by comparison: 'Orchids grow *on* trees, flaunting (a good word) their complex sexual devices. There it is again, the fluted and bulbous mechanism'. Sitting at the stuttering type-writer, he thinks of Bunk's 'autochthonous horn' growing like an orchid on the trunk which is his band. Cholly's wife catches him among these thoughts: 'You know you're not waorin working on any pay writing. You're working on play writing. And when I say PLAY writing I mean your just playing with yourself. I said playing with yourself. You know what I mean.'

In the essay in *In the American Grain*, 'The Advent of the Slaves', Williams suggested that the quality of life that the Negro had brought to America consisted in a poise which no authority could threaten. In Williams' view, the Negro owed his potency to his freedom from the narrow bonds of white morality. He enjoyed the privilege of the damned. It is an attitude which finds sensitive expression in *Paterson*, in the Negress of the scarred belly – a black contrast to the impossible white girl, Phyllis, and the queen of the Unicorn Tapestries. The Negro is nothing, which leaves him free to be something. Cholly Oldham embodies the belief that death is a meaningless blank, and that the real danger, and the cause of our irrational existence, is that the blank should be in our lives.[2] As Cholly says:

And there's religion for you. They know you can't prove nothing so you gotta believe. You gotta believe. And who says you gotta believe? The one who don't eat, don't drink, don't sleep, don't have his woman. You gotta believe. That means all you got don't mean nothing. That means all the laws you got to hold you down is made to make you believe there is something. Yes sir, SOMETHING! That's what you got to believe, that there is something – because all you got that you think you got is just nothing because your Pappy was a Greek restauranter and your mammy did some cooking.

[1] *In the American Grain*, p. 210.
[2] Cf. W. C. Williams, 'Towards the Unknown', *View* I, 11–12 (February–March 1942), 10.

The idiom of this sermon against religion is very close to the first-draft conception of the sermon in *Paterson* – originally delivered by a Negro preacher and in the printed version by the immigrant evangelist. The Negro preacher in the early version betrays his orchidean inheritance by being convinced that there is a transcendental something,[1] whereas Cholly knows, as do the coloured girls of *Paterson*, that potency of being consists in movement. To enjoy oneself at the typewriter, as Cholly's wife sees it, is to be deviant. In Dora Marsden's terms, it puts both the virgin and the whore out of business. Yet Cholly has no other aim than to appease his primitive hungers by writing.

In the second 'chapter' of 'Man Orchid' Williams returned to a favourite theme; the setback to American poetry which he considered *The Waste Land* to have been in the twenties. He compared it to the setback Negro jazz had suffered with the success of swing in the thirties.

In drawing an analogy between the course of American poetry and New Orleans jazz, Cholly – for Williams – gives voice to a dogma current in 1946, which attributed the submergence of classic jazz to the rise of 'sweet music' – the white man's orchestrated version of the black's authentic material. Rudi Blesh's *Shining Trumpets*, written while Bunk was still at the Stuyvesant Casino, epitomises such an attitude; it was the intellectual culmination of the New Orleans revival.[2] It took no account of the developments in modern jazz which Charlie Parker first recorded under his own name at just that time, and to whom Robert Creeley would later turn for an analogy for poetry, but with purist zeal strictly limited itself to the age of Johnson. Cholly is equally zealous, assigning the somewhat extreme date of 1906 for the displacement of classic jazz by sweet music. Rather like the jazz revivalists of the early forties with their recording-machines, Williams tried to find what American poetry had escaped the blight of *The Waste Land*. It had been on his mind for some time. He had spoken of a private anthology, 'an ideal anthology of singing American poems', but had no leisure for its selection.[3]

The extract Williams took from Mezz Mezzrow's *Really the Blues* for *Paterson* is representative of his belief in the general implications of

[1] Ms. (CtY).
[2] Rudi Blesh, *Shining Trumpets* (N.Y., 1946).
[3] Letter to Fred Miller, 9 July 1946.

Negro–American music for the idea of a miscegeneous American culture. But the technical details are in the two paragraphs which immediately follow his extract:[1]

What knocked me out most on these records was the slurring and division of words to fit the musical pattern, the way the words were put to work for the music. I tried to write them down because I figured the only way to dig Bessie's unique phrasing was to get the words down exactly as she sang them.

Mezzrow asked his sister to take down the lyrics in shorthand:

She was in a very proper and dicty mood, so she kept 'correcting' Bessie's grammar, straightening out her words and putting them in 'good' English until they sounded like some stuck-up jive from *McGuffy's Reader* instead of the real down-to-earth language of the blues. That girl was schooled so good, she wouldn't admit there was such a word as 'ain't' in the English language, even if a hundred million Americans yelled it in her face every hour of the day.

From correction of grammar it is but one step to correction of metrical pattern. Williams wrote to Miller, 'It's all in the timing within the lines, ignoring the grammatical divisions *but* organizing the measure to make a musical sequence... Vary the pace as much as you feel impelled to give it a jagged surface'.[2]

Mezz's success was that he was the first White Negro. At least, this was how one of the characters of Miller's *Gutbucket and Gossamer* saw him: 'Mezz, Max (Kaminsky), and Art (Hodes) – three Jewish boys sounding more Negroid than all the Harlem bebop artists put together. What do you make of that, Matt?'[3] Several things may be made of it: the Jew's identification with the Negro; the purist wish to halt the development of jazz at a historical moment in New Orleans; and the general sense of a process of acculturation accomplished. It echoes the evidence of the extract Williams took from *Really the Blues*, where Mezz identifies himself as negroid not only in idiom and in his admiration for Bessie Smith, but also expresses his belief that the coloured man's message can be reciprocated by the white man. But the detailed answer Williams would have wanted was to be found in the Negro's sense of time. Williams' notion of the variable foot bears a straightforward relation to the metrical organisation of jazz. The great rhythmic variety

[1] Milton 'Mezz' Mezzrow and Bernard Wolfe, *Really the Blues* (N.Y., 1946), pp. 54–5.
[2] Postcard to Miller, post-marked 5 August 195[6].
[3] P. 8.

of the blues depends entirely upon the varying syllabic quantity com-
pressed or expanded within the strictly temporal feet of its classic
stanza. Its variety depends upon verbal improvisation, which in turn
depends on performative flexibility within the vocal phrasing. The
blues stanza which opened a projected long poem on jazz by Miller
provides a ready example:[1]

> Well, Ah don't know any stories
>   but Ah'll tell you what happened for real;
> Said, man, Ah don't know no stories –
>   best Ah can do, tell you how things happened for real:
> Climbed up on Mountain Minnie,
>   felt about as much as Ah could feel.

In this talking blues Miller has varied the phrasing by varying the
number of syllables within the line-lengths; the local acceleration of
pace due to the extra number of syllables in the fourth line shifts the
emphasis in the second from 'for real' to 'tell you'. So the statement
becomes a confidence, a simple confession of pleasure. Where such easy
rhythmic variability is present the poem may be said to swing, or in
Williams' terms to possess the quality of measure. But swing or measure
as a perceptual phenomenon depends entirely upon the relation between
the phrasing and a steady beat, whether sounded or merely sensed. It
defies notation, or scansion, because it is derived not from a time-
signature but from performance.

What was merely 'hot' in manner was, as Williams knew, no substitute for swing, which requires not tension but relaxation in the performer. Rudi Blesh explained that this relaxation in Negro playing was
achieved by an intentional dragging: 'the delayed attack which conveys the feeling that the beat is an exterior force – almost a natural
one – which *pulls* the music after it...'[2] The obvious comparison is with
the locomotive, a favourite subject of Negro folk-song; it pulls strongly
at its start but once it gathers momentum its sheer weight swings it
along on its own steam. Analogously, when the beat appears neither to
push nor pull in jazz it can also be said to swing. Such a view, however,
has interesting applications with regard to Projective verse, which is
the product not of a relaxed performer but a tense one. Like Abstract-

[1] Ms. (CtY).
[2] *Shining Trumpets*, p. 207.

Expressionist painting, its psychic content is more closely related to the aggression and anxiety of the Beat generation than to the primitive spontaneity of a late nineteenth-century Negro peasantry.

The American Idiom

In 1932 Gorham Munson raised the question of whether there was a distinct American style. Could not American, as a language, surpass English in the way Modern English had Middle English? Was there among his contemporaries someone dreaming of actualising a perfect language, a Lyly of the American period?[1] A.R.Orage, editor of *The New English Weekly*, joined the discussion, noting that although American English was English in the sense that it consisted of words included in the English dictionary as Irish did and Scots did not, its peculiarities were much deeper than mere vocabulary or mannerism.[2] But the discussion in *The New English Weekly* did not continue so confidently. An article appeared on American style in which the writer despaired of an evolving development in style in a country where novelty was rewarded rather than originality, and where a writer who did not answer market demands was doomed.[3] It seemed as if the subject had been despaired of almost as soon as it had been raised. Then Munson wrote to Williams:[4]

One of the things we'd like to do is to thresh out the whole question of British Tradition and American Literature, and I would like to see our American contributors start the discussion, perhaps with some attacks on current British letters. You will see at once the territory such a controversy would cover – divergence in national psychology, the usable and non-usable elements in the English tradition, etc., etc. Ideally, I should like to see you start off with a paper on United States Writing, and I hope that you will not be too busy to undertake that.

Williams' reply, printed in *The New English Weekly*, was aggressive and cynical, showing an attitude of detached contempt for the British idiom, but not offering any constructive ideas with regard to the

---

[1] G. Munson, 'Stocktaking at 33', *The Saturday Review of Literature* VI, 5 (24 August 1929), 69–70;70.
[2] *New English Weekly* I, 2 (28 April 1932), 45.
[3] Henry Tracy, 'American Style', *New English Weekly* I, 11 (30 June 1932), 259–60.
[4] Letter from Munson, 2 July 1932 (CtY).

American idiom: 'I don't want to go to England. I don't care to hear their language spoken. John Gould Fletcher is a bore having been confirmed in it by having listened far too long to that which he could never have imagined.'[1] But, attacked with tart relish by an academic critic some months later, Williams responded more positively:[2]

I stand squarely on the existence and practicability of an American language – among others *like* English which are not English – and a complete independence from English literature in each case, i.e. that of Joyce and our present-day American writers for example.

With characteristic American sympathy with the Irish Williams emphasised the foreignness of English literature to both nations. By now he was roused sufficiently to search for proof. Surprisingly, he chose to review the third edition of Mencken's *The American Language* a decade after its publication.[3] Three years later he would review the substantially re-written fourth edition.[4] By then he would be in personal touch with Mencken.

A letter from Williams to Munson, referring to the first review, contained the following note:[5]

Did you notice in a recent *Time*, that one of the things Mencken plans to do now that he has quit the *Mercury* is to rewrite *The American Language*? It will occupy two volumes this time. It would be interesting to know what he thinks of my review.

His review of the book had protested against its failure to use the new poetry as evidence of the inevitable stylistic change attendant upon a new language: 'Yet in poetry lies the matter finally to clinch the argument. Mencken himself towards the close of the book invokes the time when a poet, such as Dante or Chaucer, shall appear willing wholly to risk a use of the vulgar tongue.'[6] While praising Mencken Williams also chided him for neglecting style:[7]

The inner spirit of the new language is original. Its difference from standard

[1] *New English Weekly* I, 14 (21 July 1932), 331.
[2] W.C.Williams, 'Letter to the Editor', *New English Weekly* II, 4 (10 November 1932), 90–1.
[3] *New English Weekly* IV, 1 (19 October 1933), 9–10.
[4] *Selected Essays*, pp. 170–4.
[5] Undated letter from Williams to Munson (CtMW).
[6] *New English Weekly* IV, 1, 10.
[7] *Ibid.*

English is not merely a difference in vocabulary to be disposed of in an alphabetical list, it is above all a difference in pronunciation, in intonation, in conjugation, in metaphor and idiom, in the whole fashion of using words.

Style essentially depended upon the 'new constructions of phrase and a basic pace change'.[1] Mencken, however, did not deny the importance of style. He closed the first edition with an invocation to the American dialect, drawing parallels with Chaucer, Dante, and Luther; with Whitman and Lowell; and with Synge and Lady Gregory. By the third edition he included John V. A. Weaver, Sandburg, and Anderson in his list of innovators. But in the fourth he threw them all out again, including the appendices of the third edition, 'Specimens of the American Vulgate'. These consisted of 'translations' into popular idiom of The Declaration of Independence and The Gettysburg Address, a baseball sketch by Ring Lardner with a glossary, and 'Elégie Américaine', a poem by Weaver. In a brief note to Weaver's poem Mencken claimed that the Chicago poet was the first to present the proletarian's 'most lofty and sentimental thoughts in the same tongue he uses in discussing baseball'.[2] But as Williams sharply noted, Mencken had not understood 'that because a poem's subject matter is grave the poem is not therefore serious'.[3] Nor had he realised that a self-conscious use of dialect would date so quickly.

Williams was a collector of verbal specimens himself. His correspondence files were a living museum of the spoken idiom, which he drew upon in *Paterson*.[4] But he did not revere the assumed, provincial dialects of the self-conscious so much as the telling, personal idiom of those around him. This was the true area of neglect, as he told Mencken:[5]

Formal education, as far as I can tell, is not interested. And the better the school the less the interest. I do my best to jar my sons into a realization of the cultural superiority of their native tongue over book English but even they feel a certain shame in resorting to colloquialisms in word and phrase when they have to do a 'composition'. Their letters, though, are lively when they write to me. They'd better be.

Williams' second important criticism of Mencken's book was that it

[1] *Ibid.* p. 9.
[2] H. L. Mencken, *The American Language*, 3rd edn (N.Y., 1923), p. 405.
[3] *New English Weekly* IV, I, 10.
[4] E.g. see Appendix B (*Paterson*, pp. 149–50).
[5] Letter from Williams to Mencken, 16 December 1934 (MdBE).

showed no conception of the implications of the new language for prosody: Weaver used free verse and conventional forms without discrimination. It seems likely that Mencken did see this review, for there was a brief exchange of letters and Williams offered him a three-page memorandum on the relationship between the new poetry and the new language:[1]

Poetry has to do with pace and essence. It is the final repository of language, the key to linguistic character.

In conserving the integrity of the language – the spoken language – certain restrictions are faced by the metrist which the prose artist need not feel. Forced to an analysis by the limited internal space permitted his composition, to concision – to the effect of pace on the truth of what he has to say – the poet is compelled to measure and must know why one word has to follow another, and still the sense not be distorted...

The pronunciation as spoken must make his line.

Now the line of a similar language (English) is no longer accurate. This inaccuracy (if he sticks to English) ruins his compositions. The meaning, which is the same in this case as the form, escapes...

Mencken had evaded the question of the development of an American style since the first edition of 1919. He admitted it then,[2] and he did so again in 1936,[3] and in 1947.[4] Williams' second review, of the fourth edition, barely conceals his disappointment that Mencken has done nothing with his statement. The 'Specimens' were crude examples, but they were better than nothing.

Williams' interest in prosody was not the late development in his career which the almost desperate efforts of his final years suggest. In

[1] W.C. Williams, 'Note: The American Language and the New Poetry, so called', enclosed with letter of 17 December 1934 (MdBE). The editor of *Selected Letters* (p. xviii) was correct in saying that Mencken's correspondence was sealed in the terms of his will (until 1971), but the letter cited above and memorandum were separated from his correspondence and placed with his notes on style, which is where the present writer discovered them. A letter from Williams to R.L.Latimer, 20 December 1934 (ICN), suggests he intended to supply further memoranda, but there is no evidence that he did.

[2] *Letters of H.L. Mencken*, selected and annotated by Guy J. Forgue (N.Y., 1961), p. 145: 'I had a feeling that I was shirking it while I was at work on the book, but, as I have said, the enormous mass of material rather befogged me, and at the first trial I had to evade more than one difficulty by disingenuous dodging.'

[3] Letter from H.L.Mencken to W.C.Williams, 26 September 1936 (NBuU): 'And my apologies for my failure to include the memorandum on American style that you kindly sent to me two years ago. The book became so dreadfully long that I had to omit altogether my projected chapter on American style.'

[4] Letter from H.L.Mencken to Malcolm Cowley, 6 January 1947.

1913, concurrently with the musical preoccupations of Imagism,[1] he submitted to *Poetry* (Chicago) a handwritten essay entitled 'English Speech Rhythms',[2] but Harriet Monroe returned it as incomprehensible.[3] It may have been so in its earliest form, but the typescript, entitled simply 'Speech Rhythm', which is all that remains to document his concern at that time, is in some respects his clearest statement on 'measure', although he did not use the word then:[4]

No action, no creative action is complete but a period from a greater action going in rhythmic course, i.e., an Odyssey, is rightly considered not an isolated unit but a wave of a series from hollow through crest to hollow. No part in its excellence but partakes of the essential nature of the whole.

This is the conception of the action that I want.

In the other direction, inward: Imagination creates an image, point by point, piece by piece, segment by segment – into a whole, living. But each part as it plays into its neighbor, each segment into its neighbor segment and every part into every other, causing the whole – exists naturally in rhythm, and as there are waves there are tides and as there are ridges in the sand there are bars after bars...

I do not believe in *vers libre*, this contradiction in terms. Either the motion continues or it does not continue, either there is rhythm or no rhythm. *Vers libre* is prose. In the hands of Whitman it was a good tool, a kind of synthetic chisel – the best he had. In his bag of chunks even lie some of the pieces of rhythm life of which we must build. This is honor enough. *Vers libre* is finished – Whitman did all that was necessary with it. Verse has nothing to gain here and all to lose...

The purpose I have is to clarify the practical understanding of English speech rhythms in work of highest imagination.

Each piece of work, rhythmic in whole, is then in essence an assembly of tides, waves, ripples – in short, of greater and lesser rhythmic particles regularly repeated or destroyed...

For practical purposes and for me the unit is of a convenient length, such as may be appreciated at one stroke of the attention. It must not be so small as not to tax the attention, that is, to hold it; it should be in good scale as the architects say...

The rhythm unit is simply any repeated sequence of lengths and heights. Upon this ether the sounds are strung in their variety – slipping, clinging, overreaching, triumphing but always going forward even through moments of total disorder in the advance. Yet the rhythm persists, perfect...

[1] F. S. Flint 'Imagisme', *Poetry* I, 6 (March 1913), 198–9: 'As regarding rhythm: to compose in sequence of the musical phrase, not in sequence of a metronome' (p. 199).
[2] A letter from Williams to Harriet Monroe, 29 September 1913 (ICN), mentions a ms. by this title as 'sent earlier'.
[3] The nature of her reply may be judged from Williams' own, in which he showed he intended to send the article to Pound (*Selected Letters*, p. 26).
[4] The author discovered it uncatalogued among the Viola Baxter Jordan papers (CtY).

Here then, is the touchstone to it all: though the sounds of speech, i.e. words, letters, poetic lines, what not, convey the rhythm to a passion yet the rhythm itself is a thing apart and no sound. Upon this the wordy passions string sounds as they strain toward the perfect image.

In this alone rests the principal hope, that flexibility in perfection which, absent, has blocked the way till now...

The one thing essential to rhythm is not sound but motion, of the two kinds: forward and up and down, rapidity of motion and quality of motion.

Thus the number of sounds in the rhythm unit do not because of their number give the unit any quality but only as they give motion in one of the two directions.

For this reason the poetic foot – dependent on the number of sounds composing it – cannot, except by chance, embody the rhythm unit. The motion might be given by either a greater or less number of sounds in the same unit.

By seeing the rhythm apart from the sounds clustering about it the old meter forms are enlarged into a unit more flexible and more accurate. And yet these meter forms, with their rigid stress and counted syllables are a primitive perception of the true thing. But to count the syllables is but the bare makeshift for the appreciation of elapsing time. It is as stupid as to say that every musical measure in two-four time must contain only two notes.

Besides, how can syllables of no known length be taken three and three, five and five etc., and made into a unit of rhythm? I believe it impossible, no matter what the language, unless the rhythm is first put to music. And there are other difficulties.

This makeshift of counting the syllables – only possible because we were not capable of music and because none has yet been able to count the time without it – is now expanded to meet the true necessity which is that the time, not the syllables, *must* be counted.

In the new way:
The same rhythm, swift, may be of three syllables or if two are elided, of one: whereas, slow, it may consist of four or seven or any number that the sense agrees to. This is the flexibility that the modern requires...

It presupposes a more finely attuned ear than has as yet been, a greater reserve, a quicker perception but in return it opens a way out of our word bound present. It opens a new field for the fine tools of accuracy now compelled to idleness and new places for masses that could not fit into the too rigid present forms.

But with the aid of Heaven no one shall confuse this conception with the simple stressed line; that is, three stresses, four stresses to a line, etc., this is not rhythm, this is only the half.

God preserve us all from false prophets!

Miss Monroe's article, 'Rhythms of English Verse',[1] also made

---

[1] H. Monroe, 'Rhythms of English Verse', *Poetry* III, 2 (November 1913), 61–8; 3 (December 1913), 100–11.

reference to the laws of rhythm in terms of wave-theory,[1] as did Pound,[2] and attempted to cut through the problem of quantity by defining rhythm as 'a regular succession of time-intervals'.[3] She also suggested thinking of verse in terms of music, 'it becomes less confusing to discard the word foot altogether and use instead the musical term bar',[4] and spoke of the 'measure' of the poem as its time-signature: 'each bar, like a bar of music, takes the same amount of time for utterance as every other bar, except that the reader, like the musician, varies the tempo in phrasing...'[5] Thus the stresses, rests, and number of syllables were all variable according to the phrasing. She spoke of the necessity for more scientific knowledge being necessary 'to remove English poetry from the rack of "accentual" prosody, and restore it to the great universal laws of rhythm'.[6] At this point in his career, Williams, still referring to 'English' speech rhythms, would not have disagreed, but before long he was perceptive enough to see that the racked, or rigid foot was but an aspect of the British concern to maintain unchanged standards – a hierarchy of value in poetic techniques.

In Williams' view the alien pace of English, the perfections of its achieved poetic forms, and the fixity of the idea of an elite culture, made the British model redundant. In fact, if he had read his local history at first hand, he could have found apt analogies in Paterson for European constriction and rigidity. L'Enfant, the architect of Washington, failed to design a plan for Paterson because his neat grid-system could not cope with the rough terrain; 'he proposed to run streets and avenues 200 feet in width at right angles, regardless of rock, hill or stream'.[7] And Rogers, the builder of locomotives in Paterson, wrote:[8]

Foreign built engines are as stiff as a bar of steel; the curves of the roads they run on are necessarily of a very obtuse angle and there can be no high grades. When

[1] *Ibid.* p. 61.
[2] E. Pound, 'A Few Don'ts by an Imagiste', *Poetry* I, 6 (March 1913), 200–6: 'Don't chop your stuff into separate *iambs*. Don't make each line stop dead at the end, and begin every next line with a heave. Let the beginning of the next line catch the rise of the rhythm wave, unless you want a definite longish pause' (p. 204).
[3] 'Rhythms of English Verse', p. 62.
[4] *Ibid.*
[5] *Ibid.* p. 68.
[6] *Ibid.* p. 111.
[7] L. R. Trumbull, *A History of Industrial Paterson* (Paterson, N.J., 1882), p. 34.
[8] William Nelson and Charles A. Shriner, *History of Paterson and Its Environs* (3 vols, N.Y., and Chicago, 1920), vol. I, p. 353.

3 Members of the *Others* group, Rutherford, Spring 1916. Front row
(l. to r.): Alanson Hartpence, Alfred Kreymborg, William Carlos Williams
(with 'Mother Kitty'), Skip Cannell. Back row (l. to r.): Jean Crotti,
Marcel Duchamp, Walter Arensberg, Man Ray, R. A. Sanborn,
Maxwell Bodenheim

4   *Americana Fantastica* by Joseph Cornell: front and back covers of *View* II, 4 (January 1943)

I build an engine I make it as wobbly as necessary by using trucks with a good deal of play; in other words I build the engine to suit the road. The result is that my engines turn all sorts of corners and climb grades that would be considered impossible in Europe. The cost of a road using my engines is a trifle of the cost required to build a road for foreign engines. The Englishman has always been noted for his tenacity of purpose, and his most delightful stubbornness is his refusal to learn anything from an American. He makes fun of my engines, calling them 'basket work'; I hope he will continue to do so.

It is not necessary to refer here in detail to the kinaesthetic emphasis which Charles Olson brought to the so-called Black Mountain group of poets in the early fifties. Olson's muscular conception of the poetic act belongs to an American view prefigured by Baker Brownell in 1923, and by Oliver Wendell Holmes' essay of 1879, 'The Physiology of Versification'.[1] In the company of Robert Duncan, Robert Creeley, and the prosodist among the poets contributing to the magazine *Origin*, Cid Corman, Williams was encouraged, while severely incapacitated by a series of cerebral srokes, to make explicit the tactic which he had pursued since 'Speech Rhythm' forty years before. The locomotor writing of this group is based essentially on the simple physiological functions of breathing and moving; man in general walks, the poet dances. Williams' own use of a description of the act of walking in *Paterson* catches the walker at the projective instant when the wave of energy breaks, and before the rhythmic recoil begins all over again.[2] This was the simple conception of action which he wanted. But by the time his youthful followers had taken up his cause his own physical resources were checked.

Hugh Kenner, who edited Williams' final essay on 'Measure',[3] has suggested that Williams' use of the three-part line of the late poems stemmed from his inability to read after the brain damage of his strokes:[4]

His eyes could follow a line but not jump back and locate accurately the beginning

---

[1] See M. Weaver, '"Measure" and Its Propaganda', *Cambridge Opinion* 41 [October 1965], 15–17.
[2] See Appendix B (*Paterson*, p. 59). Williams may owe something to Thoreau's essay, 'Walking', *The Writings of Thoreau* (20 vols, Boston, 1906), vol V, pp. 205–48.
[3] W. C. Williams, 'Measure', *Spectrum* III, 3 (Fall 1959), 131–57; reprinted, with textual corrections and factual annotations by the present writer, in *Cambridge Opinion* 41 [October 1965], 4–14 [33].
[4] Letter to the author, 11 February 1966.

of the next line...I'm convinced that the 3-ply typography of his late verse was originally a set of helps (with the tab stops) for just such line-finding in rereading.

But, although this suggests a physical reason why Williams increasingly used the 'triadic foot' in the last years of his life, the evidence of the publication in *Paterson* in 1948 of 'The descent beckons' must be considered. The origin of the three-part line was probably in Pound's original printing of 'In a Station of the Metro':[1]

> The apparition   of these faces   in the crowd:
> Petals   on a wet, black   bough.

To re-arrange these groups of three in a step-down line was a natural, if unconscious, development of the idea of the musical phrase:

> The apparition
>   of these faces
>   in the crowd:
> Petals
>   on a wet, black
>   bough.

This use of a line with three feet or bars is, of course, neither accentual nor quantitative, but what Williams chose to call 'qualitative'.[2] It answered the needs of the American idiom, as Malcolm Cowley described it, in part, in 1945:[3]

1. The words are simple in themselves, taken from common speech, and the authors make no effort to avoid a long succession of monosyllables. The 'phrase' – that is, the group of words – tends to be rather longer than in standard English, and the accent or changed tone of voice falls on the last word in each group, almost as in French. Thus: 'As the shadow of the *kingfisher* moved up the *stream*, a big trout shot upstream in a long *angle*, then lost his shadow as he came through the surface of the *water*.'

2. The sentence structure is generally looser than in standard English, with a number of simple statements connected by 'and' or 'but' or 'when'.

In 'The descent beckons' the changed tone falls on an apparently unimportant, but ambiguous 'even', which is in fact the pivot of the movement:[4]

[1] *Poetry* II, 1 (April 1913), 12.
[2] W.C.Williams, Statement in notes on contributors, *Poetry* XCIII, 6 (March 1959), 416.
[3] Malcolm Cowley, 'The Middle American Style: D.Crockett to E.Hemingway', *New York Times Book Review* L, 28 (15 July 1945), 3, 14;*14.*
[4] *Paterson*, p. 96.

                                        Memory is a kind
            of accomplishment
                        a sort of renewal
                                    even
            an initiation, since the spaces it opens are new
            places
                        inhabited by hordes
                                    heretofore unrealized

'Even' both refers back from renewal to memory and introduces an initiation to new places at the same instant. American intonation is what makes this possible, but the timing must also be exact if the point of balance is to be auditorily perceived.[1] Straining towards the perfect 'image', Williams, like all the Imagists, endorsed the predominantly visual emphasis of the word. Pound's 'musical phrases' and F.S.Flint's 'cadence' suggested an auditory emphasis but, as we have seen it, received little attention until the Objectivist revival of Imagism. Williams' 'measure' was inclusive; it embraced the theory of poetic structure, the perception of form, and man's objective and subjective role in the world: 'Measure is the only solidity we are permitted to know in our sensible world, to measure.'[2]

The moral conviction that the language accurately used was objectively true to reality, and that the poet must be true to his materials, led Williams inevitably to political considerations.[3] His belligerence towards British English was consistent with the surge of spirit that prompted him to write 'The Writers of the American Revolution', which asked for reconfirmation of 'a new world reconstituted on an abler pattern than had been known heretofore'.[4] His attitude towards the English iambic line was expressed as an accusation of latent fascism when called it the 'medieval masterbeat'.[5] The true government was 'the government of the words, since it is of all governments the archetype'.[6] Language, prosody, and state rested on

---

[1] For some analyses of *visually* observable grammatical ambiguity, see M. Weaver, Review of *Pictures from Brueghel*, *The Cambridge Review* LXXXV, 2078 (30 May 1964), 465–6.

[2] 'Measure', *Cambridge Opinion* 41, 13.

[3] See W.C.Williams, 'To Write American Poetry', *Fantasy* V, 1 (Summer 1935), 12–14.

[4] *Selected Essays*, p. 39.

[5] W.C.Williams, 'The American Spirit in Art', *Proceedings of the American Academy of Arts and Letters* (Second series) 2 (1952), 51–9;59.

[6] Cited from memory by Robert Creeley from Williams' speech of acceptance of the

a single democratic idea. But while Williams was composing his sequence 'That's the American Style'[1] the political style of the thirties was becoming progressively totalitarian.

National Book Award for Poetry, broadcast on the A.B.C. network, 16 March 1950, and communicated to the author by letter (31 October 1967).

[1] *Poetry* XLIII, 1 (October 1933), 1–8.

6

An Arbitrary Authority

'Blast' and the Proletarians

The woollen mills of Passaic, started by German immigrants in the 1880s, had attracted large numbers of Slavs, until in 1920 the original 6,500 inhabitants had swollen to 54,700. They flowed over into East Rutherford, and other towns across the Passaic river. Passaic had for a long time a higher percentage of foreign-born inhabitants than any other American city.[1] Living and working conditions there were substandard; the infant mortality rate was higher there than anywhere else in New Jersey; the average wage of the mill-workers was less than 1,100 dollars a year.[2] It was here, in the National Bank Building, that Williams had a second surgery from 1927 to 1935.

The year of the Passaic strike, 1926, saw the emergence of *New Masses* under the editorship of Mike Gold. Williams contributed to the first issue a story which cost him 5,000 dollars in a law-suit for defamation of character.[3] Hugo Gellert, the caricaturist, made his wood-cut portrait. But despite his feeling of identification with the socialist old *Masses*, seen largely through the eyes of John Reed, the revolutionist who had doubtless brought his ideas to the Grantwood colony in New Jersey before the First World War, Williams could not think of the *New Masses* group except as new transcendentalists.[4] They offered a social philosophy, but he had already rejected the relevance of any kind of philosophy to literature.

[1] Cunningham, *New Jersey*.
[2] Schonbach, *Radicals and Visionaries*, p. 73.
[3] In a letter to the author (23 April 1966), James Rorty noted that Williams was quite 'unrepentant', when he appeared before the editors over his story, 'The Five Dollar Guy', *New Masses* I, 1 (May 1926), 19, 29.
[4] Letter to Fred R. Miller, 11 June 1935: 'They forget that the use of the word "Soviets" indicates a plural. It means an agglomerate of various units each true *first* to its own place and necessities so to be respected by the whole.'

If Williams saw the first issue of *The Glebe*, the book magazine which published Pound's *Des Imagistes* in 1914, he would have found ample precedent for his own strike passage in 'The Wanderer'. Adolf Wolff, the proletarian poet, had self-explanatory titles like 'On Seeing the Garment Strikers March', 'To Arturo Giovannitti', 'Elizabeth Gurley Flynn', and 'The Revolt of the Ragged'.[1]

As an egoist Williams was committed to owning himself by the thoroughly middle-class habit of working for money and acquiring property. In the early twenties he was sending sums of money to a destitute writer, Emanuel Carnevali, as was Harriet Monroe, to whom he wrote:[2]

Give all your goods to feed the poor! It is a subtle hypocrisy which the world has not yet explored. I myself have been the subject of charity in small ways, the charity of fate etc. that were it not for a yellow dog's constitution I would be all dead instead of moribund. Bah.

Then again there are those who pose as mighty because they have nothing. Pride will find a coat somewhere. Intelligence is a bible in itself. Debs is the only hero.

Debs was in jail having just polled nearly a million votes as presidential candidate of the Socialist Party. He was in prison because he refused to support entry into the First War. Williams himself was evidently in two minds although, unlike Debs, he took the Allied position as soon as war was declared; an action he repeated in the Second World War.[3] When he said that if war came America would have to fight (as fight Williams' sons did), he nevertheless toasted the memory of Eugene Debs.[4] Debs, it seems, was doubly associated in his mind – with non-interventionism and socialism.

As we have seen, Williams wrote a 'Democratic Party Poem' in support of the campaign of 1928-9. In his letters he exhorted his friends to vote for Al Smith. Later, in 1936, he acted as campaign manager for

---

[1] *The Glebe* I, I (September 1913).
[2] Letter to Harriet Monroe, 13 January 1921 (ICN).
[3] Williams signed the League for Cultural Freedom and Socialism's manifesto against entry into the war (*Partisan Review* VI, 5 [Fall 1939], 125-7). A few months earlier he had favoured a military alliance with 'the democratic powers, England, France and Russia' (*New Republic* LXXXXIX, 1828 [28 June 1939], 209), but this was before the infamous Russo-Nazi pact, which thoroughly disillusioned the liberals.
[4] *Partisan Review* VI, 4 (Summer 1939), 44.

two local Democratic candidates.[1] As the campaign of 1931–2 approached he dug into his files once more and sent his poem to Louis Zukofsky, who chided him for his naivety in believing in a mythic democracy. Williams defended himself claiming that he had at one time considered an ironic ending for his poem, and had rejected it: 'I wanted to say "If this is all impossible, as you may see at once that it is, what then?" –.'[2]

His younger friends, however, were of another mind. They believed that a perfect political system was a matter for intellect not emotion. There was a clear note of determinism in that part of the Objectivist poetry programme which expressed a 'Desire for what is objectively perfect, inextricably the direction of historic and contemporary particulars.'[3] Zukofsky's acceptance of Marx at that time was an expression of his interest in dialectics. As Carl Rakosi wrote later: 'The quotations from Marx and Lenin in his work always seemed to me to be there for a literary purpose, somewhat like Thomist ideas in a religious poet.'[4] But, nevertheless, the Objectivist anthology in *Poetry* contained a poem by Whittaker Chambers. Of the other Objectivists, George Oppen had a Populist grounding in Sandburg, and Charles Reznikoff's subjects were often taken from the Lower East Side.

Just how swiftly Objectivism as a minor aesthetic sensation gave way to the rise of proletarianism in American writing can best be judged by the fate of the second series of Williams' *Contact*. When the publishers became interested in the new radicalism, and Norman Macleod undertook the editorship of a fourth issue of *Contact* on proletarian writing, Williams became positively unconcerned in the magazine's future. According to Macleod, he was just not interested in proletarian literature.[5]

It was just at this point that Fred Miller had first begun to correspond with Williams. At once Miller asked him to produce, against a deadline, a short story for each issue of his new magazine *Blast*, named not for the London magazine edited by Wyndham Lewis, but

[1] Letter to Ezra Pound, 16 October 1936 (CtY).
[2] Letter to Louis Zukofsky, 15 July 1931 (CtY).
[3] *Poetry* XXXVII, 5 (February 1931), 268.
[4] Letter to the author, 3 December 1966. Williams himself spoke of 'the poetic and theoretical solidity of Marxist teaching' (*Selected Essays*, p. 216).
[5] *Golden Goose* III, 4 (May 1952), 161; *A Year Magazine*, Section Two (1933), 14.

the war-time radical review edited by Emma Goldman and Alexander Berkman. Miller was a member of the John Reed Club of New York, whose avowed policy was to oppose any kind of cultural support for capitalism, to win over the intellectuals to the revolutionary cause, and to encourage the proletarian arts. In a mimeographed magazine, *Left Writers*, Miller described an attack made on the John Reed Club – *New Masses* group by a revolutionary Swiss editor, a Dr M.J.Olgin, at a recent meeting in New York. Olgin denied a revolutionary name to Mike Gold's *Jews Without Money*, Mary Heaton Vorse's *Strike!*, and John Dos Passos' *Three Soldiers*, which in America were regarded as the basis for a proletarian literature. He maintained that the bourgeois intellectuals who were producing these works were professional writers, and thus classless, whereas revolutionary writers would come from the workers.[1]

Miller disagreed, not only with Olgin, but with the *New Masses*. The genuine left writers were not to be found among the bourgeois journalists and liberals of the old *Masses* and *Liberator* tradition, nor solely among the workers:[2]

1. The John Reed–*New Masses* group has produced some literature that may fairly be called proletarian but that is not strictly revolutionary. With Olgin, proletarian and revolutionary are one; hence his denial of the existence of a proletarian school in U.S. writing: the 'Interbureau' also uses these terms interchangably, in its case listing as revolutionary what is often broadly proletarian and no more.

2. Workers chained to the job have not turned out the wanted satire on New York City courts nor the saga of the Ford belt-slaves because they have neither the time nor literary skill necessary.

3. Everybody cannot write. For this reason the bulk of proletarian – and revolutionary – literature will have to be written, not by the masses, but by full-time intellectuals, preferably sprung from the working-class, workers becoming intellectualized and the revolutionary bourgeois intelligentsia. At that, any proletarian guilty of an occasional poem is an occasional intellectual.

4. Why should a full-time proletarian writer be considered an 'outsider', so far as the proletariat is concerned, when a full-time political doesn't lose his standing as a worker?

5. Epics are not written between days at gruelling toil.

6. Left writers can best assist the revolutionary movement by waging

[1] F.R.Miller, 'We Want – What Do We Want?' *Left Writers* 2 (March 1931) [1–7] [*1–2*].
[2] *Ibid.* [6–7].

propaganda indirectly, thru their materials. 'Sloganization' makes for bad art, which is worthless both as art and as propaganda. Dialectic and art don't mix. This of course does not apply to the art, if it is one, of criticism.

7. Proletarian writings, tho not 100% Bolshevik (revolutionary), have a social function; they 'do good'.

8. *New Masses* has a Greenwich Village Katzenjammer and a business office respect for names. Its field is too narrow.

Miller showed himself ready to make his own way with what he called a 'mushroom mag'. In Jack Conroy's magazine, *The Rebel Poet*, it was announced more than a year later that *Left Writers* had been revived under Miller's editorship,[1] but like many another such announcements it was unsupported by funds. Meanwhile Miller would walk, for lack of the subway fare, from Union Square to the Upper Bronx to attend a Rebel Poets meeting, contributing his own poems and a translation with Philip Rahv of a poem by Johannes Becher.[2] Rahv and Miller soon went separate ways; Rahv with his critical interests to found *Partisan Review*, and Miller with his idea of embodying socialist thought in the short story to start *Blast*. Williams was not a man to join anything, but he himself believed that the creative writer could only truly clarify the problems of a proletarian literature according to his talent.

When Williams found himself named as an advisory editor of *Blast* he acquiesced, knowing that although Miller was militantly anti-bourgeois he could be counted on not to fill his magazine with propaganda. Williams had seen some notes on the short story in Europe by Samuel Putnam, who recommended a story by E.C.Fabre in the *Nouvelle Revue Française*:[3]

It is a story which, if you are at all sensitive to the *Zeitgeist* will probably haunt you like a nightmare. Yet on the surface, as you will see if you look it up – and you must look it up – it is unpretending enough. What is it, one may ask, that gives it the power it unquestionably has? The answer is: a successfully, which is to say, artistically (esthetically) transmuted social *emotion*. It is the answer to much long-winded argumentation on the subject of 'Marxism versus Esthetics', etc. It is the exemplification of the answer given by James Burnham (see *The Symposium* for January, 1933): if the *artist* happens to have *social feeling*, that feeling

[1] *The Rebel Poet* 15 (August 1932), 2.
[2] *Ibid*. p. 7.
[3] Samuel Putnam, 'Notes on the European Short Story', *The Windsor Quarterly* I, I (Spring 1933), 14–17; 15–16.

will inevitably come out. There is not a word of propaganda in the Fabre story, yet, it is, effectively, propaganda of the most terrific sort. On the side of form, too, the story is interesting, by the reason of the use that is made in it of the interior monologue.

Williams immediately translated the story in question and it appeared in the first issue of *Blast*.[1] Miller and Williams were agreed that political relevance was contained within the general cultural relevance. Accurate statement was the main requirement. But this was not the position held by the proletarians in general.

The popular front which Miller represented included *Blast*, *The Anvil* (later *New Anvil*), and *Dynamo*. The last named, originally to have been called *Fellow Traveller*, was the work of Sol Funaroff, Herman Spector, and Joseph Vogel. Although on good terms with Miller, whom they knew from *The Rebel Poet*, these city proletarians, the poets of Albert Halper's *Union Square*, chastised Williams soundly for his lack of social commitment. In Funaroff's view, the fault of Objectivism lay in the failure of the military definition in its programme:[2]

Actually, the Objectivist has no objective, has no sense of direction in the sense of movement towards a goal. His aim is really the aim of the camera, its lens focused upon an object, to snap a lifeless photograph. It is the act of the recorder and not of the creator, the man of purpose.

Spector expressed a similar criticism of Reznikoff, although this time it was properly couched in Marxist terms:[3]

Charles Reznikoff expresses in his poetry the limited world-view of a 'detached' bystander: that is, of a person whose flashes of perception for the immediate esthetics of the contemporary scene are not co-ordinated in any way with a dialectical comprehension of the life-process.

Nevertheless, Spector noted with approval signs of 'dialectical comprehension' in the Objectivists, such as Reznikoff's poem on Marx in *Jerusalem the Golden*, and held out hopes for their conversion from defeatist and negativist positions as non-partisans.

But the *Dynamo* group, as we have seen, held out little hope for Williams. When, on Miller's suggestion, he submitted his short story,

[1] *Blast* I, I (September–October 1933), 30–2.
[2] 'Charles Henry Newman' (pseudonym of Sol Funaroff) and Herman Spector, 'How Objective is Objectivism?' *Dynamo* I, 3 (Summer 1934), 26–30; 26–7.
[3] *Ibid.* 29–30.

'The Girl with a Pimply Face', Joseph Vogel rejected it on the grounds that the story showed no sense of social implications. Williams replied as follows:[1]

were the 'doctor' unaware of the social implications involved in giving the girl a fifty cent prescription when the father was earning his $10 a week for her face, when the baby is dying, that would be the precise reason for using the story in such a magazine as you contemplate. What is your purpose, to kill off all observation for the sake of monotony? I think you will miss your possible opportunity if you do. The girl *got* the fifty cents from her mother, didn't she? and without trouble.

Williams, in a staged discussion with his brother, reaffirmed this position. His brother offered the example of a Polish miner who bought his wife a 1,500 dollar mink coat, and was not perturbed to find her scrubbing the floor in it. Williams' attitude was simple: 'He got what he wanted.'[2] But his real point is that the observation of such actions as part of a totality of behaviour at all social levels is the artist's only recourse where a breaking-up of the fixed elements in society is taking place – want and luxury existing as two sides of the same coin. Williams was prepared to accept many more such maddening experiences rather than attempt to make them fit a social theory. However, a literary situation could still rouse Williams' commitment, as may be seen in his defence of a Missouri cowhand–poet.

H.H.Lewis, the author of several pamphlets published by the proletarian printer, Ben Hagglund, was one of Jack Conroy's and Ralph Cheyney's original Rebel Poets.[3] But despite, or because of, the effort of the Midwesterners to establish a literary milieu by means of their publications, the New York editors stood aloof from their fellow-radicals. When after six years or more Lewis quarrelled with his Midwestern supporters and attempted to find favour in the East, he found the pages of *New Masses* and *Partisan Review* closed to him, and told Williams of his situation.

As far as Williams was concerned the Midwest began on his side of the Hudson. His section was not Southern or Eastern in any but a relatively geographical sense. Without denying his genuine interest in

---

[1] Letter to Joseph Vogel [1933] (CtY).
[2] *Selected Essays*, p. 191.
[3] *Unrest, 1931*, ed. Jack Conroy and Ralph Cheyney (N.Y. [1931]).

Lewis's poetry, it seems also as if he was glad of the opportunity to reverse his aesthetic attitude towards social implications. *Partisan Review* had earlier called for sanctions against him because of his stance against communism in favour of American democracy. Now he consented to withhold material from the review if *New Masses* would publish an article on Lewis.[1] It was a way of rescuing the browbeaten cowhand from Cape Girardeau, and of playing the political game to Williams' own temporary satisfaction. Lewis had written of Russia in revolutionary vein:[2]

> Russia, Russia, righting wrong
> Russia, Russia, Russia!
> That unified one sovereign throng,
> That hundred and sixty million strong
> Russia!
> America's loud EXAMPLE-SONG,
> Russia, Russia, Russia!

Williams commented:[3]

When he speaks of Russia, it is precisely then that he is most American, most solidly in the tradition, not out of it, not borrowing a 'foreign' solution. It is the same cry that sent Europeans to a 'foreign' America and there set them madly free.

For Williams, as his own poem 'Russia' written in 1946 suggested,[4] it was America which was Russia's model.

The direct, natural speech of Lewis' poems also recommended them to Williams. He quoted a portion:[5]

> I'll say,
> Phew, for Crissake,
> The brains of the 'Brain Trust',
>   that's it,
> Rrrrrotten!

> Pity the poor American donkey,
> Pity the poor American farmhand,

[1] Draft of letter to James ONeal in Mrs Williams' hand, 11 July 1939 (CtY).
[2] Cited by Williams, 'An American Poet', *New Masses* XXV, 9 (23 November 1937), 17–18; *18*. The article was written in the summer of 1935 (letter to F. R. Miller, 11 June 1935).
[3] *Ibid.* p. 17.
[4] *Collected Later Poems*, pp. 93–6.
[5] *New Masses* XXV, 9, 18.

The one nervously zigzagging,
The other compelled to jerk him back
        to the row,
Plowing under cotton!
Such an 'assinine'
Torturing
Strain on the sound sense of both!

In 1941 Williams came upon the poems of Don West, 'The Sandburg of the South', in a little magazine, and marked presumably for their warmth poems like 'I Hold America to My Heart', 'I've Seen God', and 'Look Here, Georgia'.[1] Williams was impressed by such writers, not because it was easier to write about the situation of the tenant–farmer and sharecropper rather than face the urban facts of Passaic – he was doing that in the stories for *Blast* – but because these agrarian proletarians were colonists as oppressed as 'The Writers of the (first) American Revolution', the title of an essay Williams wrote at this time.[2] He said it was written for the projected magazine of an American Federation of Writers, but in the absence of traces of such an organisation we may speculate whether he was referring to the Revolutionary Writers' Federation, to which Sam Sorkin, the co-editor of *Blast*, belonged. In Williams' understanding of the term, to be a revolutionary writer was to be an American writer.

'The Lyric' and the *'red decade'*

In September 1952 when Williams was due to take up the appointment of Consultant in Poetry at the Library of Congress he was looking forward to an opportunity which he had deferred some years before. He was first offered the post in March 1948, but chose to remain in medical practice for a year or two more until his son was firmly established and he was sure, himself, of his future income. Meanwhile he was stricken with a heart attack and a cerebral stroke. Then, when he was at an extremely low ebb, the McCarthyites also struck and deprived him of the post.

The Lyric had been for many years an innocuous little magazine of 'traditional' poetry, published in Roanoke, Virginia. In 1948 it

---

[1] Williams' copy (CtY): *The Span* I, 2 (June–July 1941), 15.
[2] Letter to Roland Lane Latimer, 24 March 1936 (ICN). Misdated in *Selected Essays* as having been written in 1925.

changed hands, and passed into the control of a Mrs Virginia Kent Cummins. Her first issue was exceptionally thin in content but included an essay by a certain C.E.Burklund, 'The Treason of "Modern" Poetry'.[1] This essay-title became the key-note of Mrs Cummins' short-lived but damaging campaign. In the next issue Robert Hillyer, who led the attack on Pound's Bollingen award, appeared on the magazine's mast-head.[2] Barely three months later Mrs Cummins announced that she had established in New York, in April 1949, a Foundation for Traditional Poetry, and that its first award of a thousand dollars had been made to Hillyer, 'for distinguished and unswerving loyalty to traditional poetry'. The formal take-over of *The Lyric* was announced with Hillyer named as Vice-President, an office from which he resigned, however, in the autumn of 1950.

In the three years of her reign Mrs Cummins saw to it that Pound, Eliot, Auden, Spender, Marianne Moore, Cummings, and Williams were all dubbed either obscene or obscure whenever they received the kind of poetry award which seniority naturally brings. The same issue which announced Hillyer as a vice-president of traditional poetry contained an editorial which denounced Williams' volume *The Clouds*. 'History of Love' was obscene; 'Russia', in a shrewd selection, was treason. It was noted that, 'He is now one of the Fellows in American Letters (of the Library of Congress) which honored Ezra Pound'.[3] If the connection between the Pound case and the Williams witch-hunt to follow was not sufficiently clear from that sentence, then Mrs Cummins' quotation from Hillyer linked them certainly: '"The Library of Congress belongs to the people...it is by my authority as a citizen that I protest. *A scandalous thing has been done to the name of my Library of Congress.*"'[4] Mrs Cummins continued zealously, 'Let our battle cry be: "Truth before everything, even if it brings suffering."' She brought suffering in abundance to Williams, who was already stricken, deeply depressed, and in no condition to defend himself, but in a few months she, herself, died.

In the winter of 1951 Mrs Cummins had begun a stop-press tactic

[1] *The Lyric* XXVIII, 3 (Autumn 1948), 141–2.
[2] *The Lyric* XXVIII, 4 (Winter 1948).
[3] *The Lyric* XXIX, 2–3 (Summer-Autumn), 195.
[4] *Ibid.* p. 196.

of laying into copies of *The Lyric* mimeographed letters. The first attacked an award made to E.E. Cummings.[1] Then in the Autumn 1952 issue she inserted a separately-printed open letter, attacking Williams' appointment as Consultant in Poetry at the Library of Congress. She indicted him on the following counts:[2]

1. Dr. Williams was one of the signers of the Golden Book of American Friendship with the Soviet Union. This was a symposium of felicitations sent to Stalin in 1937 to celebrate the 20th Anniversary of the Bolshevik Revolution and the Soviet Dictatorship.
2. Dr. Williams signed a second statement in 1938 urging greater cooperation with Stalin. This was published in the Communist magazine, NEW MASSES.
3. In 1939 Dr. Williams signed an open letter urging closer cooperation with Stalinist Russia. This letter appeared in SOVIET RUSSIA TODAY.
4. In 1940 Dr. Williams signed a Communist Party statement demanding an end of the House Committee on Un-American Activities.
5. In 1941 Dr. Williams signed a public statement defending the policies and practices of the Communist Party.
6. In 1942 Dr. Williams urged clemency for the Communist Party leader, Earl Browder, then serving a prison term for perjury in Atlanta.
7. In 1951 Dr. Williams was billed, with Paul Robeson, to speak at a rally for three of the convicted 'Hollywood Ten', just out of prison.

As documentation the seven points were undoubtedly accurate, but the last was accurate only if by that it is meant that Williams was billed to speak. He himself declared that he had never given permission to be so billed.[3] There was evidently free access to more than ordinary research facilities.[4] It was stated in a syndicated column from Washington, by Fulton Lewis Jr, that the House Committee on Un-American Activities index on Williams contained fifty cards. The columnist was able to provide further bibliographical details for Mrs Cummins' seven points.[5]

[1] *The Lyric* XXXI, 1 (Winter 1951), insert.
[2] *The Lyric* XXXII, 4 (Autumn 1952), insert.
[3] Statement reported in the *New York Telegram and Sun*, 11 October 1954 (microfilm of newspaper clippings, The Free Public Library, Rutherford).
[4] The information was also used by an anonymous attacker in *The American Legion Magazine* (December 1952), pp. 18–19, 56–8.
[5] Fulton Lewis Jr, 'Literary Probe Due', *Seattle Post Intelligencer*, 24 November 1952, Section 12 (clipping kindly provided by Mr Malcolm Cowley): *1. Soviet Russia Today*, November 1937. *4.* A letter-head distributed by the American Committee for Democracy and Intellectual Freedom, January 1940. *5. Daily Worker*, March 1941. *6.* A leaflet of the Citizens Committee to Free Earl Browder. *7. Daily Worker*, 1951, sponsored by the Arts, Sciences and Professions Organization.

The line pursued by Williams through the 'red decade' was essentially that of the *New Republic*, whose editor Malcolm Cowley was also on the editorial board of *Soviet Russia Today*, the official organ of the Friends of the Soviet Union. The compilation of the *Golden Book of American Friendship* was its dazzling achievement. As Eugene Lyons wrote:[1]

Several hundred thousand signatures were gathered for that book. In view of the fact that the Kremlin was then in the midst of bloody purges which will continue to horrify mankind for generations, the size of the *Book* indicates once more how extensive the Stalinist penetration of life had become.

The Open Letter in *Soviet Russia Today* which Williams signed with 399 others, including Hemingway, Waldo Frank, Lincoln Kirstein, and F.O. Matthiessen, called for unity against fascism by means of better co-operation with the Soviet Union.[2] But it began with an attack on the Committee of Cultural Freedom founded in New York the previous spring by John Dewey, Horace M. Kallen, and Arthur O. Lovejoy, which asserted that both forms of dictatorship, fascism and communism, posed a threat to American democracy. It was Williams' own position, and he had signed the C.C.F.'s original manifesto.[3] But now he resigned.

His resignation was an extraordinary event, but indicative of the times. According to the committee's *Bulletin*, Williams was the gullible victim of a technique of disruption which took the form of intellectual terrorism. A member of the committee would either be called to the telephone and read a letter of resignation by another member and asked to resign himself, or he would be visited by a representative of another organisation of which he was a member and told that the new one he had joined was disrupting the other. Advice and cajolery would be followed by threats that his manuscripts would be rejected by a particular magazine if he continued to support the rival organisation.[4]

On 6 June 1939 it was reported in the *Daily Worker* that Countee Cullen, Williams, and a Columbia University historian had resigned from the committee. The committee wrote to them asking whether the

[1] Eugene Lyons, *The Red Decade* (Indianapolis and N.Y., 1941), p. 259.
[2] *Soviet Russia Today* VIII, 5 (September 1939), 24–5, 28.
[3] *New York Times* LXXXVIII, 29696 (15 May 1939), 13.
[4] *Committee for Cultural Freedom Bulletin* I, 1 (15 October 1939), 2.

story was true. Cullen replied that he was under the impression that his resignation had already been forwarded through the League of American Writers; 'I gave them permission to send in my resignation along with others of the League who had concluded that it would be best for them to resign'.[1] Williams' own letter was printed in the *Bulletin*:[2]

It is my intention to resign from the Committee for Cultural Freedom as one of a group who take exception to a slur upon the good name of the League of American Writers for which at its very inception the League has been responsible. I also object to the presence of certain names on your list of membership, the names of several men whom I personally cannot trust. I thought I was serving the cause of democratic freedom when I allowed the new League to use my name but almost at once, after your first meeting, I felt that the League was being seized by a group for purposes rather subversive to its published intentions. I don't like it.

As the editor of the *Bulletin* noted, the *Daily Worker* published the resignations the day after the Third Writers' Congress of the League of American Writers, to which Williams had signed the call.[3] The editor further noted that Williams had not been at the committee's first meeting, but that he had received the minutes in which no mention was made of the league. Williams, however, managed, even in the short space of his letter, to confuse the league with the committee, and his third sentence bore some resemblance to the charge levelled at the C.C.F. in *Soviet Russia Today*: '...we feel it necessary to point out that among the signers of this manifesto are individuals who have for years had as their chief political objective the maligning of the Soviet people and their government...'[4]

The League of American Writers was a Popular Front organisation closely allied with *New Masses*, having developed out of the John Reed Clubs' National Conference in Chicago in 1935, but Williams' name did not appear on the signed calls to its first two congresses in 1935 and 1937. Why, then, had he signed the call to the Third Wirters' Congress? The answer lay in the cumulative effect of several other political events of the thirties.

[1] *Ibid.*
[2] *Ibid.* p. 3.
[3] *Direction* II, 3 (May-June 1939), 1.
[4] *Soviet Russia Today*, VIII, 5, 24.

Firstly, the league had been very prominent in supporting the cause of Loyalist Spain. Williams translated some Spanish ballads for one of its publications.[1] He was on his local committee for the Medical Bureau to Aid Spanish Democracy. He read the American League for Peace and Democracy's paper, *The Fight*, and spoke in support of the Loyalists at Madison Square Garden.[2]

Secondly, the League of American Writers had become a cultural force in New York, its communist origins no longer truly obvious and its literary programme far too interesting for Williams to ignore. The discussion of 'New Mediums in Verse' at the Third Writers' Congress, which was to provide an influential background for Williams' use of documentary in *Paterson*, was extended to a further meeting held on 26 June 1939 in the George Washington Hotel. The poets present at the symposium were: Genevieve Taggard, Countee Cullen, Kenneth Fearing, Edwin Rolfe, Willard Maas, Joseph Freeman, Isidor Schneider, Sol Funaroff, and Williams.[3] This time the meeting was open to the public, which, if it knew anything at all of proletarian poetry, would have seen the gathering to be the most comprehensive in its recent history.

Thirdly, the league's unofficial relation with the Works Progress Administration, by virtue of its members' employment by the government agency, would have been noticed by Williams, who in the winter of 1938 was approached by the W.P.A., which asked him to become Director of the Writers' Project in New Jersey. He did not accept the directorship, but he did consent to be a member of the New Jersey Guild Associates, Inc., which in 1938 produced a guide to the state of New Jersey, compiled and written by members of the Writers' Project.

Finally, Williams joined a notable group of radicals who wanted to produce a 'pro-labor or pulp magazine, which will counteract the anti-labor and *vigilante* tendencies of many publishers today'.[4] His partners in this enterprise – of which there is no further trace – included Louis Adamic, Richard Wright, and the secretary of the New Jersey C.I.O. The parody in *Paterson*, 'America the golden', is evidence of Williams'

[1] *And Spain Sings*, ed. M.J. Benardete, and R. Humphries (N.Y., 1937).
[2] Letter to James Laughlin, 20 July 1938 (copy: CtY).
[3] Press release from the League of American Writers, 20 July 1938.
[4] *Direction* II, 4 (July-August 1939), 19.

own detailed knowledge of the industrial problems of the city which was at the centre of his thought.[1]

Clearly, Williams was sympathetic towards many of the causes which the league, with its Stalinist commitment, sponsored. He was, in short, a fellow-traveller. However, as a writer he was strongly opposed to the arbitrary authority of a party line, whether communist or fascist. To the publisher of his volume, *Adam & Eve & The City* he wrote:[2]

My own feeling is that the worst element we have to face is the Communistic one. They will not see straight. They are the ones that for the next few years (as for the last few) will be the major obstacle for excellence to hurdle.

What Mrs Cummins apparently did not know was that Williams' only party affiliation, outside that of the Democratic Party, was with the American Social Credit Movement. Williams' membership was part of his coherent programme for an American life.

The American Social Credit Movement

On 5 October 1938 the American Social Credit Movement was launched in New York with Gorham B. Munson as its General Secretary. The ideological involvement of most of the members of the *Secession* group whose magazine Munson had edited, was now mainly Marxist, but Munson himself had espoused Social Credit while A. R. Orage, former editor of the London *New Age*, was in New York from 1924 to 1931. In the spring of 1931 Orage gave four lectures on Social Credit at the New York School of the Theatre, then a year later returned to England to edit the *New English Weekly*. Munson became the American representative of the new paper, and formed the New Economics Group of New York.

The signatories of the group's first pamphlet, written by Munson, included Mavis McIntosh, Williams' agent at that time.[3] In 1934 Munson had the new edition of *Social Credit* by Major C. H. Douglas, the British founder of Social Credit, sent to Williams direct from the publishers, and Williams promised to read it.[4] He was therefore ready

1 See Appendix B (*Paterson*, p. 85).
2 Letter to Roland Lane Latimer, 26 January 1936 (ICU).
3 *Financial Freedom for Americans* (N.Y., [1932]).
4 Letter to G. B. Munson [1934] (CtMW).

when Pound, who always thought that Williams read too little, asked him whether he knew Douglas' ideas; Williams was able to reply that indeed he did and also those of his American backers, but that too close an organisation of theories might make it difficult to respond to actual events.[1] The local effort interested him as always.

In August 1934 Douglas' American supporters founded *New Democracy*, a Social Credit review. Not only did it publish Williams' writings on the subject, it also gave space to James Laughlin's first independent editorial efforts; *New Directions* was born within the pages of *New Democracy* and so named by Munson. In April Major Douglas had lectured in New York when Williams acted as a member of the lecture committee;[2] he now began to lend his name to various Social Credit organisations. In 1935 he joined the Black Sheep Club, a group of literary men who met occasionally with Paul Hampden, their economist, in a Sixteenth Street restaurant for cocktails and credit conversation.[3] In 1936 he went on to the General Council of the League for National Dividends, modelled on the League to Abolish Poverty in England.[4]

The increasing threat of having to choose between totalitarian alternatives in politics, the persistence of a depressed economic situation, and the surprising success of Social Credit in Alberta, inspired in Douglasites a desire for political action. John Hargrave organised the Social Credit Party of Great Britain – the Green Shirts until political uniforms were banned – and Munson campaigned hard for the drafts of the Goldsborough Bill heard briefly in Congress in various forms in 1935 and 1936, and protractedly in 1937.[5] But because the New

[1] Letter to Ezra Pound, 3 October 1933 (CtY).
[2] Letter to G.B.Munson, 18 April 1934 (CtMW).
[3] Letter to G.B.Munson, 14 September 1935 (CtMW): 'Maybe we're nominating ourselves for the firing squad when the Reds start shooting – but that's one of those things.'
[4] *New Democracy*, VI, 1 (March 1936), 21.
[5] As president of his local social club, The Fortnightly, Williams invited Munson to send a speaker on Social Credit (letter to G.B.Munson, 11 October 1935): 'But this is a bunch of Republicans, you know the type. Not interested in "crazy theories". Good guys but the back-bone-of-the-nation type, solid bone, shall I say, to anything new. They are not, however, dumb. Our host will be a well known lawyer of considerable influence in these parts – a possible candidate for Governor on the Democratic ticket (one of our few Democrats) at the next state election. He lives in Montclair!!
With these conditions in mind, looking for a practical, non-theoretical point of attack, it came to my mind that all of us of whatever stripe would be interested to hear someone speak of H.R. 9216. They can't call that theoretical.' For a discussion of the bill see

Economics Group of New York which had drafted this bill for Social Credit remained essentially a monetary reform group, uncommitted to political action, Munson seceded from it to found the American Social Credit Movement. The A.S.C.M., with which Williams registered at once as a dues-paying member,[1] issued its manifesto forthwith:[2]

The root of our economic distress is an automatic shortage of purchasing power maintained by the Monopoly of Credit.

We lay our axe against this evil root. Our mission is to destroy the Monopoly of Credit and equate Consumption to Production.

In a famous theorem C.H.Douglas identified the fundamental defect in our money system. We nail the flag of the Douglas Theorem to our mast.

We proclaim the Two Principles of Economic Democracy. 1. The power of the individual over his material environment should increase with advances in production. That is, he should find his command over goods and services steadily enlarged. 2. The choice of the individual in joining or declining productive enterprises should increase. That is, opportunity and leisure should be enlarged.

We make Three Demands: 1. Open the National Credit Account at the Treasury. 2. Institute the Compensated Price System. 3. Distribute National Dividends to All.

We announce the strategy of the fighting minority. First, recruit to the standard of Social Credit the most intelligent, boldest, most energetic members of the community. Second, propaganda and agitation to awaken the masses to the usurpation of their own credit and to raise mass-pressure for the Three Demands. Third, the election of Congressmen who will continuously bring up the Credit Question and force its precedence over all other questions in the national legislature.

We stand for Democracy, that form of society in which government and communal organization exist for the benefit of the individuals composing the community.

We are unalterably opposed to totalitarianism and collectivism, social systems in which the individual exists only for the group. No Fascism, no Communism.

We stand for the Bill of Rights and will resist all attempts to infringe upon any section of the Bill of Rights. We stand for a really free press, one in which the democratic right of criticism can be truly exercised because banker-control has been ended.

American Social Credit stands for the liberty and equality of opportunity of the individual irrespective of race, creed or color. We abominate anti-Semitism.

Gorham Munson, *Aladdin's Lamp: The Wealth of the American People* (N.Y., 1945), pp. 362–9.

[1] Roll checked (letter from Mr Munson to the author, 24 April 1966).

[2] *New Democracy* New Series, 19 (November 1938), published within the pages of *The Beacon* II, 2 (November 1935), 5.

The Money Question and the so-called Jewish Question have NOTHING to do with each other and we will let no one confuse this fact.

Social Credit or War – which do you want? All wars today are Bankers' Wars. They are bred by poverty at home. We shall fight Bankers' Wars by abolishing poverty.

Our logic shall permeate other movements – for Social Credit is the only remedy. We shall make coalition with none – for Social Credit cannot compromise.

Social Credit is the Resolvent. It resolves the sterile Left-Right conflict. It destroys the poverty-amidst-plenty paradox. It enables political democracy to work as it was intended. It brings peace and plenty, security and liberty, the rebirth of America.

Social Crediters are axemen striking at the root. Multiply the axemen!

Social Credit is coming! Shout it from the housetops!

Social Credit, as the name implies, was concerned technically with the role of credit in society. It proposed that the control of credit should be in the hands of the people instead of in those of an oligarchy of financiers, and that it should be administered by a national credit office. The government would exert its constitutional right to coin money, the consumer be provided with a national discount or credit to meet fluctuating prices, and every citizen receive a dividend based on the national credit – production against consumption – in the form of unearned income. Credit-ism, not capitalism, was at the root of a nation's ills; the bankers' monopoly of credit constituted a conspiracy to deprive man of his inalienable rights to plenty and leisure.

Douglas' proof was presented in the celebrated theorem mentioned in the A.S.C.M. manifesto. It amounted to an attack on the price system, stating that of all the payments made by factories to individuals (A), and for other manufacturing costs (B), A represented the purchasing power of individuals but $A + B$ determined the price of the goods. According to the theorem it was impossible for A (consumption) to equal $A + B$ (production). This relation of cost to purchasing power penalised the consumer and placed the factories in the hands of its creditors.

The disproving of Douglas' theorem, and its defence, need not be undertaken here.[1] Williams nowhere refers to it, although his member-

---

[1] See C. B. Macpherson, *Democracy in Alberta: Social Credit and the Party System*, 2nd ed. (Toronto, 1962), pp. 107–12, for an attack; see Munson, *Aladdin's Lamp*, pp. 142–54, for a defence.

ship in the party was accepted on the condition that he subscribed to it.[1] John Riordan, a long-standing member of the Orage group, suggests that it is unlikely that Williams had a better grasp of its technical details than any other of his fellow artists.[2] But it would have been surprising indeed if the intellectual's dilemma of the thirties could have been solved by abstract reasoning alone. As the Third Resolvent Factor in the struggle between two totalitarian alternatives Social Credit offered a radical cure for a disease which the government did not seem prepared to undertake. It did not advocate state control. It did advocate an intelligent nationalism, with the nation organised as a corporation in which the citizens were shareholders. It proposed a greater degree of socialisation without socialism; it was radical without being revolutionary. Its attractiveness for middle-class professionals who wanted a non-socialist welfare state was very great. In a speech given at the University of Virginia in 1936, Williams declared that the leftist emphasis on class war was especially intolerable since it was a manifestation of the intention to permit none of the liberty of thought which was characteristically American once power was assumed: 'Revolutions are not won by violence but by the accuracy of thought behind them.'[3]

The socialisation of credit was no less a matter of humane thought than the socialisation of medicine. In 1949 Williams was so affronted by the American Medical Association's demand that he should subscribe to fight a bill for socialised medicine that he wrote an essay to accompany a mimeographed circular, 'Health for the People', which contained statements by thirteen senators, physicians, and men of religion in favour of a federal medical service or co-operative medicine. Williams explained that without membership of the A.M.A. a physician could not join his county society and that unless he was a member of the county society he was not entitled to courtesy privileges at local hospitals. This centralised power spoke of the threat of 'regimentation'

1 *New Democracy*, New Series, 19 (November 1938), contained within the pages of *The Beacon* II, 5 (November 1938), 4.

2 Letter to the author, 1 April 1966: 'I can say that I cannot believe that Williams ever grasped the A + B theorem. Much too dry and too tightly knit. And if he ever met Major Douglas, he must have found him a living example of the theorem.'

3 'The Attack on Credit Monopoly from a Cultural Viewpoint' (NBuU), read before the Tenth Annual Session of the Institute of Public Affairs, University of Virginia, 11 July 1936. For an account of the proceedings see *New Democracy* VI, 5 (July 1936), 94.

and the loss of 'free enterprise' should the Murry-Dingman Bill succeed. Williams replied:[1]

In a republic such as ours the only alternative is Federal regulation, that Medicine, honest Medicine, may be protected from those who strive to make merely a business of it and fight off proper supervision like any business gang when the authorities intervene.

In 1942 he had attempted to thwart business power locally by becoming President of the Cooperative Consumers' Society of Bergen County, Inc.

The A.S.C.M. consciously opposed the Puritan ethic in which virtue lay in scarcity and men were more or less virtuous to the degree that they submitted to onerous labour to reap a small reward. The Bill of Economic Rights which Munson proposed was to provide a minimum of food, clothing, housing, medicine, and education. The American intellectual had done much to prepare the ground for an economics of plenty and leisure; 'it happens to be in the American tradition of expansion and aggrandizement'.[2] But another more regressive American tradition was also at work, the tradition of economic puritanism:[3]

Tribulation Wholesome, who came to power in the Age of Scarcity before Watt harnessed solar energy for the benefit of man, still thinks that there is not enough to go round, that those who get a large share are hoggish, and that one's spirit goes to sleep with the acquirement of comforts, amenities, and luxuries. He has the feeling that men should renounce riches, should work like horses and suffer deprivations, and should live in a state of artificial scarcity even if real scarcity has been abolished.

Belief in a round of work and rewards was as much the morality of the Old Economics as leisure and plenty was the morality of the New. Neither belief had very much to do with an economic system; one was pessimistic, the other utopian; one the businessman's ethic, the other the artist's. Munson proclaimed that the artist was the natural ally of the Social Crediter because, 'the epic struggle today is on a grander

[1] 'Health for the People' (CtY).
[2] Gilbert Seldes, 'The Intellectual as Savior', *New Democracy* IV, 11 (1 August 1935), 185–7; *187*.
[3] Munson, *Aladdin's Lamp*, pp. 385–6.

scale than the Marxian conception; it is literally Makers versus Brokers'.[1]

But the writing of essays was not enough. The writers produced their pamphlets,[2] but they also made a conscious effort to produce a body of Social Credit literature to rival proletarian writing. In Britain Eimar O'Duffy wrote a satirical trilogy of novels, D. G. Bridson a play, Hugh MacDiarmid some verse, and John Hargrave a novel which Williams reviewed.[3] In Italy Ezra Pound, lecturing at the Università Bocconi, used passages from the *Cantos* as the shortest possible means to an exposition of monetary problems.[4] At the same time he maintained that the difference between propaganda and literature was that propaganda was dogmatic, whereas literature was a free examination of data: '...if the result happens to confirm the opinion of any party, the work of literature then acquires a propagandist value exceeding any that a work starting with propagandist purpose can have'.[5] In his eagerness to be in the advance-guard of monetary theory, however, Pound began to be interested in reformers whose political applications were tainted by fascism. Thus, by the time the A.S.C.M. was established Pound had shifted from Douglas to Silvio Gesell, a money-reformer of French and German parentage. He had attacked *New Democracy* as a 'chappel for Douglasite methodists'[6] and issued an ultimatum: 'If Douglas really does not understand Gesell, then Douglas is done for. If his clique is afraid to discuss Social MONEY, then we must discuss them as impotent sectaries, who have had their uses in sectional education.'[7] It did not trouble Pound in the least that Gesell's ideas had strongly influenced those of Gottfried Feder, Hitler's early financial adviser. He was interested in data, not in exploring his

---

[1] *New Democracy* I, 3 (25 September 1933), 5.
[2] *Pamphlets on the New Economics* (London, 1933–4), included numbers by Orage (5), Pound (8, 9), Herbert Read (12), Bonamy Dobrée (14), and Edwin Muir (15).
[3] W. C. Williams, 'New Direction in the Novel', *New Democracy* V, 5 (1 November 1935), 81–3.
[4] Letter from Pound to G. B. Munson, 18 February 1935 (CtMW).
[5] Ezra Pound, 'Open Letter to Tretyakow', *Front* I, 2 (February 1931), 124–6;*126*.
[6] Letter from Pound to Williams, 27 October [1935] (NBuU). The spelling 'chappel' is a pun on the name of Warren Chappell, the designer of *New Democracy*'s colophon – a man taking an axe to a sickly tree with a quotation from Thoreau: 'There are a thousand hacking at the branches of evil to one who is striking at the root.'
[7] Ezra Pound, 'Intellectual Money', *British Union Quarterly* I, 2 (April-June 1937), 24–34; *34*.

political position. He expected it to be put to use in various ways by different countries. Not suggesting fascism for the United States he, nevertheless, believed Mussolini was good for Italy, simply because he seemed to understand monetary reform. He despised Roosevelt because the President appeared not to understand it.

A Gesell group had been organised in New York in 1923, but since Gesell's writings were not translated into English until much later its first American readers were German–Americans. When Hitler rose to power the membership of the group is said to have dropped,[1] but of those who remained some were undoubtedly sympathetic towards Hitler. The founder of the original New York group was a Dr Hugo R. Fack, later editor–publisher of *The Way Out*, the official Gesellite organ. In 1943 Munson produced a mimeographed report, 'The Money Reform Fifth Column',[2] in which the American Gesellites were characterised as exploiting monetary reform for subversive and anti-social purposes. Dr Fack, when investigated by the F.B.I., was shown to have compromised himself in correspondence with the Silver Shirts, an anti-semitic group led by William Dudley Pelley, and proceedings were instituted against him in 1942 to revoke the citizenship granted to him in 1931, but in 1946 he was still active, running a paper called *Freedom and Plenty*.

At the time when Pound changed his theoretical allegiance the English Social Credit movement began to be riven by internal strife. Orage was dead, and the *New English Weekly* had detached itself from the Social Credit Secretariat in London, which in turn rejected Major Douglas' chairmanship. Hargrave's party stood alone. The American movement was attacked mainly by outside forces. Munson named them as Father Coughlin's National Union of Social Justice, The Honest Money Founders, Mankind United, The United Party Movement, and The National Workers League.[3]

But if they brought monetary reform into disrepute with their anti-semitism and proto-fascism they did not threaten the A.S.C.M.

[1] Paul Ernest Anderson, 'Gesell's Free Economic System', *Dynamic America* VI, 3 (April 1938), 25–8;27.
[2] Gorham B. Munson, 'The Money Reform Fifth Column, How the Swastika was Baited to Catch American Money Reformers', *News-BACKGROUND: The Key to Current Events*, Report no. 10 (N.Y. [1943]).
[3] *Ibid.* pp. 16ff.

directly. Before long, however, a threat did come in the form of a new paper, *Money: A Mass Appeal Social Credit Paper*.

It was edited by John G. Scott, a member of the General Council of the League for National Dividends. At the time Munson wrote to Williams congratulating himself on having found a 'leading philosophical anarchist' to join the professional men on the council,[1] but he soon had cause to regret it. *Money* began to gather into its pages all the most dubious elements of the 'vermin' press. It became anti-Roosevelt, anti-British, and anti-semitic. It was banned in Canada in 1941, and refused by the U.S. Post Office for mailing in 1942.[2] Yet this was the paper from which Williams in 1950 took the 'Advertisement' for the enforcement of the Constitution on money in *Paterson*.[3]

The A.S.C.M. collapsed in 1943. For three years Munson had fought a rear-guard action against the encroachments of the proto-fascists, single-handedly running a weekly sheet, *Men First*. Having denounced the Money Reform Fifth Column publicly in a final report, he settled down in private to write his book *Aladdin's Lamp*. Then his Social Credit labour was ended. Pound, however, had not finished. Before long he was re-grouping in the shadow of St Elizabeth's Hospital in Washington. Donald J. Paquette, the Los Angeles poet whom Williams visited on his tour of the West Coast in 1950, received a characteristic memorandum from Pound in March of that year in which he suggested Paquette should contact Dallam Simpson (editor of *Four Pages*), Gary Wendleton (editor of *Mood*), and David Horton.[4] Horton, a student at Hamilton College, had started the Cleaner's Press for the purpose of disseminating the ideas of Gesell, and the monetary history of Alexander Del Mar.[5] Fack had found his way to Los Angeles where Paquette went to see him and found he still had copies of Gesell's *The Natural Economic Order*.[6] Chivvied by Pound's notes from St Elizabeth's, two of which he used in *Paterson*,[7] Williams made a special point of

---

[1] Letter from Munson to Williams, 10 February 1936 (copy, Mr Munson's files).

[2] Munson, 'Money Reform Fifth Column', p. 8.

[3] See Appendix B (*Paterson*, p. 213).

[4] Letter from Ezra Pound to Donald J. Paquette, 14 March 1950 (CtY).

[5] Alexander Del Mar, *A History of Monetary Crimes* [facsimile edn of *Barbara Villiers or A History of Monetary Crimes* (1899)], [Washington, D.C., 1951].

[6] Silvio Gesell, *The Natural Economic Order*, trans. Philip Pye (San Antonio, Texas), 1934 (*Money Part*): 1936 (*Land Part*).

[7] *Paterson*, pp. 218, 254.

advertising Gesell's book.[1] The A.S.C.M., which had rejected Pound's demand for a coalition of money groups without regard for their political affiliations in the late thirties, was no longer a force, so Pound's direct influence on Williams in fiduciary matters began to assert itself. He instructed Alfredo and Clara Studer, of Fack's group, to get in touch with Williams, and this resulted in passages in *Paterson* on the Federal Reserve System.[2] A conversation with Pound, regarding the bankers and the Cold War,[3] led Williams to misrepresent the socialisation of credit in the most ironic way. In the passage in *Paterson* on the enforcement of the Constitution on money, credit was not to be given to consumers but to producers, and the traditional enemies of monetary reformers, bankers and munition manufacturers, were to be supported by a government engaged in an arms race with Russia. The strident appeal to anti-communist feeling which the original document made was largely excised by Williams.[4]

Although it is possible to show that Pound's influence was strong in providing documents of dubious accuracy and unsavoury origin for *Paterson*, it should nevertheless be clear from our account of Williams' participation in the A.S.C.M. that Pound had no monopoly of monetary reform ideas. For if Pound's father was associated with the Mint, Williams' father was one of Henry George's Single-Taxers, and Williams' brother and son joined him in composing at least one essay on the subject of money.[5] In fact, the Hamiltonian theme in *Paterson* found its origins neither in the A.S.C.M. nor in Pound's St Elizabeth's period, but in the essay, 'The Virtue of History', in *In the American Grain*.[6] The local example was his first example; Paterson *was* 'Hamiltonia'. Pound's slogan 'LEISURE SPARE TIME/FREE FROM ANXIETY'[7] placed the emphasis on leisure, presumably for the artist, but Williams asked Pound whether the world had to be specially prepared before the artist could use it.[8] Pound, like Douglas, took a more purposive view of

---

[1] *Autobiography*, p. 340.
[2] See Appendix B (*Paterson*, pp. 90–1, 92).
[3] *Autobiography*, p. 385.
[4] See Appendix B (*Paterson*, p. 213).
[5] Mss 'What Happens to Money' (CtY; NBuU).
[6] *In the American Grain*, p. 195.
[7] Used as letter-head by Pound's father, Homer Pound, on a letter to Williams, 24 April 1936 (NBuU).
[8] Letter to Pound, 25 March 1935 (CtY).

society than Williams. His Volitionist manifesto on economics was circulated with the same kind of vigour that Williams sent round his manifesto on the American idiom twenty years later. Pound, affecting the technician and far from home, offered a blue-print for society, whereas Williams, whose will was directed towards a daily round of practice, regarded the economic situation as part of the local materials of writing.

As early as 1922 Harold Loeb, the editor of *Broom*, placed money-making in a cultural context. He claimed that in America it had given rise to a conceptual system which was neither religion nor art but was intimately related to both these human needs – The Mysticism of Money:[1]

> Money, because that which was originally but a medium of exchange and a valuable metal, has become the measuring staff of all values and the goal and reward of all efforts conventionally accepted as proper.
> Mystic because the validity of the money standard and the intrinsic merit of money making are accepted on faith, extra-intellectually.

But while suggesting a modern link between business and state as strong as the medieval one between church and state, he did admit the possibility of profoundly indignant heretics. Pound and Williams, given Loeb's premise, were heretics whose denunciations of the financiers might be seen as a form of anti-clericalism.

Thus it is that the evangelist in *Paterson* is a money-reformer, circulating his personal fortune as a local dividend. It is especially interesting that Williams, selecting a person to represent the principle of abundance chose an immigrant, Klaus Ehrens, whose apparently German–Jewish name and Christian faith embody a freely mixed culture. In a letter to Pound Williams once wrote that he had no use for Jews as Jews, or for Catholics as Catholics.[2] What he sought in both was evidence of their non-tribal, non-sectarian 'by-traits'.[3]

[1] Harold Loeb, 'The Mysticism of Money', *Broom* III, 2 (September 1922), 115–30;*117*.
[2] Letter to Pound, 6 April 1940 (CtY).
[3] 'An Essay for Martians. I. The Jew' (CtY). Williams apparently derived his title for this essay from a typical monetary reform document, *A Message from Mars to all the Earthians, including the Martians' Plan for World Peace and Permanent Prosperity via a New Monetary System* (Providence, R.I., 1924), which was tainted with anti-semitism. Munson's analysis of a survey of banking power in 1937 showed there was no relation in America between the Jewish Question and the Money Question (*Aladdin's Lamp*, pp. 377–9). As a secular or democratic humanist Williams was opposed to formal Judaism

The whole future of the American spirit in art lay in the democratic constitution of the country, not in the arbitrary institutions of outside forces:[1]

> The basic idea which underlies our art must be, for better or worse, that which Toynbee has isolated for us: abundance, that is, permission, for all. And it is in the *structure* of our works that this must show. We must embody the principle of abundance, of total availability of materials, freest association in the measure, in *that* to differ from the poem of all previous time. It will be that sort of thing, if we succeed, that shall give us our supreme distinction.

This was the truly democratic way; 'And it is important because it says that you don't paint a picture or write a poem *about* anything, you *make* a picture or a poem of *any*thing'.[2] Yet despite Williams' efforts to resolve the dichotomy between fascism and communism by means of Social Credit, and despite his public repudiation of both these absolutist systems,[3] it was possible for Williams to be suspected of being both. He was investigated by the F.B.I. as a fascist friend of Pound, and indexed by the House Committee on Un-American Activities as a communist.

---

as to formal Christianity ('Re. Sidney Hook's article, "Reflections on the Jewish Question"' [NBuU]). For a Jewish incident positively handled see a rejected portion of *In the Money* (*Hika* VI, 7 [May 1940], 5).

[1] W. C. Williams, 'The American Spirit in Art', *Proceedings of the American Academy of Arts and Letters*, Second series, 2 (1952), 51–9;57.

[2] *Ibid.* pp. 57–8.

[3] W. C. Williams, 'Social Credit as Anti-Communism', *New Democracy* I, 10 (15 January 1934), 1–2.

7

An Adjustment to Conditions

The Documentary Way

By the beginning of the thirties the aesthetic implications of capitalism were only too clearly reflected in the waste of men and materials in a ravaged country. Now the Objectivist use of documents entered upon a more public, although no less specialised phase. The magazine *Hound and Horn* published photographs by Sheeler, Walker Evans, and the Workers' Photo League;[1] the last group embodying the political turn photography now took. Williams took out subscriptions for Sheeler and himself to *The Left*, and received *Experimental Cinema*, in which there were writings and photographs by Edward Weston. The beautiful magazine *USA: A quarterly of the American Scene*, to which Williams contributed, also reproduced the work of the photographers. In *Hound and Horn* in 1931-2 there was the exciting possibility that photographs by Evans would be combined with a poem on the South-West by Dudley Fitts, and that Weston and Kenneth Rexroth would also collaborate.[2] Presenting Reznikoff's selection of Southern legal documents in *Contact*, Williams tried hard to match them with photographs by Sheeler but, for one reason or another, had to content himself with cuts from an eighteenth-century book of oratorical gestures.[3]

Erskine Caldwell and Margaret Bourke-White, the photographer, published what Cowley called an altogether new kind of book comprised of text and photographs handled in such a way that it was impossible to tell whether the text illustrated the pictures, or the pictures the texts.[4] Sherwood Anderson and Archibald MacLeish tried

[1] *Hound and Horn* III, 3 (Fall 1930); VI, I (October-December 1932).
[2] *Hound and Horn* correspondence files (CtY).
[3] Charles Reznikoff, 'My Country, 'Tis of Thee', *Contact* (Second Series) I, I (February 1932), 14-34; I, 2 (May 1932), 99-108.
[4] Erskine Caldwell and Margaret Bourke-White, *You Have Seen Their Faces* (N.Y., 1937).

this documentary structure, using the photographs made at the hands of Evans, Ben Shahn, and others for the Farm Security Administration.[1] In 1938 when two of these books had just appeared, James Laughlin predicted a great propagandist future for the medium of 'Picture Poetry'. But he made one interesting aesthetic distinction about the structure: 'It is not getting back to the ideoglyphic bases of language, because the pictures are more than simple metaphor; they are very complex descriptions, containing as much material as a prose writer would put in several pages.'[2]

The expansiveness of the new medium was more filmic than graphic. The still photographers of the American straight tradition had, in many cases, become motion-picture cameramen; Strand and Willard Van Dyke were two notable examples. As documentarists they now presented their selective and precise images in the context of a rhetorical, not to say tendentious, view of society at large. At the Third Writers' Congress both radio and film documentaries were discussed by members of the Poetry Session organised by Genevieve Taggard, the stalwart *New Masses* poet. The morning programme for 3 June 1939 had a radio documentary in which the voices of Herbert Hoover and Henry Ford were juxtaposed with the voices of the needy. In the afternoon two films were shown; the first a preview of a film based upon an investigation conducted by the Civil Liberties Committee, the other Pare Lorentz's *The River*, which was shown for those who were interested in the relation between poetry and the screen.[3] The Civil Liberties production represented one of the most tendentious and independent ventures in American documentary film of the day. *The River*, on the other hand, was a production of the United States Film Service and was a careful expression of the spirit of the New Deal. Nevertheless, the cameramen were essentially the same for both independent and government projects.

The documentary film movement had received a large impetus from Sergei Eisenstein, and his followers who edited *Experimental Cinema*. At the time of the *Que Viva Mexico!* fiasco, when Upton Sinclair confiscated Eisenstein's footage and put it at the disposal of hack Holly-

[1] Sherwood Anderson, *Home Town* (N.Y. [1940]); Archibald MacLeish, *Land of the Free* (N.Y. [1938]).
[2] James Laughlin, 'Picture Poetry', *Dynamic America* VI, 4 (May 1938), 25.
[3] *Direction* II, 3 (May-June 1939), 4, 21.

wood cutters, the magazine had been the centre of his defence.[1] But between 1935 and 1940 government support was given to films directed by Pare Lorentz, Robert Flaherty, and Joris Ivens.[2] The League of American Writers, which supported the Federal Arts Projects and the New Deal, encouraged the documentary arts in its semi-official magazine *Direction*, which Williams read.[3] In 1940 *Direction* offered a prize for documentary writing to be judged by the editors together with a panel consisting of Erskine Caldwell, Gilbert Seldes, and Edwin Seaver. There were 200 entries. Seaver, generalising from the evidence of the contributions offered a prescription: '...documentary writing should reveal facts about people united by a common social experience, although this experience may be related only in terms of one individual. The experience should be interesting not only in itself, but as it throws light on contemporary life. This is what gives it its documentary character'.[4]

The Works Progress Administration, unofficially allied to the League of American Writers and *Direction*, was also documentary in attitude. The Federal Writers' Project of New Jersey, which Williams had been asked to direct, had just produced its guide-book. The W.P.A. writers were full of suggestions as to what might be done with the regional scene:[5]

No one has yet done for New Jersey what, for instance, William Faulkner has done for Mississippi or Robert Frost for New Hampshire. Appreciation of the local scene has been left, as a rule, to the journalists. No poet has yet written a ballad on the Pineys or the Jackson Whites. An outstanding story of mill life in Passaic or Paterson remains to be written, and, save for *The Tides of Barnegat*, the fishermen and oystermen of the coast are material left unused by creative writers. This virtually unexplored field requires only the touch of skillful authors to demonstrate its value as a source of American literature.

In 1941 a new guide-book concentrating specifically on Bergen County,

---

[1] See Appendix B (*Paterson*, p. 74).

[2] See Arch. A. Mercey, 'Films by American Governments: The United States', *Films* I, 3 (Summer 1940), 7–11.

[3] *Direction* III, 9 (December 1940), 21: 'I've been receiving DIRECTION recently and have grown to look for it and enjoy it more than any print that comes into the house – and they come from nowhere! A discouraging blizzard of them, one and another, till I am bewildered.'

[4] *Direction* III, 6 (Summer 1940), 2.

[5] *New Jersey, A Guide to Its Present and Past*, compiled and written by the Federal Writers' Project of the Works Progress Administration (N.Y., 1939), p. 160.

which includes Rutherford, was added to the American Guide Series, and Williams was named as consultant for the chapter on cultural activities.[1] This time there was material on Jackson's Whites, but even so the W.P.A. who were employed to survey the region, and to give the details of their findings, could not provide him with documentation he needed for *Paterson*. They were guide-book historians, and he wanted original documents such as had been available to him in the writing of *In the American Grain*. But on this occasion there were no *Original Narratives of Early American History* available to him.[2]

Casting about for local sources, Williams heard of an authority on Jersey Dutch architecture, Herbert A. Fisher, who lived in Bloomfield. Sometime around 1940, perhaps as early as 1938, he called on Mr Fisher, and borrowed a file of notes and a manuscript, 'Legends of the Passaic'.[3] He must have appeared to Williams as an ideal source for he was a true antiquarian with a strong personal connection with Paterson. There was a picture in the family of his great-great-great-grandfather, General Abraham Godwin, standing at the Falls with Washington and Hamilton. As a boy his grandmother, a Post, used to take him to visit the Lambert family in the castle below Garret Mountain. His great-grandmother was the sister of a Lancaster, whose grandson, Edward Lancaster, died in 1942 at the age of ninety-six and was a source of information not only for Williams, but for William Nelson and William Scott, historians of the region at the turn of the century. Another distant relation on Fisher's father's side was Charles Pitman Longwell, former public librarian in Paterson, whom Williams also visited with important results. In Fisher's manuscript Williams tapped the living history of colonial Jersey. He had found a local counterpart to match his own family history of wanderings through the West Indies to Puerto Rico, which was also an essential part of his poem. Mr Fisher has emphasised that it was essentially a compilation of readings in local history, in particular the works by Nelson and Shriner, and Scott and the selections from old newspapers such as the *Paterson Intelligencer* made by William Rauchfuss, former curator of the

[1] *Bergen County Panorama*, written by Writers of the Workers' Program of the Works Projects Administration in the State of New Jersey (Hackensack, N.J., 1941), p. viii.
[2] *Original Narratives of Early American History*, general ed. J. Franklin James (N.Y., 1906).
[3] Although the ms. is now lost, Mr Fisher has indicated by correspondence with the author which passages Williams used.

Dey Mansion at Preakness, and Edward M. Graf of the New Jersey Historical Society.[1] Thus before Williams began his local researches in earnest he already had a mass of material to draw upon. He did not need to go to the histories; in fact, a comparison between those texts and Williams' versions shows that he must have followed Fisher's casual, and occasionally erratic, transcriptions, and occasionally misread them.[2]

Despite his access to such material, however, Williams was still not wanting to begin. To hasten the beginning of a poem which he had set aside as the work of his final years seemed like hurrying on to his decline. However, another person precipitated him towards further material and into action. It was his friend Kathleen Hoagland. Mrs Hoagland had helped him with plays at the Rutherford Little Theater in 1939. She had written a novel, published in 1944 with a note of recommendation by Williams on its dust-jacket. Immediately after it appeared she began a new one, 'The Rock and the City', based on the history of the Passaic region. She discussed it with Williams, and read to him from the introduction, 'The Foaming Pool'. In the summer of 1944 Williams pressed her for details of her intentions:[3]

What is your theme? Is it a man in whose character and actions the whole contemporary scene is disclosed, so that all you have to do is to tell his life in order to criticise the times? I hope so. Or is it a region whose children in their tragic blundering make it live? I don't know what it is for you have given me no intimation of it. But whatever your theme is all the scenes must be no more than an unravelling of the driving core to a tragic or other end. There can be no time for 'description' as such.

In Williams' poem the hero was to be a man, in Mrs Hoagland's it was a region. Thus they parted in formal structure along the conventional lines of poem and novel. But they shared the same background material on Paterson. It was the beginning of a literary competition conducted by two writers who were neighbours using similar materials to different ends. Now that Williams saw Mrs Hoagland busy upon a work on Paterson he intensified his own efforts. But if Mrs Hoagland was a spur to his ambitions she was also of great practical help. She answered his

---

[1] Letter to the author, 7 October 1966.
[2] See Appendix B (*Paterson*, pp. 19–20, 22–3, 45–6, 60–1).
[3] Letter to Kathleen Hoagland, 11 August 1944 (ViU).

demands for specific information when he could not obtain it, and typed the first three books of *Paterson* in all its drafts.

That same summer Mrs Hoagland went up to Lambert Castle, the headquarters of the Passaic County Historical Society. There she found for sale some copies of a run of a short-lived local history newspaper called *The Prospector*, bound in brown paper.[1] She bought one and hurried back to Rutherford to tell Williams of her find, upon which he set off immediately for the castle. There, among the pages of Paterson history, culled and paraphrased by Edward M. Graf, under the pseudonym of E. P. Erabe, he found fresh material, as well as duplication of Fisher's.[2] The multiplication of source material in *The Prospector*, and in Fisher's notes, as well as in the books on the region, makes it difficult to say exactly which source Williams used for a specific passage. He used them all, at will, although in the case of *The Prospector* he committed a curious act of second-hand plagiarism. Mr Graf's newspaper accounts of Harry Leslie crossing the Falls, and of the McNulty story were paraphrases, which Williams, in turn, altered. As museum exhibits the idiom, at least, was not authentic. Yet, for Williams' purposes, something remained.

What remained was news. In 1939 Skip Cannell, whom Williams had not seen since *Others* days, reappeared in Washington writing under the name of David Ruth. Without divulging his identity he sent Williams a manuscript, and Williams was prompted to write the following as an introduction:[3]

The truth is that news offers the precise incentive to epic poetry, the poetry of events; and now is precisely the time for it since never by any chance is the character of a single fact ever truthfully represented today. If ever we are to have any understanding of what is going on about us we shall need some other means for discovering it.

The epic poem would be our 'newspaper', Pound's cantos are the algebraic equivalent but too perversely individual to achieve the universal understanding required. The epic if you please is what we're after, but not the lyric-epic singsong. It must be a concise sharpshooting epic style. Machine gun style. Facts, facts, facts, tearing into us to blast away our stinking flesh of news. Bullets.

In 1946 Williams took his summer holiday in Paterson, visiting book-

[1] *The Prospector* (Paterson, N.J.) II, 5 (9 May 1936) – 33 (12 November 1936).
[2] See Appendix B (*Paterson*, pp. 21–2, 48, 51, 64–5, 126–7, 143, 232–3).
[3] 'Introduction to Book of David Ruth' (NBuU).

keepers in factories, and an old Swiss silk-weaver. He also made rounds with the local detectives in search of the poetry of contemporary events.[1] The editorials of *The Prospector* had denounced the writers of the Federal Writers' Project as incompetent historians.[2] Certainly Williams was not satisfied with a mere panorama; the kind of synthesis of documents which could, in his terms, be made to lie.

Williams' epic documentary style evolved over many years. As early as 1928 Louis Zukofsky had written to him enthusing over two films, *A Shanghai Document* and *Three Comrades and One Invention*, which were presented by Amkino, the forerunner of the *Experimental Cinema* group. Zukofsky wrote of his long poem *A*, '...after this evening with Amkino, I can't help but know that I will *know* what I am at'.[3] Williams, however, still conceived his canvas on the Passaic region as a narrative. In 1927 the projected story of Dolores Marie Pischak, the syphilitic child from 'Fairfield' (Garfield), a whorish contrast to that of the later *White Mule*, was intended to form part of the eventual poem *Paterson*. From 1933 Williams was occupied with what he called 'a large "canvas",'[4] the book published in 1938 as *Life Along the Passaic River*. The draft manuscripts of *Paterson* show Williams was still using the large section of Paterson history drawn from *A Little Story of Old Paterson* by Charles Pitman Longwell as a continuous narrative.[5] Only at a late stage in the poem's composition did he begin to inter-cut it with other material after the fashion of 'Man Orchid'. Separately arranged was the collection of poems he had assembled for James Laughlin as a beginning on the *Paterson* poem in 1939.[6] Joris Ivens had noted at the Third Writers' Congress that, 'The form and style of documentary film is not yet determined, there is growing art in the cutting and building up of effects integrating blood and human feeling into presentation of reality.'[7] Williams was finding it as difficult as he had predicted. Fortunately, once again, there was someone in Paterson, not an antiquarian but a very remarkable structuralist, who could help him.

[1] Letter to David Lyle, 22 August 1946.
[2] E.g. *The Prospector* II, 18 (31 July 1936), 1; II, 19 (7 August 1936), II, 21 (21 August 1936), 2. [3] Letter from Zukofsky to Williams, 22 October 1928 (NBuU).
[4] Letter to M. D. Zabel, 29 July 1933 (ICN).
[5] See Appendix B (*Paterson*, pp. 25–6, 27).
[6] 'Detail & Parody for the poem PATERSON', 9 March 1939 (MH).
[7] *Direction* II, 4 (July–August 1939), 5.

Faitoute, the Federalist Philosopher

In 1933 Pound sent an article to the *Harkness Hoot*, a Yale review of which James Laughlin was an editor, on 'Ideogramic Method'. Pound attacked 'the socalled "logical" method which permitted the methodist to proceed from inadequate cognizance to a specious and useless conclusion'.[1] Educational 'methodists' were on this occasion the object of his opprobrium; their chief fault according to Pound, with whom Williams agreed in this respect, lay in their refusal to accept any fact which did not fit their systems. Contemporary scientists, on the other hand, pursued the 'ideogramic' method; they heaped together the most heteroclitic facts, arranged them and re-arranged them, seeking organisations which would fit them comprehensively: 'Twenty-five factors in a given case may have NO LOGICAL connection the one with any other. Cf.: A definition of fever which excluded typhoid wd. be unscientific. Knowledge cannot be limited to a number of definitions.'[2] Pound urged his contemporaries to meet the challenge of intractable facts in other fields by a method consonant with the age of Marconi.

Writing to Pound soon after the article's appearance Williams said he had read it and saluted him for it. He added mysteriously that he was working on something which would eventually show that he was not insensitive to Pound's plea.[3] Williams, however, was never happy with the grand analogies Pound offered, nor was he likely to imitate Pound's practice in the *Cantos* if a local analogy could be found. There was one available soon after in the person of David Lyle, whom Alfred Stieglitz referred to as The Man from Paterson.

Lyle had had ten years of Marconi in the Merchant Marine, the U.S. Navy, and the shore-based Radio Marine. He had come to Paterson in 1938 to work as an instrument-engineer at the Wright Aero Factory, to which the old city now looked for its industrial existence. From the time he left radio service in 1931 he had been seeking some kind of connection between abstract codes of communication like Morse and patterns of human behaviour; in short, the relation between mathematics and particulars. On 4 January 1937 almost with the force of a

[1] *Harkness Hoot* IV, 4 (November 1933), 6–14; 6.
[2] *Ibid.* p. 14.
[3] Letter from Williams to Pound, 16 February 1934 (CtY).

revelation, he discovered a working method which satisfied him. Since then – for he remains active still – he has spent his life correlating the multiple networks of facts, events, and ideas, which have poured past his local vantage-point in New Jersey; first from East Twenty-fourth Street in Paterson not far from the Falls, then up in the 'back country' in Midvale about eighteen miles from the city. In 1944 he gave up his job at Wright Aero to devote himself fulltime to his method.

Lyle's hypothesis was that the world's ills could be cured not by means of newly-created political theories but by the proper alignment of thought and fact at every level of knowledge, from the concrete to the abstract. All types of organisation were based upon a system of communications, a system of organisation, and an aim or purpose. Lyle's aim was to find a common language which would illustrate the common basis of all organisation and so open the way to a sense of common purpose in the world. It was a thesis which Williams supported whole-heartedly.[1] But it is unlikely that Williams would have done so if Lyle's multiple letters had not shown him to be a thorough pragmatist working in the tradition of Charles Sanders Peirce. These letters by means of which Lyle addressed simultaneously persons often unknown to each other and in widely divergent fields, consisted of correlations of their published writings with those of other writers. In short, he was not so much a writer as a re-writer. From his correspondents' replies came fresh correlations. His aim was to bridge the gap between the alienated, whether between management and labour, or artist and audience. The more disparate the evidence the greater he found the challenge of resolution by analysis of common elements. Williams received his first letters in 1938, and continued to receive them with interest until 1947. Then, their purpose fulfilled for him, he cast them aside unopened.[2]

In the autumn of 1940, however, he was still seeking a structural method for *Paterson*. He visited Lyle to inquire further into his letters. Then he made his own correlation of Lyle's outpourings with the fact of the Falls. Standing at their head Lyle was combing the tangled

---

[1] On 25 May 1943 Williams wrote to the local draft board on behalf of one of Mr Lyle's assistants, Ronald Wood, asking for deferment of his military service because of the importance of Lyle's work.

[2] A letter from Williams to Winfield Townely Scott, 5 February 1952 (RPB), shows him wearying of the flood.

strands of first-hand experience and second-hand news into a coat of common texture. Or, to use another metaphor, the debris of New Jersey dailyness pouring over the Falls was being related in all its particulars to derive a music from their meaningless roar. It was as heroic as Sam Patch's effort to keep his head above water. Lyle was not daunted by the submarine life he had elected to lead, any more than that other Paterson man the relevance of whose story Williams may not have missed, John Philip Holland, the inventor of the first successful submarine 'Fenian Ram'.[1]

Lyle's letters did not attempt the specious logic of narration, but were arranged across the page in blocks, being indented where the samples matched. Williams went over Lyle's letters arranging them chronologically and removing the signs of Lyle's montage to make his text run in a single stream. He changed the address, 'Dear Dr. Williams' to 'Dear Noah', and the signature from 'David Joseph Lyle' to 'Faitoute'. Then he sent the material to a typist with instructions to 'run it all together in one tumbling stream by using caps or italics for special picking out of especially noteworthy bits'.[2] Williams himself prepared a portion of some 5,000 words for re-typing. What follows here is a selection illustrative both of Lyle's method and of his material:[3]

Dear Noah, December 1, 1938-Expanded Apr. 9, 1939. 'Visual Imagism' and the difficult ART of Accompaniment. Ref: NY Her Trib Apr 9...by HT and page number New Republic...June 15, 1938 NR and page nrs Elapsed writing time, 5.5. hours. In his review 'Am Fotography', and others, Nov 29th NYTimes Ralph Thompson compared it to MacLeish's 'Land of the Free' quoting Kirstein's preface to the effect...that it is nearly impossible to illustrate (i.e. accompany) pictorial ART by words. That is equivalent to saying that movie titles are impossible to achieve as meaning...that words themselves are a meaningless game (ie, the same dilemma as Math'n Russell...and his theory of types)...and that a magazine like LIFE cannot be written...(that a magazine like TIME...and what Heywood Broun calls 'Its curious SIGN language' can't exist...and therefore Williams cannot write in to approve of its poetry summary...and indicate that he feels poets are moving in mysterious ways toward a great form)...that imagism is da-da...and has NO (visible) continuity.

[1] See *Paterson*, p. 155: 'There is a drumming of submerged engines, a beat of propellers.'
[2] Sent to a Mrs H.A. De Marsico, 17 July 1942 (envelope in possession of Mrs Kathleen Hoagland).
[3] Williams' uncatalogued correspondence (CtY).

Or..it is equivalent to saying that there is some fast running, flowing continuous imagism mood..equivalent (as growth points) to Goethe's, 'fruitful moment (um), Emerson's 'ecstatic moment', Lord Dunsany's MOOD..or for a short inter-val..it is the equivalent to attaining Jeffers' express aim...to achieve the con-tinuity Boehme meant by 'Life above sense'. LIFE above sense is what a dancer means by saying that in dancing, you've got to keep your mind above (your body matter) feet...feet are taken in as instantaneously comprehensible picture setup of the 'SWAGGERING SHUFFLE' of Jap soldiers..and transferred from one picture setup to another..all known, all instantaneously comprehensible, and for convenience, sown in and out of the concrete pictures at hand. In this week's LIFE..ie, an example of the language Harold Rugg asked for in the Stieglitz essay. As continuous imagism...you can test it for yourself..The Secret behind it.....and/or all of any human acts whatsoever..concerning anything..or any length of TIME whatsoever...ie, the secret behind Maya or appearances...or quoting H.Ellis again..When all disguises have been stripped away, it is ALWAYS and EVERY-WHERE (Where is your re-al substance?) the same simple process, a SPIRITUAL FUNCTION which is almost a PHYSIOLOGICAL function, and art which NATURE makes..that is ALL, and of imagism..Ellis says..quoting Gaultier..FACULTY of drawing joy from IMAGES of things, apart from the POS-SESSION of them, is based on physiologic conditions, which growing knowledge of the NERVOUS SYSTEM may some day make clearer. That is here NOW...and involves the objective translation of that which is of the utmost permanence behind any and all possessions or appearances and creations...a substantial sameness for each and all...thru all history idea ideal, iso, oid, story, wisdom, righteousness. HT 25..a GREAT FACE..65 feet high..is pictured..the WORD and Name beneath..George Washn...It will tower above Constitution Hall. p8..Living 'GREAT FACE'. (Pope Pius 12th)..will give radio address...p9... Rabbi Goldstein asked great face Pope Pius 12th...to speak few words necessary to start the summons for world peace parley. HT..22..Many Nashville Tenn convicts get liberty thru falsified symbolic areas..the records. HT21..NYCity.. Working in full sight of 7 man, 5 woman jury, a govt agent swaps a disputed symbol area NAMED a Check entry in 1934 ledger...there is revealed a singular, simultaneous and all history, all men, all mankind, allness law...which is over-whelmingly simply and plain to see..once you know, HOW TO see the terms of the answer to the 'WHO and WHAT are the People?'..which eliminates all MULTIPLICITY...and answers the real substance question..and allows everyone, everyone...an exceptionless generality..everyone..to 'BREAK thru Humanity', together...as Dr. Canby has said Am literary men engaged in one mighty mapping of efforts to make a 'language adequate to DESCRIBE society', ie, a topological language, equivalent to Rebecca West's..Literature set out to make a map of the SEA. Describing society..involves first answering the Lynd question WHO and What are the People?' The word science roots with the Gr schizo..to split, to cleave. And also the Latin..........Scire......to KNOW. And science roots with decide, decision, precision, shade, shadow, SHINE....And where Buddha

used for utmost permanence...Nirvana...Browning used the word SHINE...
while Whitehead says that for substance becoming shadow except for man and his
lifebelts..or literal areas, where the spirit used to be..there are three stages 1. the
romantic..or Teddy Roosevelt's..lunatic or schizofrenic fringe PREceding all
great movements.2....The PREcision stage...3....and finally...with this to
literal..everyday use like radios, automats...a new generalization....the root
of this is the fact that the gravity driven period of the central nervous system is
the source of our second of time..as length..and simultaneously the source of the
idea of NUMBER. Half is pure percept..clear center and direct vision of the great
world outside..in terms of body stillness..such as when sitting at a train window
..with another train outside...the other train begins to move...and having
felt no jar jerking schism from your own train..you consult the scheduling of
your own physiologic responsings..to see which train is moving..or where the
developing movement is focused...or located. The other half is inner blindness
to the outer world tele---while struggling with the problem of ordering one's
motored members..which suddenly tend to throw themselves into the great
far out...or tele..world field beyond the space occupied by the body..This
involuntary occupational therapy plus Nirvana use of it..can be indicated by the
HT 10...Aliquippa Penn man....who felt so grateful for his WPA check...from
the overwhelming wind outside..that he voluntarily swept the streets six days
weekly, six hours daily...as an indication of gratitude at participating in a
process as vast as the USA...to sweep away war, crime,..and all the old, crude
terrors..designated by short-circuiting stockbit phrases..such as war etc....NO
acknowledgements necessary. Cheerfully, D.Joseph Faitoute

The structural method of Lyle's work remains apparent even when it is
dismounted from its original form and run as a single stream or
accompaniment, 'to heighten everything else and to stitch together
every other thing'.[1] It turned Williams' attention to the news, and the
conception of a poem as the truth of contemporary events. The
arbitrariness of Lyle's sampling, the correlation of trivia with permanence, was emphasised by his habit of giving the elapsed writing
time; he matched whatever happened to be passing over the Falls as
he wrote. The use of the letter as private speech raised to a level of
public utterance accorded with Williams' conception of language as an
exchange between two persons; an urbanity of two. The combination
of symbolic logic, the structural use of which Williams had granted in
his concern for a mathematical use of language, with time-and-motion
study, the most particular application of Einsteinian thought, represented a resolution of the problems which had beset Williams for forty

1 *Paterson* mss (CtY).

years. Lyle demonstrated that it was possible to be a philosopher of the moment and yet achieve a sense of timelessness.

But much of the roar of Lyle's material was carried into the stream of Williams' own poem. At one point in its genesis Williams was willing to share the authorship with Lyle and with Marcia Nardi, the writer of the long letters from a woman poet. As Williams gained confidence with Lyle's method of interrelating a quantity of disparate details by aligning them according to their quality of sameness, he simply credited him with his assistance. Eventually, he was able to call the poem his own. He had learnt to impersonate Lyle so well that he was completely identified with Faitoute – the man doing all all the time. Faitoute was a man through whom the whole contemporary scene disclosed itself; contained in the one individual was the social experience of a community. The community, furthermore, was no longer an aristocratic conception, 'Hamiltonia', but, 'good *Muncie*', a local 'Middletown'.[1] Paterson was at last the Federal City and no longer Hamilton's misnomer. Faitoute was doing exactly what Denis de Rougemont had recommended in 1941: 'Restore cellular entities, local radiative centers, and progressively, empirically, confederate them in multiple networks.'[2] It was a principle which, as Williams followed it, resulted in a truly federalist style.

---

[1] *Paterson*, p. 18. Cf. Horace Gregory, 'The Situation in American Writing: Part II', *Partisan Review* VI, 5 (Fall 1939), 121: 'The most reliable description of an American "audience" may be found in Helen and Robert Lynd's "Middletown" [N.Y., 1929] and "Middletown in Transition" [N.Y., 1937].' Muncie, Indiana was the subject of their studies.

[2] Denis de Rougemont, 'The Rules of Play', *New Directions* [6] (1941), 248–52;*252*.

8

Fantastic America

'America is Dada'

Just at the point when Williams was organising the manuscripts of *Paterson* an issue of *View* devoted to 'Americana Fantastica' was edited by Parker Tyler.[1] The single collage which made up the front and back covers of the issue was by Joseph Cornell, the maker of Surrealist constructions, and contained many of the motifs in Williams' poem (see Plate 4). The New World theme of discovery, Indians, Niagara, cheesecake, circus, and horror movie, suggested how much man's hopes, crushed like an aeroplane in an ape's fist or suspended in mid-air like an acrobat, were unfulfilled in America.

Gershon Legman, the editor of *Neurotica*, outlined in his banned book *Love and Death* a history of the comic book from cave-drawings, friezes (like the Elgin marbles), 'the hunting tapestries of the Middle Ages', the Tarot card-pack, and 'the crowded canvases of the Flemish peasant painters Breughel, Brouwer and Bosch'.[2] But his analysis of the modern comic book, based on a survey of more than 140 crime comic serials of the decade ending in 1947, led him to speculate whether the eight million dollars spent a year on them answered a need, or was consciously produced to draw off the energy of a citizenry which might turn to social and economic revolution were it not so diverted and perverted.[3] In his view, the popular transposition of sex by violence and death was complete.

Parker Tyler, on the other hand, did not consider the fantastic element in popular culture to be the result of a conspiracy by the

---

[1] *View* II, 4 (January 1943). An advertisement by the Gotham Book Mart proclaimed that *In the American Grain* represented 'the real fantastic America'.
[2] G. Legman, *Love and Death* (N.Y., 1949), p. 29.
[3] *Ibid.* pp. 52–3.

enemies of the Constitution but 'the real Constitution of a romantic State':[1]

This organization proceeds at a rate of leisure peculiar to someone unaware of the surveillance of the academy, the police, or God. Yet its livery of lightning, that builds as it destroys, does not cause the fantastic to appear evasive. Before everything, it is the Anti-camouflage, the enemy of self-effacement, and has the ferocity that such a total negation of deceit implies.

This element was 'the inalienable property of the untutored, the oppressed, the insane, the anarchic, and the amateur...'. It could not be attained by the professional because it came momentarily when the will had become the reflex of an unpredictable perception, and it did not depend upon a technique of communication:[2]

It is non-idiomatic and thus, while primitive, it is also sophisticated, since it makes direct appeal to that anarchy of elements which bends the most rational man to the lunatic, and enables a child to penetrate to the meaning of a cloud of words he does not understand. In this respect, the fantastic coincides with the monstrous. The monstrous is produced by desire without reason; it is the longing for the exotic satisfied immediately and symbolically, but not without a violence contrary to the world of order. The child's desire for the moon is monstrous, fantastic and violent. Mythologies are orderly, and hence they are not fantastic.

Tyler was careful to distinguish the exotic from the fantastic, for this was only its fashionable, degraded form. Unlike the exotic, the fantastic could not be transplanted like a sophisticated taste for the Gothic, but was 'earmarked with the universal because an explosion can occur at any time, any place, and is most effective when not announced'.[3] *View* documented the monstrous with a degree of relish which war-torn refugees from Europe must have found abhorrent. Robert Duncan, the poet, saw the magazine's progress as 'an exploitation of what surely originally occasioned the horror'.[4] An essay on the American macabre by Marius Bewley, designed to expose a characteristic brand of sadism not the result of Gothic aestheticism but of conditions in a pioneer society, was illustrated with a medical photograph of a face-wound, making it difficult to tell whether it was part of Bewley's moral pur-

---

[1] 'Americana Fantastica', *View* II, 4 (January 1943), 5.
[2] *Ibid.*
[3] *Ibid.*
[4] Robert Duncan, 'Reviewing *View*, An Attack', *The Ark* (Spring 1947), 62–7;64.

pose or of the connoisseurship of *View*'s editors.[1] Duncan attributed the magazine's taste for disfigurement and deformity to the personal attitude of Charles Henri Ford, its chief editor:[2]

Labelled a freak and accepting that label, suing for little more than that the world allow him his 'freakishness' (the very moment of his poetry is the irony of his suit), he came to the conscious sense of defeat before the overwhelming tide of injustice, ridicule and cruelty. It is a sense of defeat which I think it would be difficult to condemn.

Williams, in his introduction to Ford's book of poems, *The Garden of Disorder*, wrote of his 'hard, generally dreamlike poetry' as an 'active denial of all the unformed intermediate worlds in which we live and from which we suffer bitterly'.[3]

Legman was more interested in the reality than in the dream:[4]

Four million acts of intercourse are achieved in America daily. Figure it out for yourselves. Is it news? Not news that's fit to print. But if two rachitic orphans should be killed by a falling wall in a jerry-built tenement, the pictures of their mangled corpses – of no interest whatever in sickly life – are spread over every news-sheet in the country in the name of human interest.

From stories which Williams told his friends at this time we can see that the exchange of sex for death was represented in his mind by the incidence of rape and murder. He wrote to a friend about Seattle:[5]

This is a fine place for a young man or woman to grow up in. Last week a youth of 20 or so of a good family, stole a new Lincoln car, picked up a girl at a road-house, raped her, murdered her – cutting off one breast in the process. But they caught him. Three weeks ago another young man beat up his wife and threw her and their small daughter over a cliff killing the former but not the latter. It is a vigorous man's world. Very bracing!

and not long after he told a similar story to a friend who recorded it in his diary. The manuscripts of *Paterson* show he had considered using it in his poem:[6]

A girl – an orphan – was going with a boy who was sent to the army and never wrote to her. She was left pregnant by him. She lived in an attic. One night she

[1] Marius Bewley, 'On the American Macabre', *View* v, 3 (October 1945), 7, 8, 18, 20;8.
[2] 'Reviewing *View*, An Attack', pp. 64-5.
[3] Charles Henri Ford, *The Garden of Disorder* (London, 1938), p. 10. Williams' essay is dated 5 June 1937. The date in *Selected Essays* (1939) is that of the American edition.
[4] *Love and Death*, pp. 93-4.
[5] Letter to Kathleen Hoagland, 21 July 1948 (ViU).
[6] Diary of Emanual Romano, 9 October 1951, kindly provided by Mr Romano.

was awakened by a stranger who raped her and ripped one of her nipples leaving her unconscious. She was taken to hospital. In due time she gave birth to a beautiful child. A man became interested in her and married her. She became pregnant again and died in childbirth.

The significance of such stories lies partly in the persistent fertility of woman. The freakish agent is man. The essential facts match Ford's perception: 'freaks are not mothers, even to freaks'.[1]

The key to the background of Williams' attitude towards the freak is in his poem, 'The Phoenix and the Tortoise':[2]

> The link between Barnum and Calas
> is the freak
> against which Rexroth rages,
> the six-legged cow, the legless woman
>
> for each presents a social concept
> seeking approval, a pioneer society
> and a modern asserting the norm
> by stress of the Minotaur

The world of Barnum and the popular arts had provided a coarse aesthetic for the group of artists associated with the first series of *Contact*. Marsden Hartley loved vaudeville as E.E.Cummings professed to love burlesque; Hartley wrote about equestriennes and acrobats, and Demuth painted them. They did not go so far as Tod Browning, whose film *Freaks* treated the malformed complement of the athletic aristocracy of the circus world so luxuriantly. The *Broom* group, with its dependence through R.A.Sanborn on *The Soil*, promoted the wild beauty of the dime novel, the ball-game, and the billposter. In an essay on 'The Great American Billposter', as ironic a candidate for acceptance as fine art as Williams' *Great American Novel* with its Ford-car heroine, Matthew Josephson spoke of 'the unaffected beauty and wisdom of the American milieu'.[3] Waldo Frank disapproved of this manifestation of the spirit of Dada: the Dadaists reacted against the rigidities of a Europe split by war:[4]

America for analogous reasons called for the antithesis of Dada. For America *is*

---

[1] *Garden of Disorder*, p. 14.
[2] *Collected Earlier Poems*, p. 465.
[3] *Broom* III, 4 (November 1922), 304–12;*304*.
[4] Waldo Frank, 'Seriousness and Dada', *1924* 4 (1924), 70–4;*71*.

Dada. The richest mass of these bean-spillers of Italy, Germany and France is a flat accord beside the American chaos. Dada spans Brooklyn bridge; it spins around Columbus Circle; it struts with the Ku Klux Klan; it mixes with all brands of bootleg whiskey; it prances in our shows; it preaches in our churches; it tremulos at our political conventions...No wonder they imported our essential chaos to lighten the regularities of France! But we are young, and what we need is a bit of mature action. We are fantastic ourselves, and what we need is integrating thought.

The funambulists, high-divers, monsters, and preachers of *Paterson* are an expression of this 'essential chaos'. In McAlmon's view, Frank's call to maturity was itself premature; Williams, unlike Frank, did not want to develop a religious temper in American writing; Hartley's emphasis lay on the primacy of the ability to achieve a momentary vividness, which Henri Rousseau showed: 'There is imagination which by reason of its power and brilliance exceeds all intellectual effort, and effort at intellectualism is worse than a fine ignorance by far'.[1] The *Contact* group, like the *View* group twenty years later, had been committed to a magic rather than religious view of life. The unerring sense of balance disclosed by the unconscious will of the athlete, the exaggerated force exhibited by the freak, bespoke a diversion, even a perversion, of man's ability to control his energy. Tyler spoke of the celebrants of the fantastic, the uneducated, insane, and oppressed as feeling 'the apocalyptic bug of contraries': 'The fantastic is the child of unmeasured love and unmeasured hate. As such it cannot avoid being the soul's trompe-l'oeil. It is illusionist, not in the sense of representation, but in the magical sense.'[2]

In 1927 and 1928, in an extraordinarily violent piece of improvisation headed 'Rome',[3] Williams poured out his radical thoughts on the value of the murderous and perverted element in American life. He suggested to himself that it was the degenerate element, the pure products of a country gone insane or syphilitic, which was the remnant of a heroic pioneer society. The wild, decayed, and doomed represented an aristocracy of the mind whose bodies obeyed impulses which if not socially beneficent showed a wholly admirable independence of conservative thought. No perversion, no matter how shocking, was worse

[1] Marsden Hartley, *Adventures in the Arts* (N.Y., 1921), p. 69.
[2] 'Americana Fantastica', p. 5.
[3] Ms. (NBuU).

than inversion. Inversion stemmed from an exaggerated respect for given forms; whether for woman, which resulted in homosexuality in men; or for the line in poetry, which resulted in inversion of the phrase. It was encouraged by the absurd prohibitions, by the forces opposed to change. An eruption like that of Mount Pelée was inevitable since 'the pleasure of motion to relief', whether in sex or poetry, was something which could not be averted, but only perverted in its outlet. It followed that the dignity of illegality was a value for Williams. John Coffey, the Robin Hood hero of 'An Early Martyr',[1] was valuable for the authentic logic of his lawlessness.[2] Prohibition bred illegality.[3] When Williams wrote that 'the woman who throws herself from the rocks into the sea has more gist, more force than the sum of every college',[4] the handling of the story of Mrs Cumming in *Paterson* was many years off, but it shows that his attitude towards the place of the fantastic in life and in art was established earlier than the arrival of a literary movement like Surrealism in America. Mrs Cumming, Marcia Nardi (the woman correspondent), and Alva Turner,[5] are not represented in *Paterson* because they are neurotic, but because their veracity as thwarted human beings – their unimpaired though distorted vigour – finds expression in action. In a draft of the 'Author's Introduction to *The Wedge*' Williams wrote that the perfect man of action was the suicide.[6] He shared the idea with certain of the Surrealists. If Tyler spoke of the fantastic in art as 'the city of the irrational. It is the irrational plus architecture',[7] then the suicide was surely mayor.

Williams' concern was to discover the structural method of such an architecture so that he could build it in his poems. A direct Surrealist field of observation was a novel by Philippe Soupault, which Williams and his mother translated in 1929 as *Last Nights of Paris*.[8] The hero seeks the unconscious architecture of the city by prowling the streets

[1] *Collected Earlier Poems*, pp. 85–6.
[2] W. C. Williams, 'A Man Versus the Law', *The Freeman* I, 15 (23 June 1920), 348–9.
[3] W. C. Williams, 'L'Illégalité aux Etats-Unis', *Bifur* 2 (25 juillet 1929), 95–103;93: 'La prohibition...est, naturellement, un des facteurs les plus incontestablement subversifs.'
[4] 'Rome' (NBuU).
[5] Williams offered Turner's poems and letters to the editor of *View* as 'real American Surrealism' (*View* I, 11–12 [February–March 1942], 5).
[6] Ms. (NBuU).
[7] 'Americana Fantastica', p. 5.
[8] Philippe Soupault, *Last Nights of Paris*, trans. by W. C. Williams (N.Y., 1929).

at night and reading the newspapers in the morning. One of his night-companions is a sailor who is found dismembered the following morning:[1]

Inspired by a singular hope, I threw myself upon the newspapers for an explanation. But I read there only of occurrences similar to that which I had observed, similar but not the same and they seemed to me so pale, so discrete, that I cast aside the paper with a sort of disgust.

The same year that his translation was published Williams made a brief plea for the new perspective which might make poetry out of the journalism of murder.[2] A decade later, in a piece of writing calculated to out-do *View*'s favoured apocalyptic mode, he extended that plea:[3]

The feat of journalism is to give all sorts of fascinating detail, the most accurate and expensive that the imagination can buy. But that is only the beginning. This true and unprosecutable material is moulded by experts to catch in its mesh the cosmic ray of infinity. By reading we arrive at a point of imperviousness to all other news and opinion, a state of beauty of soporific sublimity is induced so that we know, finally, the truth of life. Once this is induced the rest is easy and – in fact superlatively good. It has features of the universal religious ecstasy of the 12th century. In this congeries of factual events is caught the sublime and the irrational. There the sense has, in real truth, disappeared.

Williams' sense of newspapers as a source of documents was highly developed, and he knew how important it was, 'not to twist them in order to make poetry out of them;'[4] for the substantial quality of the documents lay in the language as much as in the matter. Therefore Nathanael West's documentary evidence in *Miss Lonelyhearts* was not to be distinguished from his feeling for language, although what gripped Williams most was the witness that it bore to 'the seriously injured of our civic life – although the cases occur everywhere, even worse, perhaps, in the rural districts':[5]

The letters-to-the-papers which West uses freely and at length must be authentic. I can't believe anything else. The unsuspected world they reveal is beyond ordinary thought. They are a terrific commentary on our daily lack of depth in thought of others. Should such lives as these letters reveal never have been brought

[1] *Ibid.* pp. 121–2.
[2] W. C. Williams, 'For a New Magazine', *Blues* 2 (March 1929), 30–2;*31*.
[3] W. C. Williams, 'Towards the Unknown', *View* I, 11–12 (February–March 1942), 10.
[4] W. C. Williams, 'Muriel Rukeyser's USI', *The New Republic* LXXXXIV, 1214 (9 March 1938), 141–2;*141*.
[5] W. C. Williams, 'Sordid? Good God!' *Contempo* III, 2 (25 July 1933), 1,2;*1*.

to light? Should such people, like the worst of our war wounded, best be kept in hiding?

To discover the architecture by which the facts might be made to live off not Williams' ironical 'cosmic ray of infinity' or 'soporific sublimity' but his serious sense of poetic reality, West turned to the analogy of the comic strip. In some notes on his lyric novel he said he had originally thought of subtitling *Miss Lonelyhearts*, 'A novel in the form of a comic strip'. He abandoned the format but not the technique: 'Each chapter instead of going forward in time, also goes backward, forward, up and down in space like a picture. Violent images are used to illustrate commonplace events. Violent acts are left almost bald.'[1] In this way West combined the radical techniques of the popular arts with the naturalistic tradition of John Dos Passos, James T. Farrell, and the early Edward Dahlberg, which, as his correspondence over the second series of *Contact* shows,[2] formed his conscious literary background. *Contact* expressed this combination in the article Diego Rivera wrote on Mickey Mouse,[3] and in Charles Reznikoff's presentation of legal documents representing the seriously injured Negroes in rural districts.[4] Williams intended to supply photographs by Sheeler to go with these documents after MacLeish's and Anderson's photo-textual fashion, but when this idea could not be realised, whether because the photographs were not forthcoming or because the half-tone blocks were too expensive for the publishers, line-blocks from an eighteenth-century book of physiognomies depicting the passions were used, the formalised, European expressions of the passions contrasting neatly with the bald, American statement of the facts of violence.

The English critical response to the first issue of *Contact*, to the episode of the slaughtered lamb in *Miss Lonelyhearts* in particular, was somewhat typical of the English attitude towards American naturalism:[5]

if it really happened, then it must be regretted that Mr. West feels like that about it, if, on the other hand, it is imaginary, as it seems to be, then it is pathological, like the flogging at the end of *Eric, or Little by Little*.

[1] Nathanael West, 'Some Notes on Miss L.', *Contempo* III, 9 (15 May 1933), 1,2;*1*.
[2] File of letters to Williams (CtY).
[3] *Contact* (Second series) I, 1 (February 1932), 37–9.
[4] *Contact* (Second series) I, 1 (February 1932), 14–34; I, 2 (May 1932), 99–108.
[5] *The Criterion* XI, 45 (July 1932), 772.

West replied in general terms:[1]

What is melodramatic in European writing is not necessarily so in Am. writing. For a European writer to make violence real, he has to do a great deal of careful psychology and sociology. He often needs three hundred pages to motivate one little murder. But not so the Am. writer. His audience has been prepared and is neither surprised nor shocked if he omits artistic excuses for familiar events. When he reads a little book with eight or ten murders in it, he does not necessarily condemn the book as melodramatic.

In Soupault's novel the characters are possessed of an insatiable appetite for the bizarre. They spurn the habitual in favour of the fantastic, inventing terrifying stories for each other when their night-prowling fails to provide them with the encounters with the corpses for which they yearn ('If all at once we had encountered a lifeless form lying prostrate on the pavement bathed perhaps in his own blood, or propped against a wall, we should have come immediately to a halt and night would have been ended').[2] Violence manifests itself as daily experience in America rather than as material for flights of the imagination. The habitualness of violence in America makes Soupault's literary taste for the extraordinary seem absolutely banal. The genre of the European macabre from 'Monk' Lewis to *Maldoror*, to which Soupault inevitably belonged, is distinctly literary in a way in which the American macabre is not. The difficulty in handling the stories of Sam Patch and Mrs Cumming which Ward, the English-imitator, encountered, stemmed from the braggadocio presentation of a folk-tale, and the sentimental presentation of ballad journalism. His attempts at literary finesse aimed so high as to fall short of the primitive power of either of these sub-literary forms.

In 1937, before the French Surrealists arrived, standing before Pavel Tchelitchew's masterpiece *Phenomena* (Plate 5), Williams was asked by the painter whether he thought it was the work of a Surrealist: 'As a physician, no, I answered.'[3] Faced with the monstrous vision of a modern Bosch, he responded in a way which earned Tchelitchew's thanks for being the first to recognise what he was doing, which was

[1] Nathanael West, 'Some Notes on Violence', *Contact* (Second series) I, 3 (October 1932), 132–3;*133*.

[2] *Last Nights of Paris*, p. 41.

[3] *Selected Essays*, p. 252. The date given for the essay is erroneous; it first appeared in *Life and Letters Today* XVII, 10 (Winter 1937), 55–8.

5 Final sketch for *Phenomena* by Pavel Tchelitchew, *c.* 1937, oil on canvas; collection of Charles Henri Ford [reproduced from Parker Tyler, *The Divine Comedy of Pavel Tchelitchew* (Fleet Press Corporation, N.Y., 1967; Weidenfeld and Nicolson, London, 1970)]

not to portray the horrible so as to exploit it, but to recognise it.[1] As Tchelitchew's biographer, Parker Tyler, wrote: 'Tchelitchew *accepts* every statutory or natural irregularity in *Phenomena* as Dante accepts the sins of Hell.'[2] Williams, with his opposition to the 'interest' of the church in the *Divine Comedy*,[3] secularised the meaning of a psychological panorama of his region at the level of *True Stories* rather than that of *The Inferno*. The monstrous was a measure of the beautiful.[4] The normality of disease which Williams accepted as a doctor, could also be accepted by him as a poet.[5] Tchelitchew's use of documents – photographs from *Life* and *Look* and portraits of acquaintances and friends incorporated much as in *Paterson*[6] – must have struck Williams as he pondered the structure of his long poem, which like this painting was to be the summation of a career.

'*Antagonistic Cooperation*'

The first important piece of theoretical writing on Surrealism which came to Williams' attention was by Henry Bamford Parkes, the historian, and coincided with the announcement of Objectivism.[7] Samuel Putnam offered specimens of French Surrealism in his publications, but somewhat bewilderingly did so only to cast doubt on whether the movement could take root in America.[8] Parkes, however, went straight to the heart of the American problem. The American novelist's predilection for naturalism, reinforced by the application of the Marxist idea of the evolution of the masses, had led to the proletarian novel with

---

[1] In Williams' copy (NjFD [Rutherford]) of James Thrall Soby, *Tchelitchew* (N.Y., 1942), is the following inscription: 'To dear Dr. Williams who saw and recognised first "phenomena" as well as "hide and seek" With my best thanks Pavel.'

[2] Parker Tyler, *The Divine Comedy of Pavel Tchelitchew* (N.Y., 1967), p. 389.

[3] *Selected Letters*, p. 297.

[4] W. C. Williams, 'Cache Cache', *View* II, 2 (May 1942) [17–18;*18*]: 'Only in the monstrous do we approach the moon, the sun and the stars!...Monsters frequent the earth everywhere. Science is the accident and the accidental true...The world is monstrous, only the monstrous can be true of it. Or the world is not monstrous, only the monstrous can truly reveal that fatal error.'

[5] Cf.: '...that imponderable and enlightening element, disease, unknown in its normality to either [science or philosophy]' (*A Novelette in Prose* [127]).

[6] Tyler, *Divine Comedy of Pavel Tchelitchew*, pp. 393–7.

[7] H. B. Parkes, 'Notes on Dadaism and Super-realism', *Fifth Floor Window* I, 3 (February 1932), [1–6]. Williams wrote to Zukofsky telling him to get hold of the article, 17 February 1932 (CtY).

[8] S. Putnam, 'If Dada Comes to America', *Contempo* II, 5 (25 July 1932), 1,3,5.

its ultimately idealistic basis. But Parkes now saw the possibility of what he still called a 'Super-realism', taking its philosophical basis from nominalism:[1]

Regarding the external world as ultimately unintelligible, it considers our ideas and universals to be merely convenient ways of arranging phenomena, lacking objective validity. Theoretically, therefore, it might be possible to smash all the accepted categories and rearrange phenomena in wholly new combinations. No system would comprehend the whole of experience; but new categories might be at least as adequate as those which we have used hitherto, and they would reveal phenomena and relationships of which at present we are ignorant.

'Phenomena' was the title Tchelitchew gave to his arrangement of objects. Soupault was faced with 'a scum of objects'. One passage from his *Last Nights of Paris* presented the problem of the intelligibility of the external world prior to the nominalist's decision to name its objects and rearrange them. The need for Williams to do this was pressing, for the Passaic was as full of starved and broken things as the Seine:[2]

On the river floated a scum of objects, pieces of wood, nameless debris gliding to their destiny. Some of them, jumbled together had taken refuge in a little bay. The current disturbed them, tossed them back ironically, and sometimes seized bits of them to toss them into the middle of the stream.

My eyes ran from one bank to the other.

Now my mind would stem the current, and now abandon itself to the flow. Now I wished to look for causes, motives, and now I willingly accepted my ignorance, my simplicity.

In Paris Williams had exhibited to McAlmon a keen interest in the Surrealists, but he had little opportunity to see any exhibitions of their painting in America before 1930. The earliest took place at the gallery of an acquaintance in New York in 1932 and 1935 – Julien Levy, who published a book on Surrealism in 1936,[3] the same year that the Museum of Modern Art presented its show 'Fantastic Art Dada Surrealism'. When the French refugees invaded the city in 1940 Williams viewed every arrival of painters and poets with the same mixture of contempt and envy which he had felt for Duchamp and Picabia in 1916, noting that as they had found support from Walter Arensberg then so they found support from Peggy Guggenheim now. They managed to divert

[1] 'Notes on Dadaism and Super-realism', [3–4].
[2] Soupault, *Last Nights of Paris*, pp. 168–9.
[3] J. Levy, *Surrealism* (N.Y., 1936).

attention from the local effort once again. Charles Henri Ford started the magazine *View* with a principal aim of furthering the career of Tchelitchew, and his co-editor Parker Tyler took an opportunity of denying that it represented any Surrealist line as soon as it arose.[1] Williams applauded the magazine for not being a party organ.[2]

Nevertheless, Williams responded in spite of himself to fresh theoretical encouragement. *View*'s pre-eminence in the field of activity was challenged in 1941 by an effort of Nicolas Calas, André Breton's protégé, who intended to start a magazine, tentatively called 'Gold', then 'Midas'. Williams wrote an introduction but nothing came of it, and its energies flowed briefly into *VVV*, which, when it was first proposed to Williams that he and Breton should be senior editors with Motherwell and Calas as junior editors, showed promise of a Franco–American Surrealist pact. Thus Williams came to know Yves Tanguy, Matta Echaurren, Kurt Seligmann, and Gordon Onslow-Ford. Max Ernst and André Masson collaborated on *VVV*.

Robert Motherwell's sense of the significance of Surrealism in America was developed less by contact with Calas than with the Chilean Matta, whose South American background gave him the necessary distance to mediate in Franco-American relations, and to collate as Breton had suggested,[3] the theory of perception with the theory of chance – Gestaltism with automatism or, as is came to be known later, Abstract-Expressionism.

Matta had studied with Corbusier and shared with Motherwell 'a deep belief in what painters call plasticity, which is counter to most Surrealist painting (the notable exceptions being Arp and Miró)'.[4] In an important letter to Williams Motherwell americanised Surrealism in four propositions:[5]

A. Stimulation of the imagination – in the sense of enriching sensuous life by insisting on ignored aspects of reality, the invention of new objects of perception within reality, etc.

[1] Tyler spoke of Nicolas Calas as '*View*'s lone surrealist animator', (P. Tyler, ' "View" Objects', *Partisan Review* VIII, 3 [May–June 1941], 255). Tchelitchew had refused to be included in the 'Fantastic Art Dada Surrealism' exhibition of 1936 at the Museum of Modern Art.
[2] W. C. Williams, 'Surrealism and the Moment', *View* II, 2 (May 1942), [19].
[3] [Nicolas Calas] 'New York Interview with André Breton', *Arson* [1] [1942], 5.
[4] Letter from Robert Motherwell to the author, 22 April 1966.
[5] Letter from Robert Motherwell to W. C. Williams, 3 December 1941 (CtY).

B. The preservation of the dignity and value of personal feelings – a response to the felt need (in a world increasingly able to deal with physical nature, and potentially, with social relations) of insisting that the only possible end of science and of a good society, the *felt-content* of the organism's experiencing, must not be annihilated or be held in contempt because it is not scientifically or sociologically useful. Hence the importance of the artist, etc.

C. Revolutionism – not so much in the sense of dwelling on the material difficulties and means (though this is implied), but revolution in the sense of increased *consciousness*, of consciousness of the *possibilities* inherent in *experiencing*. Emphasis therefore on novelty, invention, the disturbing, the strange – the power of feeling to move the organism.

D. The dialectic – not so much in the Hegelian sense as constituting the metaphysical nature of reality, or in the Marxist sense as the economic nature of society, but in the sense of a weapon for interpreting and synthesizing reality, as when Breton asks for a union between normal consciousness and the unconscious.

The stress on the importance of personal feelings, which Williams shared with Motherwell, resulted from acceptance of the aggression and violence in the American character, as well as repudiation of the power of the natural and social sciences in society. Williams as physician and Motherwell as graduate in philosophy felt a compensating need for the sensual in art. Motherwell welcomed Surrealism as a relief from the political sense of revolution which had dominated the American thirties in art and literature. Yet Williams felt that the French were not sufficiently dislodged, though in exile, from their political source; he rejected their movement as a misnomer for the Fall of France. He did not reject the general usefulness of the movement, but he considered that its French originators had employed it as an involuntary diagnosis of French conditions after the First World War. They had invented a 'science of misnomers', 'misnaming of external events'.[1] In Williams' unusual view, an art of correct naming of internal events had been supplanted by a professional vanguardism which, transplanted in America, managed to exploit the weaknesses of a society not unlike the one it had abandoned.

At first he had been hopeful that the insular expatriatism of the French could be overcome ('We seek as far as we are American to take

---

[1] *Selected Letters*, p. 240.

in the difficult "foreign", identical with us in the GOLD of it...'),[1] but Breton, like Duchamp before him, showed no interest in a freshly constituted measure in poetry consonant with local conditions. Williams rounded on him in a review of his *The Cherry Trees Secured Against Hares*:[2] 'As with Catholicism and Sovietism everything is planned in Surrealism of which Breton gives here, in his new book of poems, such a balanced display. (All this is contrary to the spirit of the Constitution of the United States).' Williams' penetration of Breton's disguise, by which European conservatism of thought was simply brought up to date, was paralleled by Tchelitchew's remark about the French painters; 'They make very fine compositions. That is the French influence.'[3] Tchelitchew perceived that they were painting a planned dream. This amounted merely to a new version of the picturesque in the old frame. Thus by 1946 the closed fraternity of the French group in New York represented to Williams a new confinement of the mind instead of its hoped-for release: 'Everybody knows beforehand everything that will be said. It is completely without invention in the American sense...'[4] This American sense was founded on twin principles; the search for a new plasticity in measure, and the correct naming of objects without allegorical motive. They were, of course, the cornerstones of the Objectivist position. To americanise Surrealism effectively all one needed to do was to apply these principles to the object 'within'. The image might be deep within the individual consciousness of the poet – a personal fetish – but still remain material 'to be studied', as Kenneth Burke wrote, 'in its own right'.[5] The study of the object within, or what we might call the 'subjective object', would at best produce its proper plastic presentation. The objective quality, therefore, even when applied to the material thrown up by the automatic or improvised act of the poet, was more important to Williams than the symbolic quality. This is the source of his differences with the French Surrealists, for they were largely concerned with fulfilling the dictates of a pre-existent order as conceived by idealist philosophers. They were not nominalists. Inevitably, they were drawn towards traditional ways of

---

1 *Selected Essays*, p. 244.
2 'The Genius of France', *View* VII, 1 (Fall 1946), 43–7;43.
3 *Selected Essays*, p. 251.
4 *View* VII, 3 (Spring 1946), 46.
5 Kenneth Burke, *A Grammar of Motives* (N.Y., 1945), p. 486.

treating the most extraordinary material, until the reliance on clinical psychology made even that material predictable in its nature and its meaning. Parker Tyler spoke of the situations of the 'artist–doctor' and the 'psychoanalytical doctor' as different in their aims:[1]

The judgment of the first is that of esthetic approval, the judgment of the second that of therapeutic idealism combined with clinical realism. It was natural for the first to proceed towards the second; on the other hand, the Surrealists were slow in perceiving, and in a sense, have not yet fully perceived the contradiction inherent from the beginning in the type of artistic creation and the critical equivalent formulated for it. What the Surrealists found satisfying, no doubt, was the tragic paradox involved.

Later, Tyler also wrote of the treatment which various poets actually gave the material:

While the orthodox surrealist poem is a naive stenographic report of image-relations appearing in the subconscious, the newest movement in poetry – if it may be called such – reveals poems of a sophisticated, elaborately 'scientific' report of these relations.[2]

The newest movement was represented by Dylan Thomas, George Barker, and the poets of 'The New Apocalypse' (Henry Treece, Nicholas Moore, and others). But when we compare their 'scientific' reports with those of an Objectivist carrying his principles logically through to the object-world within his personality we find that they returned to the conservatism of fixed forms even more than the French. Plastically they had not evolved at all. In Objectivism all the 'science' was vested in new modes of organisation, but the New Apocalyptics' use of 'science' led them towards Tyler's 'therapeutic idealism' and 'clinical realism'. They were tempted by universals as Williams was not.

The psychoanalytic investigations self-consciously conducted in public by Dali and Tanguy were rejected by Williams and Tchelitchew because they believed that the examination of the ego could be made impersonally with all the force of attention falling on plastic expression. They were concerned to quarry from themselves a mythology of contemporary life consisting of the strata of events both external in the objective world and internal in the subjective world. Their whole

[1] 'Beyond Surrealism', *Caravel* 4 (1935), 2–6;3.
[2] Tyler, 'Literature and the Image', *Fantasy* VI, 4 (1940), 39–46;45.

effort lay in the presentation of these interacting worlds. They did not need to worry over responsibility to good Freudian or Jungian doctrine, for they were confident of the actuality of their own revelations.

Motherwell's fourth proposition that the American use of the Surrealist dialectical method would be neither metaphysical nor political but would psychologically effect 'a union between normal consciousness and the unconscious' undoubtedly appealed to Williams, for when he reviewed Parker Tyler's poem *The Granite Butterfly* it was its technique of juxtaposition (as well as its variable metric) which he especially noted; the juxtaposition of 'two lurid stories...a trope that might be described as allegorical overlay...it lets in the light.'[1] He borrowed his use of 'trope' from Kenneth Burke, who was concerned not with metaphor, metonymy, synecdoche, and irony as simple stylistic figures, 'but with their role in the discovery and description of "the truth"'.[2] For the old terms Burke suggested new ones: perspective, reduction, representation, and dialectic. Dialectic in a more general sense accounted for all the transformations implied in the creation of tropes:[3]

A dialectic, for instance, aims to give us a representation by the use of mutually related or interacting perspectives – and this resultant perspective of perspectives will necessarily be a reduction in the sense that a chart drawn to scale is a reduction of the area charted.

Parker Tyler defined Surrealism dialectically: 'Surrealism combines in practice the representational value of the image (imagism) and the symbolic value of the image (symbolism) in a sort of dialectical play of values.'[4] This interacting perspective on reality Williams regarded as the artistic device or trope which Surrealism offered as a means of raising to the imagination an otherwise unintelligible inner and outer world. But he insisted that the trope as dialectic be well spaced, and not 'massively, "materially", compounded';[5] that is to say, it should not be mathematically engineered after some doctrinal plan, either Marxist or Freudian. The elements of conscious and unconscious

---

[1] *Accent* VI, 3 (Spring 1946), 203–6;*205*.
[2] Burke, *A Grammar of Motives*, p. 503.
[3] *Ibid.*
[4] *Fantasy* VI, 4 (1940), 44.
[5] *Paterson*, p. 278.

material should be unified by conflict (Burke employed 'dramatic' synonymously with 'dialectic'), and not by mere linkage. He was reminded that Eisenstein's original concept of montage (outside the context of Surrealism, of course) was dialectical, and saw that under pressure of the Soviet party line it could return to mere narrative linkage.[1]

The quicker the change in perspective the more confused, 'surrealistic' in the popular sense, the representation of the world apparently becomes. Burke denied it:[2]

But on the contrary, it is by the approach through a variety of perspectives that we establish a character's identity.

Indeed, in keeping with the older theory of realism (what we might call 'poetic realism', in contrast with modern 'scientific realism') we could say that the characters possess *degrees of being* in proportion to the variety of perspectives from which they can with justice be perceived.

Science with its concern for mathematical calibration and correlation, Burke suggested, was not capable of what David Lyle called 'vivification' because it did not deal with substance as quality but as quantity: 'it is not concerned with "being", as "poetic realism" is'.[3] It was precisely of the freedom to judge qualitatively the substance of his material which Eisenstein had allowed himself to be robbed in the U.S.S.R.

In deciding the value of Surrealism to himself Williams turned not to political or aesthetic politics but to the substantial facts of his landscape; now perceived as the straight representation of the photographer, now as the Surrealist symbol of the fantasist. To the extent that *Paterson* is a poem based on the three-personed figure of N.F. Paterson (Noah, Faitoute, and the Poet/City) related to a manifold experience of women (including the woman-mountain) it is an extended trope in which the elements, conscious and unconscious, representational and symbolic, collide and recoil continuously, compounded neither into a fixed level of awareness nor into a single mode of expression.

[1] Dwight Macdonald, 'Film Chronicle: The Eisenstein Tragedy', *Partisan Review* IX, 6 (November–December 1942), 502–7;503.
[2] *A Grammar of Motives*, p. 504.
[3] *Ibid.* p. 505.

An Alchemistic Opus

André Breton, in an interview with Nicolas Calas, defined Surrealism as
an answer to two kinds of preoccupation:[1]

the first of these arising from the *eternal* (the mind grappling with the state of
man), the other arising from the *actual* (the mind witness of its own movement:
for this movement to have any value we hold that *in reality as in the dream* the
mind should go beyond the 'manifest content' of events to arrive at the consciousness of their 'latent content').

Soupault's hero's exasperated search for motives when confronted with
the actual follows Breton's prescription, but Nathanael West rejected
the use of latent content as literary psychology:[2]

Psychology has nothing to do with reality nor should it be used as motivation.
The novelist is no longer a psychologist. Psychology can become something
much more important. The great body of case histories can be used in the way
the ancient writers used their myths. Freud is your Bullfinch; you can not learn
from him.

He plainly preferred to use case histories for their literal rather than
symbolic content. Speaking of the *View* group Williams acknowledged
that they, at least, among his contemporaries, understood 'the inter-
change from the local towards the general...they have the particular in
mind, they apply their understanding in a broad symbolism. The
symbolism of the homologus (*sic*) in their lives can be taken and enlarged from that to enhance the world'.[3] Tyler wrote of the difference
between 'the readily available myth' and the 'fetish' or 'private
mythology' of the poet.[4] The strategy of Williams and Tchelitchew
was to insist on the local validity of what they represented while keeping their own counsel on its general purport. Of *Phenomena* Williams
said that it presented 'actually what is found in life',[5] but by this he
meant more than that it was capable of recognition as a social and
economic criticism of life. Parker Tyler has shown that the painting is

1 'New York Interview with André Breton', pp. 3–4.
2 'Some Notes on Miss L.', p. 2.
3 *Selected Letters*, p. 255.
4 *Fantasy* VI, 4 (1940), 45.
5 *Selected Essays*, p. 252.

underpinned with hermetic content; it possesses the most complete arcane cosmology of any modern work.[1]

In 1951 Williams wrote a reader's report on a manuscript by Nicolas Calas on Hieronymus Bosch's *The Garden of Delights*, which in discussing Bosch also invites us to consider the poet himself as a more covert writer than we might have supposed:[2]

Men do not die if their attack is kept alive by their works, hence the masters secreted their meanings in their paintings to have them live, if chance favored them, forever. And the 'longer' their meaning the longer they might expect to live, to the last day, the 8th day of Creation as Calas has pointed out. All men who have seen into their lives to this day, to the end, and so written or painted will continue to hold a secret meaning for us worth seeking as Bosch has hidden his meaning among his forms.

The synonymity of 'this day' with 'the end' is Williams' grasp of the relation between the 'actual' and the 'eternal'. The Apocalypse is now ('time having been annihilated by the jump from the last day of creation, the 7th, to the Apocalypse, the 8th').[3] The method of presentation was fully in accord with such an understanding:[4]

It can't hold itself back without pretending to be wiser or more astute or a greater painter than Bosch himself – which would be absurd. And so by these assumptions out of sheer intellectual modesty, not looseness of treatment, it must let itself go completely, not hold back, it cannot afford to be maimed by the thought that Bosch *couldn't* have gone so far. He could and *perhaps* did: one must envision everything even remotely suggested to get all the *full* truth.

Tyler is able to say: 'That Tchelitchew, at the age of 38 to 40, has seen prints of hermetic allegories goes without saying; that he saw precisely those of which I am speaking, while there is no proof that he did, seems at least plausible.'[5] Calas was able to evoke the inner meaning of Bosch's work by reference to the writings of St Gregory and St Augus-

---

[1] *Divine Comedy of Pavel Tchelitchew*, pp. 397–403. In writing about Tchelitchew's *Hide and Seek* Williams showed he was aware that he 'does not treat lightly the tenets of magic and necromancy', but chose to emphasis the 'plain sense' of its origins as a tree sketched in England ten years before, and how it had become 'monstrous'. ('Cache Cache', *View* II, 2 [May 1942], [17–18]).

[2] 'Nicolas Calas' illumination of the significance of Hieronymus Bosch's *The Garden of Delights*', typescript and letter to Gertrude Myers, 3 September 1951, kindly provided by Miss Vaun Gillmor of the Bollingen Foundation.

[3] *Ibid.*

[4] *Ibid.*

[5] *Divine Comedy of Pavel Tchelitchew*, p. 403.

tine. How, then, may we evoke the 'full' truth of *Paterson*, stopping short of interpretation?

Williams first encountered Nicolas Calas through his book *Foyers d'Incendie*,[1] which he welcomed saying that he acutely felt the need of such a book, 'a book of general criticism touching all the relationships between the artist's impulses and the world about him'.[2] He saw it as a landmark: it was a powerful synthesis of the Surrealist argument for a radical approach to man in society. He asked for a copy to be sent to one friend and wrote to others about it.[3] But it was another book by Calas, *Confound the Wise*,[4] which ultimately was to have the most covert influence upon Williams. He saw portions of it from 1941 onwards, when he and Calas were attempting to launch the review 'Midas'. Alchemy offered an analogy for the quality of mind which could transmute all matter into gold,[5] even if at Columbia the physical search for the philosopher's stone was over.[6] He felt a profound intellectual attraction for Calas' mind: 'I know what your graphs and glyphs are about. They agree perfectly with my own code – unexpressed with any satisfaction to myself'.[7] When the published book came he was glad to have it, but it was not until almost three years later, in 1945, that he referred to it in a letter, when he praised its ideas as 'sound and welcome and valuable'.[8]

Later in the year Williams encapsulated a 'review' of it in the second half of 'The Phoenix and the Tortoise',[9] making a plea for a book which was as good as boycotted by reviewers at the time of publication. To draw attention to the specific chapter, 'The Salutary Image', on the three-faced portrait of the Trinity in the Museum

[1] Nicolas Calas, *Foyers d'Incendie* (Paris [1938]).
[2] Letter to Nicolas Calas, 15 July 1939.
[3] Letter to Madeleine Boyd, 25 August 1940 (in Mr Calas' possession): 'I think the book is likely to have a lasting formative interest on me and what I shall do with writing hereafter. The last part is even better than the first.' Postcard to Louis Zukofsky, 19 July 1939 (CtY): '...that takes the object up into its final place in the sun'.
[4] Nicolas Calas, *Confound the Wise* (N.Y., 1942).
[5] *Selected Essays*, p. 244.
[6] Letter to Nicolas Calas, 15 November 1940: 'Gold has been transmuted from quicksilver by bombarding the atoms in a cyclotron (a small one would cost $60,000 to produce microscopic amounts of gold). The work was done here in N.Y. by Dr. Urey of Columbia University in collaboration with Colin V. Fink.'
[7] Letter to Nicolas Calas, 15 October 1942.
[8] Letter to Nicolas Calas, 13 January 1945.
[9] *Collected Earlier Poems*, pp. 465–6.

WILLIAM CARLOS WILLIAMS

Loverdo in Athens, would have been to betray too obviously the
secret source of the triadic whole composed of 'Noah Faitoute
Paterson'. What Calas says of the portrait of the Trinity applies
equally to Burke's 'perspective of perspectives', and to the composite
hero of *Paterson*: 'On whatever part of the picture the gaze first falls, be
it on the central one or either of the side ones, the image is complete
and yet it is manifestly only part of a larger whole.'[1] Referring to a book
which we know Williams to have owned,[2] Calas observed that the
Christian Holy Trinity was the only religious one in which the third
member, the Holy Ghost, was an abstraction. The Greek Christians
overcame this element by emphasising the human aspect of Christ,
while the Roman Christians humanised Christ by means of Mary. He
interpreted Mariolatry as the transference of personal feelings of love
from one person to another, whereas the emotion expressed by the
monstrous three-faced Trinity was depersonalised.[3] In a paragraph
which could not have but been pleasing to Williams he explained the
neglect of demonology and magic as the result of theological persecu-
tion:[4]

Priests and professors have reason to be afraid of the disturbing effect abnormal
beings (cyclops, three-headed monsters, demons with missing limbs) and the
irrational behaviour of the inspired and the insane, can have upon all who live in
a society where triadism has produced a fourth figure, the Church for the
Christian and, for the belivers in the triad of Montesquieu, the State.

This fourth figure for Williams is the City.

In 'The Phoenix and the Tortoise' Williams cited Calas' opposition
to positivism and dualism; in the book we find Calas' preferred monism
taking triadic form:[5]

It is my firm belief that one of the principal tasks of the artists of our day who
breathe the air of philosophic (Hegel), political (Marx), and psychological
(Freud) triadism is to discover a pictorial expression that corresponds to the need
of this world.

Through Calas Williams came to meet Kurt Seligmann, most
learned in the occult sciences of all the Surrealists in New York. There

[1] *Confound the Wise*, p. 191.
[2] Levi Leonard Paine, *The Ethnic Trinities* (Boston and N.Y., 1901) (NjFD [Rutherford]).
[3] *Confound the Wise*, pp. 195,198.
[4] *Ibid.* pp. 195–6.
[5] *Ibid.* p. 197.

148

6 *Fata Morgana* by Pavel Tchelitchew, 1940; collection of Mrs Zachary Scott [reproduced from Parker Tyler, *The Divine Comedy of Pavel Tchelitchew* (Fleet Press Corporation, N.Y., 1967; Weidenfeld and Nicolson, London, 1970)]

7 *William Carlos Williams* by Emanuel Romano, 1951; oil on canvas,
32″ × 26″; collection of Gotham Book Mart and Gallery Inc.

is no evidence that the historian of magic and the poet conversed about alchemy or Gnosticism on the recorded occasion of their meeting,[1] but Calas was quite capable of relaying information and sustaining any interest Williams might have had. Seligmann was the warm friend of Tchelitchew, and in Tyler's words, 'knows enough about the background of magic to interpret Tchelitchew's big masterpiece'.[2] Conveniently summarising his current preoccupations, Seligmann wrote in *View* about the sun and moon as male and female emblems, the Gnostic trinity of father, mother, and son, the philosopher's stone, and the Gnostic serpent or alchemist's dragon.[3] Of this latter, the Ouroboros or snake which bites its own tail, it would be tempting to say that Seligmann's article was the source of the motif in *Paterson*, had it not been in Williams' mind a long while already.

The earliest notable example of Williams' interest in the Ouroboros is in an unlikely place – on the dust-cover of *A Voyage to Pagany*, which he tells us was designed by his brother.[4] Depicted on it is the Gnostic Serpent circling the Mundane Egg. The source of this design in 1928 was D. H. Lawrence. It is not hard to explain Williams' willing interest in the English writer who had been so warmly taken up in the Stieglitz circle. His review in 1926 of *In the American Grain* was one of the most generous notices Lawrence ever wrote,[5] and two years later the book was one of the very few that he was recommending.[6] Williams was sorry to the end of his days that Lawrence never replied to a letter from him.[7] Thus, when Lawrence published *Reflections on the Death of a Porcupine* in Philadelphia in 1925 it is unlikely that Williams did not read it; in particular, the chapter called 'Him with His Tail in His Mouth'.[8] Lawrence's own reading was undoubtedly in Madame Blavatsky's *The Secret Doctrine* and Sir James Frazer's *The Golden Bough*, but from Lawrence the myth was readily available to Williams as an

---

[1] Letter to Nicolas Calas, 10 November 1940.

[2] *Divine Comedy of Pavel Tchelitchew*, p. 422. Tyler's illustrations of Hermetic engravings are partly drawn from Kurt Seligmann, *The History of Magic* (N.Y., 1948).

[3] Kurt Seligmann, 'Heritage of the Accursed', *View* v, 5 (December 1945), 6–8.

[4] *I Wanted to Write a Poem*, p. 46.

[5] Reprinted in D. H. Lawrence, *Phoenix* (London, 1961), pp. 334–6.

[6] Edward Nehls, *D. H. Lawrence, A Composite Biography* (3 vols, Madison, Wis., 1959), vol. III, p. 290.

[7] *Autobiography*, p. 51.

[8] Reprinted in D. H. Lawrence, *Phoenix* vol. II (London, 1968), pp. 365–475;427–36.

immediate talisman, to be worked out in full in the last book of *Paterson* much later.

Lawrence's chapter contains much with which Williams sympathised; the attack on religion and philosophy, which imagine that 'the end is one with the beginning',[1] and the belief in 'the spark between man and the living universe...the third thing, the spark which springs from out of the balance...'[2] Lawrence, in a passage which had significance for Tchelitchew as well as Williams, insisted on plurality and multiplicity as the principle of balance:[3]

Creation is a fourth dimension, and in it there are all sorts of things, gods and what-not. That brown hen, scratching with her hind leg in such common fashion, is a sort of goddess in the creative dimension. Of course, if you stay outside the fourth dimension, and try to measure creation in length, breadth, and height, you've set yourself the difficult task of measuring up the Monad, the Mundane egg. Which is a game, like any other. The solution is, of course (let me whisper): *put his tail in his mouth.*

The living relationship in nature is not a closed circle but a live circuit. The serpent's tail fastened into its mouth 'with the padlock of one final clinching idea',[4] is Williams' 'enchained dragon', which must find egress if it is to maintain contact with the sensual world.[5] But as Williams wrote:[6]

Enchained by whom? By ourselves, naturally, who else?...And there it IS, crouching within us – a mould packed with the images of ten million minutes before we have learned so much as to drink from a cup.

The art is to get through to the fact and make it eloquent. We have to make a direct contact, from the sense to the object (within us) so that what we disclose is peeled, acute, virulent...

Williams' attack on clerks is related to Lawrence's attack on philosophers. The academics 'lock' knowledge when they put a padlock on a rounded idea. They substitute 'righteousness' for what is 'good' for

---

[1] *Ibid.* p. 427.
[2] *Ibid.* pp. 434–5.
[3] *Ibid.* p. 431.
[4] *Ibid.* p. 428.
[5] In *Paterson* the dragon splits into two – the tiger in the brakes (p. 33), and the shark which snaps at its own tail (p. 234).
[6] W. C. Williams, 'Advice to the Young Poet', *View* II, 3 (October 1942), 23.

poets.[1] Most interesting of all, perhaps, is Williams' translation of Lawrence's attack on Plato: 'He popped the Logos into the mouth of the dragon, and the serpent of eternity was rounded off.'[2] The logos represents to Williams the words a poet uses to release the power of the 'unlying dragon'; 'only a channel of words will release it, words related to the senses, not learned at school – whose witness will be the instinctive movements of a nascent thing, a variety, living and firm – not those of a hack or a seal trained to say papa'.[3]

A chance phrase like this last against saying 'papa' identifies Williams' sympathies with the Gnostic rather than the Catholic Trinity; Christ was sacrificed by the Father who had sent him not to cleanse the world from sin but to reveal the secret doctrine, and then sowed dissension among the Jews so that they destroyed their seer. In alchemical allegory the Father (the Body) devours the Son (the Spirit).[4] But the Gnostic doctrine is extremely ambiguous on account of the number of ideas imposed upon the serpent of paradise: the good head nourishing itself on the bad tail; the continuous metamorphosis of bad into good, good into bad; the serpent as emblem of knowledge without sinful connotation. The first of these ideas Williams rejected with Lawrence as incestuous and onanistic; the others he retained. He probably accepted the Gnostic version of the Trinity and its alchemical extension: 'According to the alchemists, the philosopher's stone could be made only through the union of the male and the female, the fixed and the volatile, day and night, Sun and Moon, etc.'[5] But his insistence on the conflict of polarities, the coition of opposites, aligned him not only with Lawrence, but also with Breton who disapproved of the homosexuality of the *View* group.

Williams' rationale in support of heterosexuality was based, of course, on his early, Weiningerian sense of the dialectic between the sexes.[6] Revolutionary potency depended upon the sexual relation,

---

[1] Cf. Lawrence, *Phoenix* vol. II, p. 432: 'I don't want to be "good" or "righteous" – and I won't even be "virtuous", unless "vir" means a man, and "vis" means the life-river.'

[2] *Ibid.* 426.

[3] 'Advice to the Young Poet', p. 23.

[4] K. Seligmann, *The History of Magic* (N.Y., 1948), Fig. 54.

[5] K. Seligmann, *View* v, 5 (December 1945), 7.

[6] In a source for *Paterson* Williams read about the drowning of 'two little girls firmly locked in each others' arms' (see Appendix B, *Paterson*, p. 120). In the poem this is rendered, 'Two others, boy and girl, clasped in each others' arms.'

which the poet should carry through into his relation with the whole world. He opposed the domestication of the male element because, as he said, 'Man has been mother to woman so long that he has forgotten her function (and his own) in large measure...with a throwback of female elements in the arts and in affairs: anti-revolutionary, complacent, quilted.'[1] The significant conjunction of man and woman, city and mountain, before the cavern at Passaic Falls provides an alchemical setting for the poem:[2]

In Michael Meyer's *Chemical Secrets of Nature* (1687), a curious etching shows Sun and Moon embracing in front of a cave which symbolizes the hollow of the retort. The etching is explained thus: 'He is conceived in water and born in air; when he has become red in color, he walks over the water.' The offspring of the Sun and Moon is the philosopher's red stone, floating upon the liquid in the crucible.

In *Paterson* the generative imagery of condensation which is so notable in the first part of Book I results in 'a grasshopper of red basalt, boot-long', which 'tumbles from the core of his mind',[3] like an ingot of the precious metal. The manuscripts of the poem show Williams thinking of Ymir, the giant of the Norse creation myth:[4]

> Of Ymir's flesh
> the earth was made and of his thoughts
> were all the gloomy clouds created.

These lines occur in the immediate context of '– Say it, no ideas but in things –', which line is followed in the manuscript by:

> and factories, crystalized from its force
> stand like ice about the chimney rocks.

The anthropomorphic landscape was, of course, a common subject in Surrealist painting. André Masson began his metamorphic series of pictures in 1937, and Williams had ample opportunity to see them in the New York galleries as well as in *View* and *VVV*.[5] Tchelitchew made many anthropomorphic landscapes based on Derby Hill in Vermont, the best known of which is *Fata Morgana* (Plate 6). The im-

---

[1] *Selected Essays*, p. 243.
[2] Seligmann, *History of Magic*, p. 145.
[3] *Paterson*, p. 62.
[4] Ms. (CtY).
[5] At the Bucholz Gallery (1942, 1944, 1945), or the Paul Rosenberg Gallery (1944); in *VVV* I (June 1942), 10–11; in *View* III, I (1943), 9.

mediate source of such a topographical conception of man was probably Antonin Artaud's *On a Journey to the Land of the Tarahumaras*, which appeared – for these French-speakers – in 1937, but was not available to Williams in translation until 1948,[1] when *Paterson* had already appeared.

In 1958, mentioning an illustration in a magazine, Williams wrote: 'the figure of the boy facing the bull, with its accompanying text, summarizes a whole age of Surrealism.'[2] Tchelitchew's *The Bullfight* is a perfect example; and the centre of *Phenomena* depicts a triumphant fighter and a dead bull. But in 1915 Williams wrote a poem which is a zoömorphic as well as anthropomorphic confrontation of the oedipal struggle for the female. The father, whether bull or goat, is related to the porcine mother:[3]

$G^{RoT}E^{sq}U^e$

The city has tits in rows.
The country is in the main – male,
It buts (*sic*) me with blunt stub-horns,
Forces me to oppose it
Or be trampled.

The city is full of milk
And lies still for the most part.
These crack skulls
And spill brains
Against her stomach.

A notable difference between this conception and that of *Paterson* is the lack of differentiation between the social and economic values of the male city as opposed to those of the female country. Here the country is the implacable father and the city the nursing mother. But Williams later found no obstacle to referring to the city of Paris as a woman's body.[4] What counts, here as in 'The Wanderer' and 'The City',[5] is the simple conjunction of opposites.

1 *Transition Forty-Eight* I (January 1948), 56–9; 2 [June 1948], 76–85.
2 Letter to Jonathan Williams, 15 February 1958; the illustration and text are in *The Black Mountain Review* 6 (Spring 1956), 115. The death of Lorca on the horns of a fascist firing-squad in his home-town of Granada is an analogous image (*Selected Essays*, p. 229).
3 Ms. (Viola Baxter Jordan papers: CtY).
4 W. C. Williams, 'Picasso Breaks Faces', *The General Magazine and Historical Chronicle* LIII, I (Autumn 1950), 40–I.
5 *Collected Earlier Poems*.

In *Phenomena* the differentiation is at once clearer and more obscure. As a Tchelitchew scholar writes: 'The city stands for the man-made environment in contrast to that fashioned by Nature. The emphasis is on waste, inhumanity, and literally, insane energy. The idea is conveyed by the titles of several studies for *Phenomena* titled "Garbage-town".'[1] Yet Tchelitchew's 'city' is an androgynous combination of possible kinds of community. Williams referred broadly to the 'background of mountain, classical ruin and Mexican adobe house, with sea and sky going off toward the top and back'.[2] Parker Tyler's name for Williams 'mountain' is the City of Glass, which Williams calls a 'glacier prospect'. But the city of glass is a literal description also of the skyscrapers on the right of the painting, which side is extensively permeated by male emblems (testicular forms, diver, soldier, car junkyard, painting of gold, etc.). The shadow of the skyscraper falls upon the base of the mountain which is shored with brick. Yet this side in the Hermetic Cosmos is the half of the Moon, which it is partly here with its emblems of water stretching beyond the city, and in the lake and seminal sac. The left-hand side is the Sun's half, and the 'city' now is a cave-dwelling and a shanty-town. The baked-brick is as uneven as desert stone (which presumably left in Williams' memory the idea of an adobe house; the 'classical ruin' is not evident). The Gnostic ladder, however, is surmounted by a female figure, and the guardians of the Gateway to Eternal Wisdom are Gertrude Stein and Alice B. Toklas. The Phoenix is a Rhode Island Red hen.[3] In the centre, the Lion-Man's legs are surmounted by 'the face of an old woman, a tormented, wrinkled face'.[4] 'N. F. Paterson', however, is not androgynous at all. Sex differences are kept clear in *Paterson*, with the exception of the episode of Corydon and Phyllis.[5]

In Tchelitchew the Hermetic Androgyne suggests completion; the abnormal perfection is compounded together. But Williams was strenuously opposed to completion, and to perfection as 'composi-

[1] Letter from Stephen Prokopoff to the author, 11 December 1965.
[2] *Selected Essays*, pp. 251–2.
[3] This description is indebted for its basis, if not its emphasis, to Parker Tyler, *Divine Comedy of Pavel Tchelitchew*, who does not, however, distinguish the breed of hen, which is that of Lawrence's female Phoenix in 'Him with his Tail in his Mouth', *Phoenix* vol. II, pp. 431–2.
[4] *Selected Essays*, p. 252.
[5] *Paterson*, pp. 177 ff. (See Appendix B).

tion'. He was equally opposed to the incompletion of the broken object. In an essay on the painter Emanuel Romano, he suggested that the fragmentation of images in Pollock, Michaux, and Artaud (whom he called, in 1957, 'the Ultra-Moderns'), and in René Char's *Leaves of Hypnos*, was 'part of the schizophrenic picture that men and women cohabit with their sex unproductively, as in the days of Socrates and Sappho'.[1] He defined these men's work as 'the non-representationalism of incompletion'. Tchelitchew, we are told, used to repeat Gertrude Stein's charge not to 'break the object' like Picasso: 'He was impelled to agree with her that breaking an object (she apparently did not distinguish between life and painting) was a confession of impotence in relation to it.'[2] The fractured object was to Williams an indication of a disintegrated personality; the androgynous form indicated an inverted personality. Thus Williams, unlike Tchelitchew in this respect, maintained the sense of dialectic relationship between the sexes which the Surrealists also shared.[3] This conjunction throve on the 'antagonistic cooperation' of opposites,[4] rather than an idealistic union of opposites.

Jung was also among those proposing a dialectic relationship between conscious and unconscious life based upon 'open conflict and open collaboration'.[5] But his fresh contribution to the *View* group was the demonstration of parallels between Gnosticism and alchemy and the psychological process by which a man becomes whole or individual. The attraction of alchemy for an artist is best explained by Jung's perception that the alchemist, unlike the Christian mystic, recognised in external facts and events an internal psychic reality. He does not believe in correspondence on theoretical grounds, but 'because he experiences the presence of the idea in the physical order':[6]

I am, therefore, inclined to suppose that the true root of alchemy is less to be sought in transmitted philosophical views than in certain experiences of projec-

---

1 'The Broken Vase', typescript kindly provided by Emanuel Romano.

2 Tyler, *Divine Comedy of Pavel Tchelitchew*, p. 31.

3 In this respect it is interesting to note that Motherwell's favourite mythological creation was the Unicorn (a not irrelevant choice for *Paterson*), whereas his least favourite was Narcissus ('Concerning the present day relative attractions of various creatures in mythology and legend', *VVV* I [June 1942]).

4 *Paterson*, p. 208 (see Appendix B).

5 Carl G. Jung, *The Integration of the Personality* (London, 1940), p. 27.

6 *Ibid.* pp. 212–13.

tion of the individual researchers...He experienced his projection as a characteristic of matter; but what he actually experienced was his own unconscious.

The way in which the alchemist tried to bring the spirit to light by means of a search for materialisation in the laboratory was analogous to Williams' arrangement of phenomena to let in the light of the imagination. Alchemistic method was also good Objectivist practice. Furthermore, the belief in the redemptive power of the philosopher's stone may have produced a parallel between the *lapis* and Christ, but it did so with one important difference:[1]

for the Christian *opus* is an *operari*, to the honour of the redeeming God, on the part of the man who needs redemption, while the alchemistic *opus* is the labour of man the redeemer in the cause of the divine world-soul that sleeps in matter and awaits redemption.

The difference is between the religious and the artist. Until the alchemistic imagery of *Paterson* is analysed in full,[2] we must allow Jung a final word:[3]

It was not for nothing that alchemy called itself an *art*; it was right in the feeling that it was dealing with creative processes that can be fully grasped only in experience, although the intellect may designate them. Let us not forget that it was alchemy that coined the admonition:

Rumpite libros, ne corda rumpantur.

('Rend the books, lest your hearts be rent asunder.')

[1] *Ibid.* p. 270.
[2] Jung's discussion of the *anima* ('she embraces the degraded woman and the *femme inspiratrice*, Faust's Gretchen and the Virgin') (*ibid.* p. 23) is clearly relevant to Williams' theme of the Virgin and the Whore in *Paterson*. His analysis of Faust, 'which from beginning to end is saturated with alchemistic forms of thought' (*ibid.*), is also of interest since we know that Williams was reading Goethe's play throughout the period of the composition of *Paterson* (letter to Jim Higgins, 6 February 1942; also *Selected Letters*, p. 249 [1946]).
[3] *Ibid.* p. 276.

9

The Core of a Man

In May 1946 Williams underwent an operation for a hernia, which had to be re-done just before Christmas. The downward motion had begun, but it was not serious enough to impede the publication of *Paterson: Book One*. In February 1948, however, he was confined to bed for three weeks after a heart-attack. In March 1951 he suffered a light stroke. But still these jolts were not sufficient to throw the locomotive poet off the track. Then in mid-August 1952 he was severely stricken, and the damage done to mind and body was profound. In October he was doubly hit, with a fresh physical attack and with the troubles over his appointment at the Library of Congress.

Earlier, in about 1944, in response to an inquiry from Kathleen Hoagland about the effects of a stroke, he had written: 'the use of paralyzed limbs can be completely regained if the injury to the brain is not too great, that is if the clot is absorbed. It has occurred. I've heard of people having five or six strokes and surviving'.[1] He was almost exactly right with regard to his own case. In 1947 he wrote to Fred Miller that he was 'convinced at the moment that my right arm is rapidly becoming paralysed: probably hysteriacl (see what I mean?)'.[2] His premonition of paralysis in his right arm was also accurate. In 1952 he lost the power of this arm, the writing arm, and the power of speech, by which a poet tests the efficiency of his ear. Whether or not the damage done to his sensual life of writing was self-induced as much as suffered, his nervous temperament and worried disposition sank him deeper into depression than other men might have gone. The petty torment of his daily medical practice had brought with it the

[1] [Answers to questions of a medical nature], four-page typescript, *c.* 1944, kindly provided by Mrs Kathleen Hoagland.
[2] Letter from Williams to Miller, 2 May 1947.

157

mobility which fired his mind and left it spent. Now the man who had owned nine cars had run off the road. Shuttling backwards and forwards between the worlds of medicine and writing had made him complete, but now he was confined to the house for more than a year; he spent two months at Hillside Hospital, Glen Oaks, N.Y. in the spring of 1953,[1] and was still receiving psychiatric treatment in 1957. His derangement caused him the same kind of deprivation and anguish he had known in his youth.[2] The restraint which led to hell then had come as the result of the infection of his mother's idealism; now it was from his enslavement to the doctor's life.

Referring in the *Autobiography* to Vercingetorix,[3] the leader of the Gallic resistance against Caesar, he implied that the lesson to be learned from his story was that a man is inevitably betrayed by his own people, but in the manuscript he chose to emphasise that the followers of such a man had their right hands cut off at the wrist.[4] It is this latter emphasis which occurred again in 1957, where he remembered the 'Roman conqueror who cut off the hands of the Gauls to make them impotent'.[5] In the literary sphere Williams thought of Eliot as Caesar and of himself as Vercingetorix, but in the personal realm the tyrants were family and career. They represented his bad, and punishable, conscience.

The 'immoral virtues', the serious success with women, 'the springtime of the soul' which Aaron Burr embodied, were the themes of 'The Virtue of History'.[6] But just as Williams identified part of himself with Burr, so he identified another part with Hamilton. Had not Hamilton come up out of the West Indies, with a French mother and an English father and a trace of Negro blood? With his 'bold face and pop-eyes',[7] was it not his desire to make Paterson, or any similar place where he had an interest, the merchandise capital of the world, just as Williams wished to redeem its provinciality and capitalise it poetically?

---

[1] See *Pictures from Brueghel*, pp. 97–100: 'The Mental Hospital Garden'.
[2] In a letter to Fred Miller (9 January 1953) Williams spoke of his 'mental hell', and to Robert Creeley (8 October 1953) of 'unadulterated hell'.
[3] *Paterson*, p. 170.
[4] 'Autobiography', p. 210 ms. (CtY).
[5] 'For Broadcast', typescript (September 1957) kindly provided by Mrs Mara Ritums of the Office de Radiodiffusion-Télévision Française, New York.
[6] *In the American Grain*, pp. 200, 196, 204.
[7] 'Paterson' ms. (CtY).

Williams, like Hamilton, wanted success. The one chose finance, the other medicine; both equally closed, professional, shops. As doctor and householder Williams was true to his family's idea of success but could not practically attain it as a writer.[1] His Unitarian father offered him *Noble Lives and Noble Deeds* to read,[2] but Williams chose to portray the passionate, individualistic heroes of the American tradition rather than the successful ones. Yet Hamilton's determination to succeed in order to free himself from the demands of 'the great beast' was also shared by Williams. Williams would not give away his house or his money. They were his check against abandonment to the life he desired. When Charlotte, with a face like Garbo's, eloped to Germany with her soulmate, Ferdinand Earle, Williams' father-in-law, a Prussian from Breslau, disowned her with Williams' compliance.[3]

But the volatility of Williams' personality was derived from his mother, whose life he began to write in 1939. He hoped it would prove his 'major' work at that time,[4] and later suggested that it would explain his own nervous disposition, 'how I got that way: honestly out of my mother'.[5] It was twenty years before it appeared as *Yes, Mrs. Williams*, and it was hardly the book he had intended.[6] Meanwhile, most of its preoccupations with family history had found their way into *Paterson*, freshly prompted by his visit to Puerto Rico in the spring of 1941.

The parallel between Williams' own life and his mother's was close. The reason her brother, Carlos, had sent her to Paris was to recover from a broken engagement: 'She got over it, quick – or never.'[7] But she came back, married, and moved to Rutherford: 'Her heart was broken'.[8] Williams' atonement for having desired Charlotte, the

1 In 1949 he calculated his literary earnings over a twenty-year period as approximately $200 a year (letter to Harry Roskolenko, 5 April 1949 [CtY]).

2 *Noble Lives and Noble Deeds. Forty Lessons by Various Writers, Illustrating Christian Character*, ed. Edward A. Horton, 3rd edn (Boston, 1895) (NjFD [Rutherford]).

3 Letter from Ferdinand Earle to W. C. Williams, 28 October 1915 (CtY).

4 Letter to Louis Untermeyer, 8 March 1939 (InU).

5 Letter to Fred R. Miller, 18 July 1958.

6 Letter to Winfield Townley Scott, 11 April 1959 (RPB): 'I can't keep from telling you that it will be far from a finished book when it is finally released – too many people have had a hand in its composition and I am powerless to do anything about it. At that Dave [McDowell, the publisher] has done what he has had to do or there would have been no book at all.'

7 W. C. Williams, 'From My Notes About My Mother', *The Literary Review* I, 1 (Autumn 1957), 5–12;10.   8 *Yes, Mrs. Williams*, p. 5.

artistic life, and Europe was achieved in marriage to Florence and committal for life to Rutherford. He took his wife on their honeymoon to Concord, where she was sick in a grave-yard.[1] Watching him prepare ground for rhododendrons in Rutherford a girl, whose father grew orchids, asked him if he were happy.[2] He had not realised that atonement meant substitution of the temperate rhododendron for the tropical orchid.

It was from his mother that he inherited the idealistic aspirations of the torrid island of Mayagüez. The strength of his identification with her is transparent:[3]

What did she mean by 'the truth'? That's what her story is. For what does any man care about the truth, in her sense, especially what does a writer care, an artist, compared with his convictions? Nothing. Perhaps that's why she never got very far with painting. She wanted to be a portraitist. The truth was curiously at war with her sensibilities. One had to report the world according to one's perceptions of it, willy nilly. But this meant serious denials. There was another truth, the truth of self, of angry demands, of satisfaction, of love. She had rejected love for truth's sake. But she had denied herself in that crisis. What truth could there be in that?

The truth of egoism meant the affirmation of the priceless values of idealism. The photographic sharpness of the Puritan vision denied this truth and put a price upon every material object. Williams and his mother were formed in the matrix of this incongruity. It was their special integrity. Kreymborg explained it as the result of mixed blood,[4] as did McAlmon: 'No wonder he was up in the air most of the time, with a feminine will and intuition thrown in upon his impulses...'[5] With his masculine will Williams believed in hybridisation and mongrelisation as the future of the country, but with his feminine intuition he superstitiously feared the consequences of 'bad blood'. He championed the outlawed, the ignorant, the diseased, and the untouchable, even as he tried to 'cure' them as a doctor, because he

[1] *Autobiography*, p. 130.
[2] *Ibid.* p. 133 (the girl is not identified as belonging to the orchid-grower's family (p. 177), but Mrs Hoagland, who typed the manuscript, informs me that Williams told her that she did).
[3] 'From My Notes About My Mother', p. 9.
[4] Alfred Kreymborg, *Troubadour* (N.Y., 1925), p. 243.
[5] *Post-Adolescence*, p. 14.

sensed in their physical state the condition of his mind, tortured and deformed with denials and duties. Even within his own family he valued the pariah. His grandmother's untraceable birth made her proud. Her son, his Uncle Godwin, told the policeman who came to arrest him after he had insanely terrorised the family: 'Don't touch me. I'm a gentleman',[1] and proved he was his courageous mother's son.

The Baroness Elsa von Freytag-Loringhoven, who offered her venereal disease and insanity as if it was a precious gift,[2] was wisely refused by Williams, but he cherished the idea of 'Complete insanity, complete competence', and wrote of 'The magic of four which all trinities miss, leaving a blank for insanity',[3] confessing that 'the trinity always seemed unstable. It lacks a fourth member, the devil'.[4] He appreciated the authentic untouchability of the baroness as a challenge to the phantom ideal of purity which Lewis Mumford described: 'The ideal maiden of adolescent America was a sort of inverted pariah: untouchable by reason of her elevation. In defiance of Nature, her womanliness and untouchability were supposed to be one.'[5] The dual aspect of Jung's *anima* is constantly present in Williams' work. A single example will suffice. The 'editor' of *Paterson* recalls that Williams often used to refer to the mother of Christ as Miriam,[6] as if implying that the habit was a mild aberration on the poet's part, whereas Williams' reference to both Miriam (Matthew) and Mary (Luke) within one citation is intended to juxtapose the 'tagged' figure (Miriam) with the 'saintly' virgin (Mary).[7] The grandmother, refusing Williams' questions about the past, invites her grandson's speculation whether she was 'caught' with child when her man went off to the Crimea.[8] It would mean his own father was, like Hamilton,[9] born out of wedlock. Yet Columbus Day was his father's birthday and a saint, Abbess

[1] *Autobiography*, p. 26.
[2] 'The Baroness Elsa von Freytag-Loringhoven' (ms. CtY).
[3] 'Towards the Unknown', p. 10.
[4] *Selected Letters*, p. 333. Jung also noted that the quaternity, including the devil, was prefered by some alchemists in order to include 'the black substance of evil' (*Integration of the Personality*, p. 48).
[5] L. Mumford, 'The Metropolitan Milieu', in *America & Alfred Stieglitz*, ed. Waldo Frank *et al.* (N.Y., 1934), p. 36.
[6] *Paterson*, p. 266.
[7] See Appendix B (*Paterson*, p. 277).
[8] *Ibid.* A reference to the Crimean War was cut out of the final printer's copy (MH).
[9] *Paterson*, p. 283.

Hildegard, who wrote the choral for her own funeral,[1] died on Williams' birthday. He felt destiny at work in these dates.

The underlying purity of Williams' mind was implicit in the very promiscuity of his thought, just as the affirmation of his wife was contained in the seriousness of his dalliance with women.[2] His boyish light-heartedness, carelessness, recklessness, and humour were the measure of the strict seriousness with which he took life. The quality flared up as the two tendencies, improvisatory and precisionist, rubbed ceaselessly against each other. He checked himself by remaining in Rutherford the better to abandon himself in the face of the severest opposition:[3]

desperately scattered, he had remained *still*; whereas they, Jack and the rest, being always collected, could go loose. But if he should go loose, he would die, of this he was convinced, to go loose to him was to go totally ungoverned, drunken, syphilitic, starved, jailed, murderous: Finis. The rest were pikers really – careful schemers, really. This had been his excuse. Not an excuse. It was the wall over which he could not climb, short of annihilation. This kept him enslaved. He could see himself running, hitting against the bushes madly; bruised charging against Moresco the giant back: going against insuperable odds. – Yet that is the only thing worth going against. He was willing but he couldn't – that was all. If they wanted to be damned fools, all right. Yet, that was what he wanted to be – really; abandoned.

McAlmon and the expatriates in Paris ('Jack and the rest') were of purer stock and less nervous in temperament.[4] They were better 'collected' than he was. It was why the English society girls needed to be so profligate.[5] But Williams was uncollected. In McAlmon's *Post-Adolescence*, Marsden Hartley ('Brander Ogden') gave his opinion:[6]

He just never will know [how] to handle the many different qualities and personalities within himself. My, I ceased long back ever asking him what he thinks about anything, because that puts him in a panic, so he has to run home

---

[1] *Ibid.* p. 212.

[2] Williams' nine African women, 'astraddle a log, an official log to be presumed', shows an interesting departure from the picture he saw twenty years before in which six women are seated on individual stools (see Appendix B [*Paterson*, pp. 22–3] and Plate 8). The log – a phallic invention of the memory – unifies the chief's sexual life like imagination unifies the poet's.

[3] *A Voyage to Pagany*, pp. 70–1.

[4] *In the American Grain*, p. 105.

[5] *Autobiography*, pp. 220–4.

[6] *Post-Adolescence*, p. 14.

immediately to try and think out what he does think, and that means another siege of trying to calm him down for Nellie [Florence]. There is so much wild imagination, audacity, and timidity, mixed up in him indiscriminately that nobody can ever know where he is, least of all himself.

To the prediction that he would never know how to reconcile his incongruities should have been added a proviso – *outside his poems*. Hartley showed he realised this in a letter: 'he has made a very splendid struggle to plasticize all his various selves & he is perhaps more people at once than anyone I have ever known, not vague persons but he's a small town of serious citizens in himself'.[1]

But Williams was never confident in his struggle. On receiving the galley proofs of *Paterson: Book One* he confided feelings of panic to Fred Miller:[2]

Perhaps I should chuck the whole mess, just burn it up. But I'm not sure enough of myself to do that. As a result I've slashed the galleys unmercifully...

Do I have to let it appear? I could pay the printer and quit. But I can't quit. Maybe the finish. I hope not but I'm desperately afraid.

His initial disgust with himself passed after further work on the galleys,[3] but his insecurity was extreme. Wallace Stevens described him a few years later as 'a man somehow disturbed at the core and making all sorts of gestures and using all sorts of figures to conceal it from himself'.[4] But if Williams was confused in his life he used the gestures and figures of his poetry for self-revelation rather than self-concealment.

His capacity for projection was very great. He employed it both alchemistically to identify himself psychologically, and pictorially to reproduce, in the cinematographic sense of projection, the daily passage of time.[5] In the last years of his life, his memory gone and painstakingly collected details of his life falling away, bafflement returned. His speech had failed. The ideas in his mind could not find a match in his unfocusing eyes, and his hesitant tongue could not speak

[1] Letter to Alfred Stieglitz, 9 October 1923 (CtY).
[2] Letter to Fred R. Miller, 8 September 1945.
[3] Letter to Fred R. Miller, 21 September 1945.
[4] *Letters of Wallace Stevens*, selected and edited by Holly Stevens (London, 1967), p. 592; letter to Barbara Church, 29 April 1948.
[5] Gorham Munson told me how remarkably successful Williams was in performing the mental exercise of 'unrolling the film of the day' (see A.R. Orage, *The Active Mind* (N.Y., 1954), pp. 91–5).

them. Yet the urge towards the projection of art remained. He learnt, at seventy-four years of age, the word 'solipsism',[1] the meaning of which he had expressed in 1926:[2]

I must look and digest, swallow and break up a situation in myself before it can get to me. It is due to my wanting to encircle too much. It is due to my lack of pattern. For if I were working inside a pattern, everyone working in other patterns beside me... would be understood by me at once – and they are not so understood by me. As I exist, omnivorous, everything I touch seems incomplete until I can swallow, digest and make it a part of myself.

But my failure to work inside a pattern – a positive sin – is the cause of my virtues. I cannot work inside a pattern because I can't find a pattern that will have me. My whole effort... is to find a pattern, large enough, modern enough, flexible enough to include my desires. And if I should find it I'd wither and die.

The final truth came to him in terms of his mother's failure to become a portraitist. She had thought that to paint one truth was to deny another, not realising, as he now did, 'The artist is always and forever painting only one thing: a self portrait.'[3]

He died on 4 March 1963, just a few days into spring.

---

[1] Letter to Ethel M. Albert, 22 November 1957. Williams writes about *Paterson 5*, 'a poem that may be concerned with the whole problem of solipsis'.
[2] Letter to John Riordan, 13 October 1926.
[3] W.C. Williams, 'Emanuel Romano', *Form* 2 (1 September 1966), 22–5;22.

APPENDIX A

A Selection from Thomas Ward's 'Passaic'[1]

—————

PASSAIC,

A GROUP OF

POEMS TOUCHING THAT RIVER:

WITH OTHER

MUSINGS:

BY FLACCUS.

—————

NEW-YORK:

WILEY AND PUTNAM, 161 BROADWAY.

1842.

[1] From pp. 10–41, 44–8, 66–8, 125–40.

APPENDIX A

INTRODUCTORY MUSINGS
ON RIVERS

Of shallow brooks that flowed so clear
The bottom did the top appear;
Of deeper too, and ampler floods,
Which as in mirrors showed the woods.
DRYDEN

I

BEAUTIFUL Rivers! that adown the vale
With graceful passage journey to the deep;
Let me along your grassy marge recline
At ease, and musing, meditate the strange
Bright history of your life; yes, from your birth
Has beauty's shadow chased your every step:
The blue sea was your mother, and the sun
Your glorious sire: clouds your voluptuous cradle,
Roofed with o'erarching rainbows; and your fall
To earth was cheered with shout of happy birds –
With brightened faces of reviving flowers,
And meadows, while the sympathising west
Took holiday, and donned her richest robes.
From deep mysterious wanderings your springs
Break bubbling into beauty; where they lie
In infant helplessness awhile, but soon
Gathering in tiny brooks they gambol down
The steep sides of the mountain, laughing, shouting,
Teasing the wild flowers, and at every turn
Meeting new playmates still to swell their ranks;
Which, with the rich increase resistless grown,
Shed foam and thunder, that the echoing wood
Rings with the boisterous glee; while o'er their heads,
Catching their spirit blithe, young rainbows sport,
The frolic children of the wanton sun.

Nor is your swelling prime or green old age,
Though calm, unlovely; still, where'er ye move
Your train is beauty; trees stand grouping by
To mark your graceful progress: giddy flowers,
And vain, as beauties wont, stoop o'er the verge
To greet their faces in your flattering glass:
The thirsty herd are following at your side;
And water-birds in clustering fleets convoy

166

Your sea-bound tides; and jaded man, released
From worldly thraldom, here his dwelling plants –
Here pauses in your pleasant neighborhood;
Sure of repose along your tranquil shores.
And when your end approaches, and ye blend
With the eternal ocean, ye shall fade
As placidly as when an infant dies;
And the death-angel shall your powers withdraw
Gently as twilight takes the parting day,
And, with a soft and gradual decline
That cheats the senses, lets it down to night.

II

Bountiful Rivers! not upon the earth
Is record traced of God's exuberant grace
So deeply graven as the channels worn
By ever-flowing streams: arteries of earth
That widely branching circulate its blood:
Whose ever-throbbing pulses are the tides.
Amazing effort for the weal of man!
The whole vast enginery of Nature, all
The roused and laboring elements combine
In their production; for the mighty end
Is growth – is life to every living thing.
The sun himself is chartered for the work:
His arm uplifts the main, and at his smile
The fluttering vapors take their flight for heaven,
Shaking the briny sea-dregs from their wings:
Here wrought by unseen fingers soon is wove
The cloudy tissue, till a mighty fleet,
Freighted with treasures bound for distant shores,
Floats waiting for the breeze: loosed on the sky
Rush the strong tempests, that with sweeping breath
Impel the vast flotilla to its port;
Where, overhanging wide the arid plain,
Drops the rich mercy down: and oft when Summer
Withers the harvest, and the lazy clouds
Drag idly at the bidding of the breeze,
New riders spur them, and enraged they rush
Bestrode by thunders, that with hideous shouts
And crackling thongs of fire urge them along.

As falls the blessing, how the satiate earth
And all her race shed grateful smiles! – not here

The bounty ceases: when the drenching streams
Have inly sinking quenched the greedy thirst
Of plants, of woods, some kind invisible hand
In bright perennial springs pumps up again
For needy man and beast: and as the brooks
Grow strong, apprenticed to the use of man,
The ponderous wheel they turn, the web to weave,
The stubborn metal forge: and when advanced
To sober age at last, ye seek the sea,
Bearing the wealth of commerce on your backs,
Ye seem the unpaid carriers of the sky
Vouchsafed to earth for burthen; and your host
Of shining branches, linking land to land,
Seem bands of friendship – silver chains of love
To bind the world in brotherhood and peace.

III

Primeval Rivers! ancient as the hills –
From immemorial ages have ye run
From mountain unto sea: your busy brooks
Still singing endless songs; your solemn falls
Pealing aloft their ever-during hymn
Unwearied – mightiest thine, Niagara!
The loudest voice which Earth sends up to Heaven.

Back to the primal chaos fancy sweeps
To trace your dim beginning; when dull earth
Lay sunken low, one level plashy marsh,
Girdled with mists; while Saurian reptiles, strange,
Measureless monsters, through the cloggy plain
Paddled and floundered; and the Almighty voice,
Like silver trumpet, from their hidden dens
Summoned the central and resistless fires;
That with a groan from pole to pole upheave
The mountain masses, and with dreadful rent
Fracture the rocky crust: then Andes rose,
And Alps their granite pyramids shot up
Barren of soil; but gathering vapors round
Their stony scalps condensed to drops, from drops
To brooks, from brooks to rivers, which set out
Over that rugged and untravelled land,
The first exploring pilgrims to the sea.
Tedious their route, precipitous and vague,
Seeking with humbleness the lowliest paths:

Oft shut in valleys deep, forlorn they turn
And find no vent; till gathered into lakes
Topping the basin's brimming lip, they plunge
Headlong, and hurry to the level main
Rejoicing: misty ages did they run,
And with unceasing friction all the while
Frittered to granular atoms the dense rock,
And ground it into soil – then dropped (oh! sure
From Heaven) the precious seed: first mosses, lichens
Seized on the sterile flint, and from their dust
Sprang herbs and flowers: last from the deepening mould
Uprose to heaven in pride the princely tree,
And earth was fitted for her coming lord.

Thus in those ancient channels still ye run
Enduring rivers! thus will run till earth's
High places be laid low – ye haughty hills!
Had not the Almighty word the solemn truth
Elsewhere revealed, I know your days are numbered:
Yes! streams, the gentlest of God's messengers,
Though late, yet sure shall bow your stubborn heads,
And bring your honors level with the plain! –

Whenever upon mountain peaks I stand,
And mark the broken and disordered scene –
The wreck, the crumbling crags, that stone by stone
Have tumbling piled the rubbish heaps that choke
The deep ravines, while up their hoary sides
Rash vines and bushes clamber where they can,
Clinging with hungry, desperate roots – it seems
To fancy's eye that earth is one wide ruin,
And vegetation but the ivy wreath
That crowns, and beautifies its mouldering walls:
Unworthy dwelling for aspiring souls
That crave perfection: yet there be who deem
The charms of earth enhanced by ruggedness –
That without contrast beauty's self were tame:
If true of nature, yet that better land
Exists, where order without change can charm;
And universal beauty needs no foil
To yield perpetual rapture to the soul.
Not unattainable this perfect clime
Even by the weakness of ignoble man,

169

If rightly sought, as rivers seek the sea:
With humbleness that loves the lowliest ways –
With patience under crosses, and withal
Enduring courage, faithful to the close –
The crowning close! when on the wondering sight
Opens the eternal sea! lit by the Sun
Of Righteousness, whose vivifying ray
Cheers the awed spirit, quickens, purifies,
And lifts it like a virgin cloud to heaven!

Tale I

THE GREAT DESCENDER

Canto I

Since he, miscalled the Morning Star,
Nor man, nor fiend hath fallen so far.
BYRON

WILD was the night; fast flew the hurrying cloud,
Mantling the heavens with many-folded shroud;
The baffled moon kept struggling, though in vain,
Through the rent gloom to smile upon the plain.
Out stood the cliffs, still blacker than the sky,
Whence rushing, tumbling, foaming from on high,
PASSAIC, driven with impetuous sweep,
Sprang with a scream of horror down the steep;
And in the depths of sternly-girdling rock,
Muttered deep groans of anguish at the shock:
To whose lament, the snarling winds on high
Yell back their surly howlings in reply:
And not a voice disturbed the air, beside
That clamorous quarrel of the wind and tide;
Whose loud dispute – for wranglers never spare –
With ceaseless brawling tires the sleepy air.
Dark, savage scene – wild as a murderer's dream –
Which to the moon's dim-gazing eye might seem
Like a sick beast, that, fretting as it lay,
Growled, frowned, and fumed the sullen night away.

Now from the west upheaves a denser gloom;
Red lightnings gleam, and coming thunders boom
Portentous: starts the sleeper in his bed,
Blessing the shelter that protects his head;
And mourns the hapless traveller's piteous plight,

Who bears the tyrannous fury of the night.
Bursts the big cloud, the gushing deluge pours,
That ev'n the cataract outrains and roars:
When lo! a flash, and quick successive shock
Quivers and thunders; high upon a rock,
Lit by the lightning's momentary blink,
A human form sits dangling o'er the brink!
And by his side, lo! darkly crouching there,
A red-eyed monster, black, with shaggy hair!

Oh! who is watching at this awful hour?
What murderer hides him from law's iron power?
What unchained madman shows his daring form,
Or madder poet, amorous of the storm?
The glancing moonlight, as the clouds roll by,
Reveals the startling phantom to the eye.
His dress and mien a lowly man display,
Whom fortune owes much, but neglects to pay:
Yet his fixed lip shows firmness not to blench;
His eye, a fire no cataracts can quench.

From his drenched hat the spray-drops, gathering slow,
Drip one by one far down the gulf below:
Like tears they seemed, that 'scaped his bended head –
Alas! the only tears he knew to shed.
His care-worn features, wild, and fever-tinged,
Bespoke a soul ambition's fire had singed:
High resolution flashed from every look,
And trying thoughts his rigid sinews shook;
As if some mighty purpose swelled his mind,
Big with results to science and mankind.
No murderer he, that shunned the meed of crime –
No madman loose, nor madder child of rhyme:
No! 'tis the Great Descender, mighty PATCH!
Spurner of heights – great Nature's overmatch!
Lone, strange, and musing on his deeds unborn,
Of youth the laughter, and of age the scorn;
And the fell fiend that crouched so darkly there,
Was but his pet and follower, a bear:
For his was far too bold, too wild a mind,
To mate with creatures of a common kind.
Thus great Columbus idled on the shore,
Dreaming of worlds his genius should explore:

Thus Newton, child-like, blew his bubbles bright,
To give the sneering world the laws of light:
Thus Franklin flung his line and kite on high,
Angling for lightnings in the liquid sky;
By all the jeers of gaping fools unchecked,
Whose very heads his wit would soon protect.
Oh! ever thus, short-sighted man decries
The startling projects of the great and wise:
And Science' self seems doomed to wander here,
Scoffed, scorned, and pelted, through her long career:
Yet nobly gives for sneers new powers unborn,
And with protection pays the debt of scorn.

What wonder then our hero should evade
The face of man, and court the lonely shade?
What wonder his congenial soul should seek
The spot where daring waters leap and break?
There breathed a spirit round that wild abyss,
Of storm and energy, akin to his:
The strife of tortured waters, groaning there,
Seemed but the struggle of his own despair;
While their calm progress after trials passed,
Typed the sure triumph he should find at last.

But hark! – he lifts his voice, and thus proceeds;
Turning his thoughts to words that shall be deeds:
'Ill fated lot, to grovel yet with pride,
To thirst for fame, with power to win denied:
From my sad birth, to toil and ignorance doomed,
Cursing my days ignobly thus consumed.
And yet ofttimes the question stays my sighs:
Can grovelling ignorance ne'er hope to rise?
Can the wide world, in all its paths of care,
No instance show to hold me from despair?
Are none unlettered at this very hour
Treading the heights of wealth, of place, of power?
Are there none such, great Gotham! wear thy crown,
And sway the topping circles of the town?
Find we none such among our noisy great,
Holding the high – ay, highest chairs of state?
Oh, Law and Physic! – mid your dregs and lees,
Have ye none such that fatten on the fees?
Mid Physic's apes, than with her sons no less,
Are there none such? – great BRANDRETH! answer yes.

Ah yes! – too many such the prize obtain:
So many seek, it kills my hope to gain.
Alas! then whither shall my spirit turn,
To quench in deeds these fiery hopes that burn?
Teach me, ye stars! some method, short of crime,
Some untried ladder lend me now to climb!'

With lifted head and proudly soaring eye,
He scanned, as sage diviners wont, the sky:
At once, a sudden meteor, trembling there,
Slid down the sky, and quenched itself in air:
The hero started: 'Ha! I will obey!
Renown is mine! – the heavens have marked the way:
Yon meteor whispers: wherefore climb at all,
Since fame as well irradiates things that fall?
Yon earth-born meteor, spawn of slime and mire,
More wakes the vision by its dropping fire,
Than the world-sprinkled heavens, whose lights sublime
Have cheered the darkness since the birth of time.
And more: does not the monarch of the skies
Go down in glory too, as well as rise?
How many watch him as he sinks away!
How few pay homage to his rising ray!
The lightning's self may glitter as it likes,
'Tis ne'er gazetted, save it stoops and strikes.
How many, smitten with the fame it gave,
Have dived in bells far 'neath the ocean-wave!
Or from balloons in parachutes gone down,
Stooping to catch the jewel of renown.
We pass unpraised the stones that round us lie,
But hail them when they tumble from the sky:
The Arch-fiend's fame no poet's tongue would tell,
Nor history chronicle, until he fell;
And Pisa's tower, so bending, and so tall,
We laud – that only makes a threat to fall.
'And thou, Passaic! of clear streams the queen –
How many pilgrims at thy shrine are seen!

Why gather thus these strangers at our walls?
To see thy flood – and why? – because it falls!
Ignobly else thy gentle tide had flowed,
Nor won the worship of th' admiring crowd:
Thy very mists, whose silver-drizzling spray
Bears rain-bow blossoms in the sun-bright day,

173

Have first to fall, before they mount and glow,
With glory's garland wreathed around their brow.
Oh! thus the world, for its applause, demands
Some perilous deed—some trial at our hands:
A life of peace, though better worth a name,
Is barely whispered by the breath of fame;
While trumpets shout at every daring leap,
Which Danger ventures from his dizzy steep.
Forgive me, Heaven! – if that which I pursue
So warmly now, be sought too rashly too:
Ambition drives me – urging, pushing still –
I have the bump, and cannot use my will.
Floods, tempests, quicksands, rocks of blackest frown,
Line the sole route life opens to renown.

'Thou stubborn stream! that from thy fount dost sweep
Downward, unswerving to thy goal, the deep;
Nor even pausest at yon giddy height,
But run'st in eager rapids at the sight,
To gain sure headway for the leap profound,
Then clear'st the horrid barrier at a bound,
Lighting in triumph on the vale below –
Canst thou rush on where I would fear to go?
Canst thou by leaping win immortal praise,
And I not reap with like success the bays?
Yes! here I'll prove, at midnight, and alone,
Some things, as well as others, can be done!
I hang a cloud, a blot upon the sky:
For heaven too low, for worldly use too high,
Till my rich fall, like rain upon the dearth,
With wisdom's increase gladden all the earth.
Thou gaping chasm! whose wide devouring throat
Swallows a river – while the gulping note
Of monstrous deglutition gurgles loud,
As down thy maw the huddled waters crowd,
I to thy hungry jaws devote me too!
My hour is come – my steady nerves keep true!
I toss my body from these giddy rocks,
'To bring up drowning honor by the locks.'
I dive for glory's rare and pearly prize:
I stoop to conquer, and I fall to rise!
Cavern of savage darkness, foam, and roar,
Where never mortal plunged, and lived before!
Oh! cast me safe, as erst, within him hid,

174

The great Leviathan the prophet did!
Sons of renown! who seek a deathless name –
Mount, if ye like! I will *descend* to fame!'
He ceased, with dignity in every look:
Then from his head his dripping hat he took,
And whirled it proudly in the boiling sea,
Saluting thus: 'Old friend! I follow thee!'
With one rude bound he rushes madly on
To the dark brink's sharp edge – and – is he gone?
Not yet – not yet; he halts in mid-career –
What sudden thought, what shock arrests him here?
Ah! wherefore seek the anguish that oppressed,
In hour like this, his big, tumultuous breast!
Condemn him not! – we cannot know the strife
That shakes a mortal on the verge of life.

Again he's roused – first cramming in his cheek
The weed, though vile, that props the nerves when weak.
Once more he rushes! Stay – he stops once more,
With more spasmodic quickness than before;
Envy would say, fright checked his bold career –
Vain, ignorant sneer! – for heroes know not fear.
Perchance he thought upon his parents, lone,
Childless, all hope of future issue gone;
Himself, last scion of the house of Patch,
Tossed like the tide, for every rock to catch!
Perchance he started, thinking on his debts;
Perchance – but see! all danger he forgets,
And from his breast a vessel doth remove,
Charged with the nectar heroes ever love:
With one long draught, the fiery tide he quaffs –
Feels a new vigor – leaps, and shouts, and laughs:
Now! – now! – he springs! he clears the final stone,
Shoots down the darkness – gracious heaven! – he's gone!
No shriek is sent, no sound is heard, beside
Th' eternal thunder of the falling tide;
And Bruin's growl, who prudent turned about,
Following his master by a safer route.
Mad, reckless man, to brave sure ruin so,
And stake his body on so rash a throw!
Ambition's fool – none saw the death he braved –
All's lost with life, even to the fame he craved.
But hark! – far down yon water-flooded vale,
A voice swells faintly on the evening gale:

175

He lives! – he lives! – his feeble voice it is –
His, first survivor from that black abyss!

On a green isle, which seems so sweet asleep,
That the rude waters, ere its shores they sweep,
Fork gently, touched with charms that helpless lie;
And pass unwaked the dreaming beauty by –
The hero lies, left by the hurrying steam:
Though spent, his eye is bright with victory's gleam –
Battered, and worn – still conqueror of the fall,
Exhausted – yet triumphant over all!

Canto II

THERE are, to tempt our mortal search and aim,
Two rival peaks that crown the hill of fame:
One sought by those in love with temporal power,
Who court the certain glory of the hour:
Who posthumous honors deem not worth the strife,
And plant no crops they may not reap in life.
Such are the rich, the placeman of the day,
Professor, judge, all worthy in their way,
But who more love live plaudits in their ear,
Than all the praises dead men can – not hear;
And this their epitaph when live is o'er:
'They filled their place – as it was filled before.'

The steeper summit of the glorious hill
Is clomb by spirits of a loftier will;
Who beaten routes and vulgar custom shun,
And aim at deeds by mortals yet undone:
Fame's forlorn hope, who tread her fright fullest ways –
The samphire-gatherers of her cliff-born bays –
Who scorn renown which threescore years can span,
Which bounds the glory with the frame of man;
Whose sun-struck sight one dazzling maxim blinds:
'No mortal fame can sate immortal minds.'
So lost in longing for perennial bays,
They slight as dross contemporaneous praise;
And bid intruding worshippers return,
And hoard their homage for their senseless urn.
How wild soe'er their hopes – their schemes immense,
One must admire their lofty confidence,
Who scorn the pittance of the shores to reap,

And bound for glory, launch upon the deep:
Freighted with stuffs by cunning genius wove,
Devised to tempt some distant trader's love –
Since goods at home as cheapest trash despised,
In ports remote and foreign, may be prized –
Consigned to strangers in an unknown clime,
To barter there for honors of far time.

What different paths these rival ranks divide!
Those trudge the road – these course the mountain side;
Those till the lands by others tilled before,
These clear new fields on some untrodden shore;
Those ride on jades of sorry speed and power,
These back wild steam, at fifty miles the hour;
Those mount the hill, to catch the breezes there,
These in balloons spring up at once to air;
Those by safe steps descend the rocky steep,
These clear the dreadful barrier at a leap!
Oh! none can doubt which rival throng of fame
Our own bold hero of the fall may claim:
Mate of the few, too rare in every age,
Who blend at once the hero with the sage;
Who mighty thoughts with mighty brains conceive,
And mighty deeds with mighty hands achieve.
He stopped at nought his daring spirit bid;
Whate'er his mind conceived his body did.
Oh! rarest union of all mortal powers!
Oh! pride – that such a paragon is ours!

We left him fainting on the grassy bank;
His frame unstrung, his garments dripping dank:
Unconscious violets bore his noble head,
And mossy cushions lent his limbs a bed.
O'er his pale brows green laurels brushed the air,
As though they sought to twine in chaplets there:
While trump of frogs, sole heralds of his feat,
Seemed but the foretaste of applause more sweet.
Revived at length, he seeks his humble home;
Full of past deeds, but more of those to come.
At every step, lit by the moonlight beam,
The trickling drops like sparkling jewels gleam:
And gems they are in Science' eye that shine
More precious than the rarest of the mine.
The tears of pity, or the soldier's blood,

Match not those drippings of the conquered flood.
Triumph is his and ever bright renown –
Ranked with immortals shall his name go down!
He proved a fact that science never knew,
And did a deed which none had dared to do.

Next morn, the sun awakes the busy town,
To learn of feats and miracles unknown:
On every post, pump, pillar, corner, tree,
This startling card the awe-struck people see:
'On Wednesday next, from yonder rocky height,
Whence falls the flood – unwinged, unaided quite –
Near where the dwarf pine lives, yet cannot grow –
One PATCH will leap into the tide below;
And in his body prove to every one,
Some things as well as others can be done.'
Some pity melts, some horrid fears appal;
But soul-absorbing wonder rouses all.
Some that had chanced his moody ways to know,
And feared him mad, now deemed him truly so.
Some as a hoax the matter feigned to treat,
And foully called the hero wag and cheat.
The Deacon said, as God no wings had given,
Such flights by man seemed like defying heaven:
PATCH he denounced, and on his head did pour
Such doom as Galileo met before.
The Doctor thought the case was doubtful; true,
If safe he reached the water – safe went through,
Unhurt by rocks, why – he must own, for one –
He thought the feat might – possibly – be done:
Especially – if he were standing by –
The limbs to rub – the stomach-pump apply –
Then put to bed – then purge a week – then bleed –
He felt quite sure – he must – perhaps – succeed.

At length the day of awful trial came;
Momentous morn! – big with disgrace or fame.
And neighboring farms, and distant cities, all
Disgorge their throngs, to mingle at the fall.
There stand at least, on mountain-height and glen,
Ten thousand women, and one thousand men –
For woman seeks and shines in trial's hour,
When pity, her own balsam, she can pour –
And measuring glances many an eye would throw

From the tall cliff to yon black lake below,
Streaked white with suds from many a well-washed rock;
Oh! who could mark that depth, without a shock!
Schools are let loose – the merry urchins scream –
Bestride the sharp-backed rock, or wade the stream;
And many a tree around that craggy shore
The precious fruit of mortal bodies bore:
Among their leaves that quivered in the breeze,
A thousand hearts were fluttering more than these.
Loud shouts the tumbling river, 'till it frights
To shrieks and quakings, all the rocky heights.
Oh glorious spectacle! – oh noble stage!
Whereon to bare bright science to the age;
A heaven-set trap appears this rocky glen,
Where chasing wit may corner truth, and pen;
And waft its prisoner by its magic power,
O'er tardy centuries in a single hour.
Who would not seek it even through yon abyss!
Or die to prove it on a scene like this!

But where is he? – the hero of the day –
Whose call this thronging multitude obey?
Why ask? When genius oft its face displays,
'Tis tanned and cheapened in the public gaze:
It were unfitting his should be attacked
By vulgar vision, till the hour of act.
But where is he? Approach yon humble shed,
Behold him there! – his frugal dinner spread –
His active jaws their motion quick repeating –
And PATCH the hero, PATCH the sage, is eating!
You smile! – as if a wit could live on stone –
'As if God meant his fruits for fools alone;'
As if a genius of the mightiest ken
Had not teeth, stomach, throat, like other men.
Even Satire might forgive him a repast
All human reason feared would be his last.

The compound, man, none better knew than he:
And knew the body still supplies must find,
Despite the nausea of the haughty mind:
Ungrateful mind – the very means to slight,
Whence through corporeal channels springs its might.
Full well he knew the courage food instils –

179

The heart grows bigger as the stomach fills:
Full well he knew, where food does not refresh,
The shrivelled soul shrinks inward with the flesh –
That he's best armed for danger's rash career,
Who's crammed so full there is no room for fear.

Now from the gathered and still gathering crowd,
Impatient murmurs swell, and burst aloud;
And threats arise – which soon to whispers sink –
For look! at last he stands upon the brink:
'PATCH!' shouts the mighty multitude around,
And 'PATCH!' 'PATCH!' 'PATCH!' hills, caves, and skies rebound!
Now! hero – now! – one trial, and the last,
To build thy fortune, or forever blast;
Ere one young hour be born from time's full womb,
Thy fame shall find a trumpet, or a tomb!
No time he wastes; from the brown jug he brings
One draught he takes – thrice claps his hands – then springs!
He's off! He whirls! with flutter, rush, whiz – dash;
Cleaving the foam with gurgle, spatter, splash,
Down-sinking! – Through the hushed and choking crowd,
The breath grows thick, and cannot shriek aloud:
All feel his gasping pangs – increasing still –
The breathless spasm – the epigastric thrill;
As fast, and faster hurried to the stroke,
He strikes! – all start as from wild dreams awoke!
In that dread moment of uncertainty,
Ev'n envy's sneer dies down to pity's sigh;
While the cold doubter, whom no pangs can thrill,
Prepares to croak – he knew 't would end in ill:
But soon to sneers and fears is put an end;
Through the dark lake behold his face ascend!
Ruddy, and welcome as the second sun
To Adam rose, who feared his race was run.
When genius shoots his lightning through the soul
Applause the recognizing peal should roll:
Loud shouts and long, the roaring flood outroar,
When safe he finds, and stands upon the shore!
Through the glad heavens, which tempests now conceal,
Deep-thunder guns in quick succession peal;
As if salutes were firing from the sky,
To hail the triumph, and the victory:
Shout! trump of fame – 'till thy brass lungs burst out!
Shout! mortal tongues! – deep-throated thunders, shout!

8   The 'better halves' of a Mangebetou chief, lined up in order of preference [reproduced from *The National Geographic Magazine* XLIX, 6 (June 1926), 716]

9 *A View of the Falls on the Passaic, or second River, in the Province of New Jersey*...Sketch'd on the Spot by his Excellency Governor Pownal. Painted and Engraved by Paul Sandby, London. Hand-coloured etching, 20¾″ × 14¼″

For lo! – electric genius, downward hurled,
Has startled science, and illumed the world!

Now rushing winds and thunderbolts engage:
Chaos of sounds, and dust, and flame in rage;
That the firm frame-work of the heavens on high
Rocks wide, as if an earthquake shook the sky.
While from the brimming and o'errunning cloud,
The ominous drops, big, scattered, rare and loud,
Tinkle like dropping pebbles on the lake –
Beat dust from earth – on rocks, wide spattering, break.
Each friend of science gazes upward – wheels,
And prudent, takes for shelter to his heels:
Not even the hero, dripping from the flood,
The general panic of the time withstood.
Oh! strange infatuation of the mind:
To flinch at trifles, though to dangers blind.
So the hot heroes of the barricade,
When, tired of laws, and kings themselves had made,
They met defying fire, and sword, and slaughter,
Were by Lobau dispersed with muddy water.

A knot of savans, huddled 'neath a shed,
Discussed the feat; one rigid sceptic said
There was some trick – but where he could not see:
Enough for him to know it could not be;
What was impossible for man t' achieve,
Ev'n though he saw it, he would not believe.
A learnéd sage from Gotham that had come,
Who bared some falsehoods, and believed in some,
Declared, with boldness common to the wise,
Possible, or not – he must believe his eyes.
The doubter cried 't was humbug, humbug all –
Believers ever into error fall;
The world was full of humbug; he, for one,
Could not so tamely be imposed upon.
The hero vowed – with anger justly moved,
To hear disputed all that he had proved –
To prove it still, on that, or any ground –
On taller heights, could taller heights be found;
Ay, hotly swore to leap through all the air,
From the moon's horns, would any hang him there.
Take not his boasting in the literal sense –
Success and whiskey gave him confidence;

And in the heat, and triumph of the hour,
He felt no bounds to his presumptuous power.
The doubter, warming, said, he must repeat
He deemed him all a humbug, and his feat.
Redder than morn the hero's life-blood rose,
And tinged his cheek still brighter than his nose:
Then fell his vengeance on the slanderer's head –
Fists flew – claws clenched – teeth gnashed, and noses bled;
And struggling, tumbling, rolling, on they go,
Till Patch is parted from his prostrate foe:
Victor alike in battle and th' abyss,
The day, the triumph, now is doubly his!
'T were vain to trace the toils the hero passed,
Through each repeated trial, to the last:
From towering masts to Hudson's tide the leap,
Or from Niagara's more appalling steep:
Till that dark day of sorrow's blackest frown,
When the bright sun of leapers last went down;
And that great light so many streams had drenched,
Oh, Genessee! – was in thy waters quenched.
No cloud – no gloom that morn the heavens o'erhung,
Yet dark forebodings rose from many a tongue;
And warning voices bade him shun the shore,
And tempt the horrors of the leap no more.
But with that fatal bias which has led
So many a hero to his doom, he said:
'Could danger fright, I ne'er had braved th' abyss:
If death must come, what fitter hour than this?'
He ceased, and leaping from the fatal shore,
Dropped like a stone, and sank to rise no more!
When to the crowd the awful truth grew plain,
That daring form would ne'er be seen again,
They spoke not, shrieked not, wailed not; with dismay,
Each gazed on other, dumb – then turned away.
And oh! most said, most touching sight – the mate –
The widowed comrade of his wandering fate –
His bear, returning with the mournful throng,
There led, all friendless, masterless, along!
He fell! – the Great Descender of his time –
The only traveller in his route sublime:
Forewarned, like Nelson, of his doom, too well;
Like Nelson, mid his scenes of glory fell:
By that last mortal effort of his mind,
Enriching truth, but beggaring mankind.

Dropping too often – for his zeal was such –
He yielded, vanquished by a drop too much.
Think not I mean to hint the hero quaffed
Too oft for health the soul-inspiring draught:
Though some there be who slanderously contend
He thus was basely hurried to his end.
Weak, ignorant fools, then know ye not, indeed,
That souls of fire on fiery food must feed?
That what would burn your feeble nerves apart,
Is natural diet to the great of heart?
As well the dull and browsing ass might sneer
At locomotive in its swift career;
Unthinking, in the folly of his ire,
That such tremendous energies require
A drink of scalding vapor, and a food of fire!

There are, who hold this dread belief, beside:
That by design the mighty leaper died;
That of earth's common, tame abysses tired,
His soul some wilder, bolder plunge desired;
And thus, all braced to brave the final pang,
Down the deep gulf that knows no bottom, sprang.
Such were an end – howe'er the heart it thrill –
More in accordance with his daring will.
Why should he further here prolong the strife?
He had fulfilled the mission of his life;
And ran art, science, and the world in debt:
A mighty debt, alas! uncancelled yet –
Oh! my sad pen with tears of ink could weep,
To find such worth left unrenowned to sleep.
His class immortal, who possess, combined,
Th' heroic body with th' inventive mind,
Too rarely run with triumph to the goal,
Till from the clay-clog death has loosed the soul.
Then shall their fame rush brightly into day;
What present owes them, future time shall pay;
And all, who erst their living fires did spurn,
Shall throng to hail the ashes of their urn.

No living laurel on their brows may bloom,
But chiselled garlands shall enwreath their tomb:
No praise shall swell, their lonely course to cheer,
Till poured unheeded in their marble ear:
Their very features to the world unknown,

Till carved by glory in the pallid stone.
'Tis only from the chilly air of death
Fame, like the soul, first draws enduring breath;
And genius, when from earthly fetters freed,
First grows immortal, when it has no need.
Like rays phosphoric that surprise the night,
'Tis death's corruption fires its hidden light:
Death's tongue of thunder tells us, when gone by,
Some flash of wit has shot along our sky.
The world to merit wakes not till 'tis past,
And notes no struggle, till it makes the last:
Nor knows the skies a genius deigned to rain,
Till like a cloud it blooms on high again:
Learns not a spark astray from heaven has come,
Till the bright wanderer finds once more its home;
And, like a star life's day-time has concealed,
Stands, by the darkness of the grave revealed.

Martyr of science! – in whose glorious cause
Thou'st lost thy life, and gained the world's applause,
To the historian of thy deeds sublime,
Thou seem'st a fossil monster of old time:
Huge, shadowy, lone, of mighty race of yore;
But now on earth extinct for ever more.
Mine be the boast thy relics to have stirred!
Mine the Cuvierian hand that disinterred,
And classed thee monarch of a giant reign,
Whose mammoth like we ne'er shall see again.
Farewell! Great Heart! Thou'rt doomed to bright renown,
And like thy body shall thy fame go down
To the deep sea which rolls without a shore,
Farther than fame or body went before.
Oh! happy chance that gave thee for my theme!
Now, linked together, will we sail the stream;
Thou shalt be called the PATCH whom Flaccus sang,
Or I the bard who PATCH's praises rang:
Yes! I shall buoy thee on th' immortal sea,
Or, failing that, thyself shalt carry me!

Tale II

THE WORTH OF BEAUTY: OR, A LOVER'S JOURNAL

From Canto I – First Love

Oh who can tell what cause had that fair maid
To use him so, that loved her so well?
Or who with blame can justly her upbraid
For loving not? – for who can love compel?
SPENSER

Bloom of the earth! my pride, my bane,
My spring of rapture, and of pain;
Bright BEAUTY! – child of starry birth,
The grace, the gem, the flower of earth:
The damask livery of Heaven,
To earth for choice apparel given,
From its own stores of rosy light:
A sample sent to tempt our sight,
That brimming fount of light to gain,
Whence only scattered drops will rain:
But ah! whose drops so gem the air,
And shed such rain-bow tintings there!
It seems as if some angel-hand,
To mark it with the owner's brand,
Had in that fount its pencil dipped,
And every pet of Nature tipped;
Which by the master-touch illumed,
At once the barren landscape bloomed.
As morning clouds of chilly gray
One dull disordered mass display,
Till the awakening beams aspire,
And crest each wavy ridge with fire,
So gloomed the hueless world in night,
Till Beauty rose, and all was bright!

Now roses blush; and violets' eyes,
And seas reflect the glance of skies;
And now that frolic pencil streaks
Now jewels bloom in secret worth,
Like blossoms of the inner earth:
Now painted birds are pouring round
The beauty and the wealth of sound;
Now sea-shells glance with quivering ray,
Too rare to seize, too fleet to stay,

And hues out-dazzling all the rest,
Are dashed profusely on the west,
While rain-bows seem to palettes changed,
Whereon the motley tints are ranged.
But soft the moon that pencil tipped,
As though, in liquid radiance dipped,
A likeness of the sun it drew,
But flattered him with pearlier hue;
Which, haply spilling, runs astray,
And blots with light the milky way;
While stars besprinkle all the air,
Like spatterings of that pencil there.

But queen of flowers, of gems, of skies,
Now WOMAN opes her peerless eyes:
Last work the heavenly artist planned,
The rarest of that master-hand;
For there is pencilled in her face
Of all his works the hue and grace:
All brightest, purest things of earth,
Are mingled to compose her worth;
All lights that spot the evening sky,
Are clustered in her starry eye;
All sunset hues the west that streak,
Blend in the blush that lights her cheek;
All notes of sweetest song-birds' choice,
Swell the rich chord of woman's voice:
All flowers that mortal sense beguile,
Twine in the wreath of woman's smile.
And while so richly dowered her face,
She teems with every inward grace:
All thornless flowers of wit, all chaste
And delicate essays of taste,
All playful fancies, wingéd wiles,
That from their pinions scatter smiles,
All prompt resource in stress or pain,
Leap ready armed from woman's brain.
While every virtue that can bless,
Truth, honor, mercy, nobleness,
All joys that kindness can bestow,
All faithful tenderness in wo,
All holy hopes that woo the sky,
All precious tears of sympathy,
All sweet affections gushing start

From the full fount of woman's heart.
But Heaven, to other creatures free,
Denied the charmer's gift to me;
And formed me as for other's scoff,
Or foil to set their beauty off;
With features coarse, and stature low,
Ungainly gait, and accent slow;
But not deformed; for, humbled then,
My pride had kept me back from men;
And Pity then had stayed the sneer,
And soothed my burnings with her tear.
Such was my wavering, trying state,
Too poor for love, too good for hate;
With too much ugliness to please,
Nor yet enough my hopes to freeze;
Now drawn to seek, now driven to shun,
As shame or passion urged me on.
All this with nerves so finely strung,
That every touch of Beauty wrung;
And all the ravished chords would thrill,
When swept by their fair mistress's skill:
Nay, scarce a scent-breeze stirred the air,
But wakened some vibration there.

So much in love with Beauty's face,
I sought her glance in every place;
My busy eyes no spot let rest,
Exhausting Nature's round, in quest;
No tints the sunset cloud could dye,
But I was ever watching by:
No bow could span the stormy air,
But I stood, dumb with homage, near:
No lonely moon could walk the sky,
But I must keep her company;
Nor could she swim the glassy tide,
But still I followed by her side.
Ne'er passed me spangled butterfly,
But straightway on the chase was I:
No flowers, whose garland wreaths the year,
Could at their stated hour appear,
But far through wood or marsh I'd toil,
To greet and cull the brilliant spoil.

APPENDIX A

Snake-Hill, July 4th

BELLS, drums, shouts, cannons, wakened me,
With all the roar of jubilee:
But I escaped the din and stir,
To climb the hills and dream of her;
My journal and my stick the sole
Companions of my lonely stroll;
But Nature brightly smiled on me,
And lent me her sweet company;
And strewing beauties for my gaze,
Amused me in a thousand ways.
Yet Anna – hence with jealousy!
She could not win my thoughts from thee:
No! all of bright my eyes could find,
But waked thy image in my mind!

The winds were fresh, the heavens were fair,
Azaleas spiced the brushing air:
And orchis in the grassy seas
Bowed princely to the passing breeze:
And rows of weeds in tangled plight
Stood wov'n with threads of parasite,
In golden meshes prisoned quite.
Bees buzzed, and wrens that thronged the rushes
Pour'd round incessant twittering gushes;
While thousand reeds wheron they hung,
Bent with the weight of nests and young.
Like a huge bear, alone and still,
Crouched on the meadow, lay Snake-Hill;
Shaggy with bushy forest-hair,
Wild as the savage left it there.

Now on its giddiest cliff I stand,
Victorious o'er the prostrate land:
Oh! boundless view – oh! wondrous scene!
The marsh a velvet carpet seems,
Broidered with silver-threaded streams:
Before me, stealing through the green,
Passaic, bashful, strives to hide,
As shy to meet the stranger tide,
That wooing, keeps so near her side;

But soon, coquetting o'er, they blend,
Like lovers blest, and down the bay,
New-wedded, take their golden way:
As there the honey-moon to spend:
Before they enter on the strife –
The dangerous world of ocean-life.
Far off, with heads blue-veiled, and high,
Dim mountains bank the distant sky;
Here opes the high-road to the deep,
And here the city's banners sweep;
And streamer's fluttering lengths are sent
From mast, and tower, and battlement...

Tale III

THE LAST LOOK

She vanished, we can scarcely say she died;
For but a now did heaven and earth divide:
She passed serenely with a single breath;
This moment perfect health, the next was death!
DRYDEN

MORN slowly lifts the curtain of the night,
And shows to man earth's wondrous scenery:
Who stand, a pair, on yonder rocky height,
To watch the brightening of the eastern sky?
Arm linked with arm, in fond security,
He darkly clad, and she in robe of snow:
Noble his mien, and soft her honoring eye,
That worships his, and fair her cheeks that glow
With the awakening east, where roses bud and blow.

II

Lovers they seem, and never lovers' feet
A fairer spot at fairer season trod:
All round is poured a solemn voice and sweet,
For Nature here is talking with her God.
'Tis where Passaic leaps with all his flood,
Trampling the vale with heavy-thundering tread,
That the stout rocks all stagger with the load:
Yet are there soft delights as well as dread –
Wild-flowers and shady trees the shattered cliffs bespread.

III

With hearts long linked, their fates are newly bound:
Love's port is gained, all storms of courtship o'er;
The chill of pride, the sharp and jealous wound
Of rival's favored eyes, so galling sore,
The rack of absence following smiles before,
The idly-anxious day, the feverish night,
Now lash the billows of their breasts no more:
Calm as a level lake, the currents bright,
Deep, clear, and brimming, sleep in dreams of golden light.

IV

Oh! softest ray that cheers benighted earth!
The moon among our twinkling starry beams:
The sweetest flower is marriage, that found birth
Within the rich first garden's wide extremes.
Young hearts, Passaic, like thy mountain streams,
In frolic morn shout on awhile and leap;
Till wearied all of sports and noisy screams,
They drop into each other's arms asleep,
And wake like thee more fit to tug with danger's steep.

V

But danger's steep by these is rapture found;
Their eyes are fed with such indwelling light,
That the rent rocks and dizzy cliffs around,
Seem smiling gardens to their happy sight.
Love makes the rough place smooth – new gilds
        the bright,
And even roses dies a rosier red;
And from all tears and vapors, by his might,
Gives out such hues as on yon mists are spread:
See! how they cling and smile – have I not truly said?

VI

His was the peerless sway of eloquence;
His throne the pulpit, whence his power he dealt;
Strange, mastering power, of energy intense,
That more than music knows to rouse and melt:
'Twas not the might of reason in him dwelt –
His written thoughts would fail – but Oh! when heard,
All hearts, like seas the tempest's breath that felt,

Quick into wild tumultuous life were stirred,
Then rolled in billowy waves, submissive to his word.

VII

How did that voice our captive bosoms raise
To throbbing life! as on its tones we hung,
When met our freedom's stormy birth to praise,
Of all our fathers' woes his faltering tongue
Told the sad tale; and tears like rain-drops sprung
Down droughty cheeks, long strangers to their flow:
But when with trumpet-note he told the young
Theirs for defence henceforth must be the blow,
How did our spirits leap, and long to find a foe!

VIII

But hark! – he speaks – he calls his happy bride:
'Look up! dear heart – the day-break hovers nigh:
The moon drops down behind the earth to hide,
And bashful stars outrivalled yield and fly;
For the young east is winning every eye:
See! yon rose cloud that sails so meekly there,
Bound like a ransomed spirit to the sky:
Up the blue deep it fades – dissolves in air!
Such be thy gentle fate, when death no more will
        spare!

IX

'The drowsy morn is stirring from his dream –
Warm on his cheek the waking blushes play,
Through lash of trees now peeps his trembling
        beam,
Now opes his awful eye upon the day!
Loosed on the night, and eager for their prey,
The scattering sun-beams chase the flying gloom –
Couriers of light, bright-rushing far away
To spire and hill-top, met with as they roam,
News-telling, that the king of light and life is come!

X

'He comes! triumphant in his car of gold!
Waken, ye clouds! put on your crimson dies;
Ye mists! haste up the hill-side to behold!
Ye breezes! jog the slumbering leaves with sighs!
Deep breathing water-falls! salute the skies,

And wreath fresh rainbows round your brows of
spray!
Ye beasts! – birds! – insects! – all awake! arise!
To greet the coming of the lord of day:
Thou, too! oh, man, shouldst wake – but wake to
praise and pray!

XI

'God of this wondrous scene! whose iron hand
Tore ope the lion-jaws of chasms – this strait
Of warring waters, this high mountain-land,
Yon flaming globe, all tell me thou art great;
And oh! with all my raptures, this dear mate
To share and sweeten, shows me thou art good:
I cannot thus unthankful bear thy weight
Of unbought bounties – let this gushing flood
Of happy tears say all my failing accents should!'

XII

Long do they kneel, and pour their silent prayers,
Awed by the roar of falls, and dizzy brow
Whereon they rest – still showering April tears:
When hearts are full, the eyes will overflow,
Be the deep burthen one of joy or wo:
But soon those eye-born dews the breezes drink,
Sooner than those which on the mosses glow:
And now he leads her to the slippery brink,
Where ponderous tides headlong plunge down the
horrid chink.

XIII

Shuddered the solid frame-work of the rock,
Down the black gulf the waters, crushed, amazed,
Shivered to snowy atoms by the shock,
Shrieked dreadful: that her giddy head, half-crazed,
Hid in his sheltering bosom while he gazed.
Damp, with a scent of stricken flint, the spray
Rushed like a wind, and high in air was raised;
Drenching the lovers on its drizzling way:
'Lo! how it soars,' he cries, 'and blossoms in the day!'

XIV

'A fairy bridge of azure, gold, and flame,
Where water-sprites might pass from shore to shore,

Spans the dread gulf: the cataract's wreath of
    fame –
The worn stream's smile of patience, trial's flower –
Heaven's early mark of promise, that no more
The passing curse the drowning earth should wear:
Proof to the stream its trial-storm is o'er –
The seal of God set o'er the waters there,
To stamp the act as his, and bid them not despair.

XV

'Nor need they groan; soon, guided by his hand,
Through rocky perils to yon flowery vale,
Long shall they journey through a pleasant land;
While freighted barks upon their bosom sail,
And briny tides their welcome face shall hail,
Sent half-way up the coming guests to greet;
Soon at their sea-home, whence they did exhale,
The kindred streams once more in peace shall meet:
Oh! thus through storms to rest, our God will guide
    our feet!'

XVI

Now down the hill-side, o'er the valley-bridge,
Their venturous feet the wildest paths pursue:
They cross the village – near the southern ridge,
Passing the gap, whence, startling to the view,
Tall cliffs wide-parted brightly bursting through,
The whole wild beauty of the fall is seen –
Gray rocks, black pools, and foam of snowy hue;
While far away, the cloven crags between,
The fleecy waters curve, with amber striped, and
    green.

XVII

They seek cool shelter from the sunny glow,
Where trees, leaf-thatched, an emerald roof have
    made,
Whose trembling shadow blots the turf below:
For quivering heat and dazzling glare pervade
All save the woodland's ever-evening shade:
There by the bank they rest, above the foam,
On tufted moss, thick sown with blossoms, laid;
Around, the laurel showers its rosy bloom,

Wreaths the bare-headed crags, and lights the
    forest-gloom.

XVIII

Clear-throated birds perpetual concert keep:
Their treble pipes relieving the bass thunder
From the hoarse lungs of caverns groaning deep;
While dainty insects peeping flower-bells under
Give honied sounds, for honied sweets they plunder:
Coolness from streams, and odors ever new
The breezes bring, blending delight with wonder:
Songs, odors, blossoms, gales their souls subdue,
Balmy as Eden's bliss – alas! as transient too.

XIX

Oh, Love! no starry jewels of the night,
No breezy blessing of the balmy spring,
No thrill that gives to mortal sense delight,
Such dreamy rapture as young Love can bring,
When first he fans us with his downy wing:
Love on! – love on! young revellers, while ye may!
Life o'er your dim, benighted path can fling
No light more precious than his moonlight ray,
Till love immortal breaks, and blends it with the day!

XX

Now gently gliding from his twining arm,
To pluck, and bring him forest-flowers she goes;
He bids her mark the Kalmia's changing charm:
Red starry buds, and whitely opening blows,
Where each bent stamen, as it loosens, throws
With sudden spring its quickening powder there.
'Beware the cactus-flower!' he cries: 'it grows
Bristling with stings that guard its blossoms fair:
I would not have thee harmed, even by the tiniest
    hair.'

XXI

Smiled her meek eyes, and shone her happy brow,
Stirred her soft tresses in the gentle blast;
His doting eye pursued, as, playful now,
Bright flowers and branches in the tide she cast,
To mark their fatal voyage, sailing fast
From peace to ruin, in the swallowing foam:

194

Upon the stream he muses, gliding past
Calmly asleep, unconscious of its doom –
So might himself sleep on, nor dream of wreck to
 come!

XXII

Wearied at length, she seeks once more his side,
To list his accents, leaning on his breast:
'Oft have I dreamed, by some such stilly tide,
Ere age comes on, we'll build our cot of rest;
Of love, of peace – oh! then of all possessed:
With happy children, sporting, or asleep –
With daughters, blooming as their mother, blest:
Thus stream-like gliding to the solemn steep,
To wake in happy fields, where storms no more shall
 sweep.'

XXIII

She answered soft: 'The picture is most bright,
But oh! with thee all scenes alike I prize!
Love, like the sun, bedazzling all with light,
Alike to bloom and desert blinds my eyes:
The din of towns, that once I did despise,
Would charm like mellow music, heard with thee;
And 'neath thy step would verdure ever rise!
Though sweet these birds we hear, these flowers
 we see,
Still would I meet them all, wherever thou mightst be!'

XXIV

Thrilled to the quick, he clasps her with a start,
And straining, fastens on her lips a kiss
That seemed to suck the life-blood from her heart:
She pales! she droops in those dear arms of his;
But oh! 'tis nothing but excess of bliss:
She dreams she floats mid girdling rainbows, driven
Half-whirled, half-wafted, glancing down th' abyss;
Buoyed by the foam to spirit-shores, forgiven:
He speaks – an angel-voice confirms her shadowy
 heaven.

XXV

'Come, love! 'twere rapture thus to wear the time,
Yet must we yield when duty bids us go:'

'Ah! yet,' she cries, 'from yonder height sublime,
One long, last look still let me cast below!'
Thither he guides with cautious feet and slow;
Across a chasm they step, of blackest frown –
So deep, so strait, as if with sudden blow
Split by the axe of thunder – on the crown
Stands a lone starving pine, where, clinging, they
  look down.

XXVI

'Awful!' he cries: 'how the bewildered tides
Stunned, battered, frightened, madly, vainly flock,
Now here, now there, along their prison's sides;
Where towers of square-hewn and intruding rock,
That rear their fronts, all outlet seem to block:
Some, angry-black, slink sidelong in a bay,
Sullen, or palsied by the dreadful shock:
At length, o'er heaps of tumbled fragments gray,
Out of the hideous pit they make their hurried way.

XXVII

'Close underneath us bend thy shuddering sight,
To yon black underlying lake; so clear,
It seems a floor of marble, veined with white;
Upon whose polished glass almost appear
Our overhanging faces mirrored there –
Cling closer now! How deep! – yet still more deep
Sinks the full pool; what sharp rocks, never bare,
What caves, there lurk! – Come hence! the frightful
  steep
Dizzies my steadier brain, and numbs my will to
  sleep.'

XXVIII

They leave the brink and bend their steps for home:
'Follow,' he cries; 'this narrow path we take' –
He moves before her, trusting she will come,
When sharply is his ear stabbed by a shriek!
He turns – he stares – he gasps – he cannot speak;
For she is – *where?* – swift to the rocky brow,
Where late they stood, he springs, he flies, to seek
Horrors too wild for thought! – and far below
Sees sinking in the gulf her fluttering robe of snow!

XXIX

'Screeches on screeches burst convulsive out! –
Bewildered, stunned, he hurries to and fro –
Maddening at length, as each repeated thought
Confirms his ruin with its hammering blow –
With ringing brain, and eyes all blind with wo,
Forth to the brink he rushes with a bound,
That soon had quenched his torments far below –
Had not a stranger's hand by Heaven been found,
To drag him from the crime, and spare his soul the
        wound.

XXX

Ah! why not leave him to that easier fate,
Sweetly to death within her arms to yield;
Safe from his present torture, and more late
His reason's wound, which never wholly healed!
That inky lake no cavern had revealed
More drear to him than life's lone wilderness;
The flintiest fragment of sunk rock, concealed
Within its dankest, jaggiest recess,
Were downier bed, alas! than he again may press!

XXXI

I never look upon that fiendish pool
Without a thrill, though years have rolled away;
With smile so grim, with glance so deadly cool,
It seems still watching with hushed voice for prey.
Down to the shore they wound – and there it lay,
Unbroke by wave or bubble on its gleam,
As though its breast no murder hid from day:
Like the false smile, of calm yet treacherous beam,
That cunning Guilt puts on, when guiltless it would
        seem.

XXXII

Now frantic threats of rash self-sacrifice,
Now sobs and prayers his frame alternate shake:
Oh! 'twere enough to thaw a heart of ice,
To mark his sorrows like a flood o'ertake,
And on his head in pitiless masses break!
Soon gathering friends, with ready kindness, flew,

And for the corse long dragged that fatal lake;
At last, all dripping on the shore they drew –
Oh! agonizing sight, for lover's eyes to view!

XXXIII

Hushed as a dreaming statue, there she lay,
In all the soft abandonment of sleep;
Her clinging robes her marble limbs display
As nature chiselled in their graceful sweep:
Still round her cheeks her damp locks closely creep,
Where a smile hovers, like a sweet surprise –
One charm unstrangled by the heartless deep!
He sees – he kneels – he clings, with piteous cries:
All feel his choking pangs, and hide their brimming
        eyes.

XXXIV

'Back! – back! – and let my kisses break her
        trance –
She is not dead – I will not lose her so:
Wake, dearest! – speak! – give but a sign – a
        glance! –
Wilt thou not heed? – and must thou from me go? –
Pity me! friends – thus left alone with wo:
When I had griefs her dear arms would relieve,
When bruised my balsam was her tears – ah! who
Clings round me now? – who now can solace give? –
Oh God! my heart is broke! – why am I left to live!' –

XXXV

Droop not, poor mourner! o'er those perished
        charms:
She fell not wholly with her falling clay,
For underneath 'the everlasting arms'
Caught soft and bore her better part away,
Where treacherous steeps no more shall fright or
        slay:
Bear well this cutting trial of his dart,
And God thy patience with her sight will pay –
Patience, the fragrance of the bruiséd heart,
Incense best loved of Him, who knows to heal the
        smart.

XXXVI

Oh! blessed knowledge, that all tears that shower
Enrich the heart, and make its harvest sure;
That all our sighs are gales of favoring power
To waft the soul to starry port secure;
That every groan He dooms us to endure,
Is of His voice indwelling but the call
To guard our steps when danger's snares allure;
And every bruise His kindness sends to gall –
The close grasp of His hand that would not let us fall.

XXXVII

Now from his fever dull collapse ensued,
With chill and torpor, both of heart and brain –
Oh! better far, than such unnatural mood,
His frenzy's fire were kindled there again:
They bear her thence – he follows with the train,
And all unconscious quits the fatal ground:
Friends give him words and tears – but all in vain;
Earth has no balsam for a heavenly wound:
He only finds the balm that the fell weapon found.

XXXVIII

They lay the lovely ruin in the grave:
He draws him nigh with measured step and slow –
Ah! who can mark unmoved, however brave,
His precious jewel sunk in earth below –
While pitiless heaps on heaps of clay they throw,
All rescue closing with the load profound? –
But there he stands with stony heart and brow,
Nor shudders once, when all are weeping round –
Save when the first-dropped clod sends up its dull
cold sound.

XXXIX

They lead him home – oh! chamber desolate –
There is the hearth, and there the vacant chair:
The empty cup of joys, o'erturned by fate –
The blooming garden, desert now and bare:
No child, no image of his lost one, there –
And this is home – oh! mockery of home!
Lone, dark, he sits, the prisoner of despair;
Without a ray to cheer his dungeon-gloom,
Save the pale star of hope that trembles o'er the tomb!

XL

Passaic! ever when the generous sun
Unprisons Nature from her wintry gloom –
Waking young brooks to praise him as they run,
Winning all flowers to offer grateful bloom,
And pour their gushing worship in perfume –
Gay hearts shall haunt the wild and fatal steep
Where thy brave current, rushing to its doom,
Grows instant famous by a dazzling leap;
And, shuddering on the brink, pause o'er the mur-
    derous deep.

XLI

There young Romance the deepness shall look down
Sacred to passion, and to passion's wo,
And thrill with pangs and trials not his own;
And Mirth, light-tripping on the fatal brow,
Grow dumb for her whose joy was hushed below;
And Love, lone-wandering in his sweet unrest,
Or linked with Beauty, there shall overflow,
At the sad tale, with sorrows unrepressed;
And clasp his treasure close, and closer to his breast!

APPENDIX B

Notes to 'Paterson'[1]

[11] *Rigor of beauty is the quest...*
This 'quotation' is from a longer prefatory note by Williams (ms. CtY), which answers the question: 'It is not in the things nearest us unless transposed there by our employment. Make it free, then, by the art you have, to enter these starved and broken pieces.'

12 *It is the ignorant sun...*
'All I mean by the sun coming up in the slot of old sun's risen is that it has all happened before – many times, it's the old groove. Every morning when I am shaving, these days, I see the sun coming up behind the houses on the little rise in the ground behind our house. In summer the sun rises far to my left as I look out of the window. But at this time of the year the sun has drifted more and more to my right until at last it comes up in a narrow slit between the two houses in our rear. When it gets to that point I know it won't go any further, that's the finish. From there it turns north again toward the heat of the year. I wait for that turn. It happens every year' (letter to Fred R. Miller, 21 December 1945).

15–16 *In regard to the poems I left with you...*
This portion of a letter, and of subsequent letters on pages 59–60, 63, 80–1, 93–4, 101, 105–13 (*q.v.*), came from Marcia Nardi whom Williams had introduced to *Botteghe Oscure* and *New Directions*. Her collection, *Poems*, was published by Alan Swallow (Denver, 1956).

17 *communications from the Pope and Jacques | Barzun*
As a by-product of research into the Paterson textile strike of 1913 eventually published in *Kings Crown Essays* IX, 1 (Winter 1961), Howard A. Levin wrote to Barzun, whom he had known at Columbia, and to Williams for an explanation: 'Williams said, "It is hard for a poet to say exactly what he means... in this I hoped to get something of the universal academic". Barzun replied, "I do not know exactly what Williams means... but I presume some anti-catholic bias"' (letter from Mr Levin to the author, 13 May 1966).

18 *PISS-AGH! the giant lets fly!*
One of the many variations in spelling of Passaic given by Nelson and Shriner
[1] The figures at the left refer to the page numbers of the standard 1963 edition.

(*History of Paterson*, vol. I, p. 81) is *Pissaik* (1686): 'Heckewelder says the word means "valley". But it has always been applied only to the river, not to the land. It is doubtless derived from the root *pach*, "to split, divide".'

18 *A gentleman of the Revolutionary Army...*

Taken from Herbert A. Fisher's notes on the history of Paterson, which in turn drew upon J. W. Barber and Henry Howe, *Historical Collections of New Jersey* (Newark, N.J. [1855]), p. 407; and Trumbull, *History of Industrial Paterson*, p. 20. Trumbull's version is free of the incorrect use of inverted commas and gives 'on large pillows' for 'in pillows'. Barber and Howe italicise the *twenty-one inches* of the monster's head, and spell Whig and Tory without capitals. Thus although the text is originally, and principally according to Barber and Howe, improvements have been made, most likely by Mr Fisher who notes further: 'The natural curiosity was Peter Van Houten ("Big-headed Peter"). If I recall correctly, his father's name was Cornelius, who was a Tory, who evidently later changed his viewpoint. Cornelius lent Capt A. Godwin money to maintain the Passaic Hotel; Van Houten owned it at the time of the Revolution and then it was bought back by General A. Godwin, the Captain's son.' (Notes supplied to the author, October 1967.)

19 *From the ten houses Hamilton saw...*

From Herbert A. Fisher's notes on Paterson census records.

19–20 *The twaalft, or striped bass...*

The first sentence, to be found in Nelson and Shriner (*History of Paterson*, vol. I, p. 142) almost certainly came from Mr Fisher's notes, as did the last sentence, which is taken from C. P. Longwell, *Historic Totowa Falls* (Paterson, 1942), pp. 57–8. The 'and' between '*Bergen Express*' and '*Paterson Advertiser*' should, of course, also be in italics.

21–2 *If there were not beauty, there was a strangeness...*

The Prospector for 3 July 1936 was a special Ringwood Manor issue, including illustrations of the chains made to block the Hudson. The last paragraph is taken almost word for word from Seamus MacCall, *Thomas Moore* (London and Dublin, 1935), p. 94, where 'to mate with others' reads 'to mate with the negro slaves'.

22–3 *I remember / a Geographic picture...*

See Plate 8, from *The National Geographic Magazine* XLIX, 6 (June 1926), 715–16.

23–4 *Mrs Sarah Cumming, consort of the Rev. Hopper Cumming...*

From Barber and Howe, *Historical Collections*, p. 412. On page 24 two words, 'which was', are omitted between 'event' and 'to ensue' (l.3), and the name in parentheses (l.4) of the stairs, '(the Hundred Steps)', is added presumably by Mr Fisher.

25 *"Jersey Lightning" to the boys*
   See Cornelius Weygandt, *Down Jersey* (N.Y. and London, 1940), p. 91: 'Jersey lightning is so nearly extinct that young Jerseyites, even those well versed in all wickedness, do not know what it is. It is the most potent sort of applejack, and applejack, let me say, if there are any so benighted as not to know what it is, is cider brandy.' The book was reviewed by Williams' friend Kathleen Hoagland in the *New York Sun*, 25 July 1940, under the pseudonym of K.R.E.Hood.

25 *N for Noah...*
   'The Minsis had a legend that in the beginning they dwelt in the earth under a lake, from which they accidentally discovered a way to the surface – to the light. The other Lenâpé tribes had the same story, except as to the lake. Bishop Ettwein says: "They had some confused Notion of the Flood, and said: All men were drowned, only a few got on the Back of an old big Tortoise, floating on the Water; that a Diver at last brought them some Earth in his Bill, and directed the Tortoise to a small Spot of Ground, where they alighted and multiplied again. Therefore has the great Tortoise Tribe the Preference among the Tribes." This deluge myth is known to all the Algonkin tribes, and to most others in America. "Others say, the first Person had been a Woman, which fell from Heaven • • • and bore Twins, which peopled this Country."' Nelson and Shriner, *History of Paterson*, vol. I, p. 51.

25–6, 27 *That day was a great day for old Paterson...*
   In the ms. (CtY) these pages are part of a long narrative in the person of an old man of Paterson, the latter portion of which Williams did not use until he came to Book IV (pp. 226–32), where he changed the form from prose to strophe: 'A little story of Paterson: as told by an old man – The city of Paterson owes much of its importance to its historical associations. So to the past this little volume is dedicated. Although it is not written simply to give facts, it does give the correct facts about what it says.
   The birth and life of a city is likened in many respects with the birth, infancy, growth and development of a human being. First the period of infancy, when it knew no recognition from the outside world, but was confined to a little world of its own.'
   This is taken from the opening chapter of a very rare volume by Charles Pitman Longwell, *A Little Story of Old Paterson* (Paterson, 1901), referred to by Longwell himself in a later book, *Historic Totowa Falls* (Paterson, 1942), where he speaks in a preface of his grandfather: 'It was he who gave me the story of Sam Patch. He being present at the placing of the first bridge across the falls chasm. I have made use of it in one of the chapters, taken from my little book, A Little Story of Old Paterson, published over forty years ago. Now out of print.'
   A photo-copy of the only known copy of this little volume was kindly provided for the present writer by its author's son, Edward M. Longwell, who was found in response to a request to the editor of the 'Call for Action' column of the

Paterson newspaper, *The Morning Call* (see Edward J. Gorin, ' "Paterson" Muse Traced', *The Morning Call* CLXXII, 122 [21 May 1968], 13). Mr Longwell informed the writer that his father was assistant librarian at the Paterson Public Library, where he had worked for fifty-seven years before retiring in 1945 at the age of seventy-five, and that the name of his great-grandfather, the old man of Paterson, was John Duchess (letter to the author, 3 June 1968). The story of Sam Patch is taken from pages 37–41, with some minor alterations in style (e.g.'…a great day *in* old Paterson,' '…under arrest at *different* times'), and with a few factual errors: The man of 'large, rugged stature' was one Sam Pope (not Patch), and Sam Patch's fatal leap at Genessee Falls was in 1829 (not 1826). The theme of failed speech is Williams' own.

31 *put myself deliberately in the way of death?*
    Ms. (CtY):
Why have I not
long since (answer before the question)
long since put myself deliberately
in the way of an oil-truck? out of contempt,
rather than in my own mind
to be denied and contemptible (a phrase!)
I was afraid. I was afraid: a phrase. Is
that news? Stale as a whale's breath. Paid
Paid for it. Over and over again: paid…

37–8 *I was over to see my mother today…*
    The *T* with which this letter is signed stands for Alva N. Turner, whom Williams had known by correspondence since 1919. In the last paragraph of the letter Turner refers to his mother's disquiet at the thought that he should remain in their wooden house after her death, because of the danger of fire. In the summer of 1954 Turner filled the oil-stove to heat some water and went into town. When he got back the house was blazing, and all his belongings destroyed. Williams sent him his second-best typewriter, an Underwood.

40 *I positively feel no rancour against you…*
    'Read Dahlberg's new book, *Will* [sic] *these bones lives*? It seems incredible that he should have had difficulty finding a publisher. It's a book to swear by' (letter to Louis Untermeyer, 14 March 1941 (InU)).

44 *He was more concerned, much more concerned…*
    Cf.: 'Can you blame us then if we say, with Freud and perhaps Plato, that the poem is an objective unworthy of a man, the resort of a cowardly disposition: that a poem is wish fulfilment, empty of sound good. And so it is if we are, as we are taught, to take our prosody without invention and on loan from another language: you take the bottle with its label already applied and fill it with any rot-gut you like. If it fulfils the *rules*, o.k.' ('Some Hints Toward the Enjoyment

of Modern Verse', a talk given by Williams at Bard College during the Second World War and printed in *Quarterly Review of Literature* VII, 3 [1954], 171–5;*172*).

45 *In time of general privation...*
'Once, after Willie Hansen had been let go from the now despoiled Lowe estate, he took a job for the Princesse de Talleyrand, née Gould, who had a much larger place at Tarrytown, which we were privileged to visit (In the orchid houses hardly a soul cuts a flower.)' (*Autobiography*, p. 334).

45–6 *Cornelius Doremus, who was baptized at Acquackonock...*
Errors in transcription, or in Williams' reading of Mr Fisher's handwriting, must be responsible for the changes made from the list in Nelson and Shriner, *History of Paterson*, vol. I, pp. 138–9, where, for instance, *two* handkerchiefs cost 75 cents, shoebuckles are two words, the word 'cents' is largely omitted, the pair of andirons cost *two* dollars, and the 'Kastor hot' is a castor hat! Acquackonock should read Acquackononk.

46–7 *By nightfall of the 28th, acres of mud were exposed...*
From *The Prospector* II, 22 (28 August 1936), 4. Mr Fisher writes that this lake was on the south-east edge of Paterson, in the Crooks Avenue area, and extended well down into Clifton. The 'cars' mentioned were, of course, horse-drawn street cars.

48 *Shortly before two o'clock...*
From *The Prospector* II, 32 (12 November 1936), 1, 4. Verbatim, except for the last paragraph which is partly rewritten.

50 *Your interest is in the bloody loam...*
P is Ezra Pound; I is Williams: 'When I was at the University of Pennsylvania, around 1905, I used to argue with Pound. I'd say "bread" and he'd say "caviar". It was a sort of simplification of our positions. Once, in 1912 I think it was, in a letter (we were still carrying on our argument) he wrote, "all right, bread". But I guess he went back to caviar' (Harvey Breit, 'Talk with W.C.Williams', *New York Times Book Review* XCIX, 15 January 1950, Section 7, 18).

51 *"The 7th, December, this year..."*
From *The Prospector* II, 17 (24 July 1936), 1. The newspaper account is historical. By introducing inverted commas Williams has attempted to give it credence as a document contemporary with the event.

52 *Earth, the chatterer, father of all speech...*
Cf. C.G.Jung, quoted by Count Keyserling in *America Set Free* (London, 1930), p. 43: 'The extraordinarily lively temperament of the average American, which shows itself not only at baseball games, but more particularly in an

astonishing passion for verbosity (the most instructive example is the boundless and interminable torrent of words in the American newspapers), can hardly be traced back to a Germanic ancestry; it resembles much more the "chattering" of the negro village.' Keyserling's thesis was that '*the American scene is to a greater extent determined by the Earth as such, than by man*' (p. 31); however, Earth was to him the traditional mother, not father.

59   *The body is tilted slightly forward...*

From Beckett Howorth, 'Dynamic Posture', *Journal of the American Medical Association* CXXXI, 17 (24 August 1946), 1398–404; *1402, 1403* (fig. 6B):

Dr Howorth in reply (16 May 1967) to an inquiry from the author, writes: 'Dynamic Posture relates not only to walking, but is in a sense a way of life. You may find other sentences, especially toward the end, which will interest you, and which possibly interested Dr. Williams.'

A few such sentences are given below:

'Precision and smoothness are essential to good muscle action and low energy output. Timing is one of the most important and delicate phases of movement. Good timing makes the movement easier and more effective. Alternating contraction and relaxation with balanced timing produce rhythm in movement and increase the capacity for sustained action ...' (p. 1402).

'Correct walking is done with a smooth rhythm, the muscles contracting gently with a brief wavelike action and relaxing in the interval. It is characterized by free muscle and joint action, momentum, balance and rhythm. Effort becomes much greater if the speed is increased or if momentum and rhythm are disturbed.

Walking is often done badly, with the body erect and stiff, with sudden jerky movements, tense muscles, precarious balance, needless jolts and a lack of rhythm. The steps lack spring and the flexibility needed to meet unusual situations. The good walker should be able to change pace, stop, start, turn, step up or down, twist or stoop, easily and quickly, without losing balance or rhythm...' (p. 1403).

'Crowded city pavements and dirty fume-laden air usually promote bad walking posture, whereas the varied topography and surfaces and the clean air make good walking posture easier...' (*ibid.*).

60–1   *No fairer day ever dawned anywhere...*

From *The Prospector* II, 33 (12 November 1936), 5. Mr Fisher says that the

Dalzell story was among his notes, which may explain the editorial parentheses
'[to]'. In *The Prospector* the sentence reads, 'Some of the Paterson police rushed
Dalzell out of the house and he succeeded in reaching the house of John Ferguson
some half furlong away.' The last two sentences of the passage can be found in
identical form in Nelson and Shriner, *History of Paterson*, vol. I, p. 501. It is
interesting that Williams breaks off suddenly. The final sentence remarks on
'...his display of Christian charity, for he was the highest prelate of the Catholic
Church in Paterson and the man he was befriending had been prominent among
the Orangemen'.

64–5 *Shortly after midnight...*
   From *The Prospector* II, 31 (29 October 1936), 4.

74 *the peon in the lost Eisenstein film...*
   In October 1933 a version of Eisenstein's projected film 'Que Viva Mexico'
opened at the Rialto Theatre, New York, under the title *Thunder over Mexico* (see
Marie Seton, *Sergei M. Eisenstein* (N.Y., 1960), p. 281). But the image which
Williams remembered comes, as Miss Seton informed the author in conversation,
from the version she edited – *Time in the Sun*, shown at the Fifth Avenue Play-
house, New York, late in 1941.

78 *I see they – the Senate, is trying to block Lilienthal...*
   This is almost certainly from a letter from Fred R. Miller, who as editor of
Blast often engaged Williams in defence of the communists (Williams stated in a
letter to Miller, 21 December 1945, that he intended to use a portion of one of his
letters in the poem). Mr David E. Lilienthal, in reply (14 December 1966) to an
inquiry, wrote: 'I am pretty sure he was referring to the hearing before the
Senate Committee on my confirmation as Chairman of the Atomic Energy Commission. But the background of my TVA battles was probably also in the poet's
mind. "The bomb" surely must mean atomic energy broadly speaking, and not
simply its application to a weapon.'

85 *America the golden!*
   George Zabriskie, one of Williams' friends brought up in the Paterson region,
volunteered the following information in a letter to the author (24 June 1966):
'In the first place it is a serious, although bitter, parody of Katherine Lee Bates'
America the Beautiful. Before the *Star Spangled Banner* became our national anthem,
America the Beautiful was one of the three serious candidates, the other two being
America (sung to the tune of *God Save the King*) and the *S.S.B.* which won,
although its tune is equally British. When I was in grammar school we generally
sang *America* and *America the Beautiful* more or less in alternation. If I'm not
mistaken, *America the Beautiful* was written sometime in the 1890's – a date
germane to its use as the basis for the parody.
   "America the golden!" as you will discover when you try to sing it, uses the

last half, not the first half of *America the Beautiful*'s music, so that

We bow our heads before thee	To crown thy good with brotherhood
and take our hats in hand.	from sea to shining sea.

The content of "America the golden" relies on events of the Populist movement and the 1890's as reflected in the poetry of Nicholas Vachel Lindsay... The
first line echoes the theme of Bryan's speech "You shall not crucify mankind
upon a cross of gold." Employers in Paterson and elsewhere encouraged their
employees to vote for McKinley by promising a lockout if Bryan won. McKinley's
vice president, during his first term, was Garret Augustus Hobart, a Paterson fat
cat whose mansion was still a showplace in my youth although its owner died in
time for Teddy Roosevelt to become McKinley's second vice president. The
Hobart Mills prospered until the strikes of the '30's and the removal of the silk
industry to Scranton, Wilkes-Barre and elsewhere. Hence the second line of the
poem.

John Peter Altgeld was governor of Illinois during the period of the early
1890s, shortly after the Haymarket Riots and during the Pullman strike. The
surviving Haymarket rioters were pardoned by Altgeld in the face of opposition
by the press and the wealthy. During the Pullman strike, in which the strikers
were joined by Eugene Debs' American Railway Union, Altgeld refused to call
out the National Guard "to protect the rights of property." President Grover
Cleveland (born in Caldwell, N.J.) a true believer in the sanctity of ownership,
the right of an employer to do as he pleased, and the duty of the government to
combat lawlessness by the working classes, denounced Altgeld, and used troops
to break the strike. Not only were the Pullman workers crushed, but Debs'
A.R.U., "The One Great Union," was hopelessly crushed. The railroads fired
ARU members as quickly as possible, giving them service letters watermarked
with a crane with a broken neck. Until the ruse of this watermark was discovered,
the men were unable to obtain other employment.

The line about the mourners refers to both the victims of the Haymarket
riots and those of the Pullman strike, which erupted into violence around
Chicago. Altgeld, who in retrospect seems to have been a more able man than
Bryan, ended his political career by upholding the cause of the workers. Naturally
he was not reelected.'

90   *The Federal Reserve System is a private enterprise...*
From a mimeographed single sheet put out by Alfredo and Clara Studer,
dated January 1947 (NBuU).

92   *In other words, the Federal Reserve Banks...*
From 'Tom Edison on the Money Subject', referred to as an enclosure on the
Studer's sheet.

105–13   *My attitude towards woman's wretched position...*
'I did not compose it. It is, as you see, an attack, a personal attack upon me

by a woman. It seemed a legitimate one. It had besides a certain literary quality which was authentic, that made it a thing in itself worth recording…

The five or six friends to who[m] I then showed it, men and women, were divided in their opinions but, watching their reactions, I decided that [there] were more reasons for putting the letter in than there were for leaving it out: In the first place it was a reply from the female side to many of my male pretensions. It was a strong reply, a reply which sought to destroy me. If it could destroy me I should be destroyed. It was just that it should have its opportunity to destroy. If I hid the reply it would be a confession of weakness on my part' (letter to Robert D. Pepper, 21 August 1951).

112 *La votre C.*

'A metropolitan softness of tone, a social poetry that Chaucer had long ago to such perfection. You remember how Chaucer had Cressida sign her letters to the man she left behind her in Troy? "*La votre C.*" Marvellous!' (*Selected Letters*, p. 233).

117 *A fortune bigger than | Avery could muster…*

Samuel Putnam Avery (1822–1904): 'It was not long before this self-taught descendant of English Puritans was a collector of rare paintings and etchings, advising Americans who had money to spend in the importation of such works from the galleries of Europe. These well-to-do Americans gave Avery the opportunity to accumulate a fortune' (*Dictionary of American Biography*).

120 *Old newspaper files…*

From *The Prospector*: 'clasped in each others' arms', II, 15 (10 July 1936), 6; 'The Paterson Cricket Club, 1896', II, 21 (21 August 1936), I, 7; the two millionaires who moved to Chicago to make their fortunes were Martin Ryerson and Charles T. Crane, II, 28 (9 October 1936), I, 4; 'Another Indian rock shelter', II, 27 (2 October 1936) 2, 7; 'Rogers Locomotive Works', II, 22 (22 August 1936), I, 5.

122 *Rose and I didn't know each other…*

'My wife, Rose, and I had been radicals, let us say I.W.W. sympathizers or anarchists, since we never joined either the Industrial Workers of the World or the Socialist Party. For a quarter of a century we had sided with the workers, most of that time in South America, where we had gone to escape war black-listing for not helping keep the world safe for Mister Morgan' (Bob Brown, *Can We Co-operate?* (Pleasant Plains, Staten Island, N.Y., 1940), p. 13). Williams knew Bob Brown from Grantwood colony days, and in 1934 invested 500 dollars through him in oil-prospecting at the Llano colony in Newllano, Arkansas: 'But it was a dry hole and all we got out of it was a headache' (*ibid.* p. 208).

126–7 *From 1869 to 1879 several crossed the falls…*

From *The Prospector* II, 19 (7 August 1936), I, 4. The newspaper version, of which this is a condensed paraphrase, gives the earliest date of a crossing by tight-rope as 1860, not 1869.

131   *Sing me a song to make death tolerable...*
    Mary Ruvolo Lyle died of cancer on 20 March 1947. Six weeks before her death Williams wrote to David Lyle, who was not yet her husband: 'I'm almost afraid to ask you, but – How is Mary? Would she want to see me? It's late, my trained imagination doesn't help me in any way. All I can say – is that I have thought of you and of her constantly, every day, but I have shrunk from calling on the phone or even sending a letter. But if it would give her the least satisfaction to have me go to the hospital with you – if it is not already too late – call on me. I will go.' Williams had recently undergone a hernia operation: 'I tell you, even to have gone thru the minor surgery I went thru, made me think hard of the fate of others, that even after they have been treated to the best of all abilities must know that they have not been basically cured. I admire those that can take it. My writing goes on. I am starting on Paterson, Part 2. In fact, I have been working on it tonight' (letter to David Lyle, 4 February 1947). On 10 February, with Mary confined to her hospital bed, the Lyles were married. Williams visited her: 'As he was readying to leave (Flossie was waiting in the car outside), steadying a decision on a woman vibrant and joyous yet knowing fully death was but a few weeks away, he spoke of a gift to be wrought for her by him..." And you, my dear, will be right in the middle of Paterson, Book 3"' (letter from Lyle to the author, 7 October 1965). The overt candidates for the man and the woman who stare death in the face are the Volunteer of America and his proposed wife (p. 126). The ms. (CtY) shows she died, aged forty, after the blood test and even before its result could be known.

133   *to New Barbadoes came the Englishman...*
    Williams' father, William George Williams, came up from the West Indies (possibly evoking the 'old' Barbados) to the area between the Passaic river and Hackensack meadows called in revolutionary times New Barbadoes Neck.

138–9   *With due ceremony a hut would be constructed...*
    From Nelson and Shriner, *History of Paterson*, vol. I, pp. 51–4.

142   *An iron dog*
    An account of 'The Brass Dog' is given in the *Passaic County Historical Society Bulletin* III, 5 (November 1944), 19–20.

143   *The Library?*
    The Prospector II, 25 (18 September 1936), 1, 4–5, carried pictures of the ruins of the Danforth Library which burned to the ground in February 1902.

149–50   *Hi Kid...*
    Gladys Enalls, a sixteen-year-old Negro maid who lived with Mrs Kathleen

Hoagland, who as Williams' friend typed *Paterson I–III*, absconded in 1942 taking with her some of Mrs Hoagland's clothes. She left behind some letters from her friend Dolly who lived in Paterson, and when Mrs Hoagland showed them to Williams he asked if he could use them. The originals are at the University of Virginia.

162–3   *It was a place to see, she said, The White Shutters.*
This story was told to Williams by Kathleen Hoagland. She knew the band-leader of *The Clipper Crew*, Lester Wadsworth, who earned his living as the Traffic Manager of the Barrett Company in Paterson.

165   *S. Liz 13 Oct...*
Letter from Ezra Pound (CtY).

166   *SUBSTRATUM*
From Herbert A. Fisher's notes; data obtained from the files of the SUM office facing the Falls.

167   *American poetry is a very easy subject to discuss...*
From a review of a group of American poets by George Barker, 'Fat Lady at the Circus', *Poetry (London)* 13 (June–July 1948), 38–9;39. Williams probably heard of it in the reply of Kenneth Patchen and others, 'Mr Barker's Fat Lady', *Golden Goose* I, 2 (Autumn 1948), 32–6. Mr Barker has since confessed: 'Certainly it is a remark that, in and out of my cups, I made several times too often in those days. Myself I don't think it disputable that an American poetry is beginning to happen now. More power to its elbow' (letter to the author, 22 September 1966).

171   *When an African Ibidio man is slain...*
For *Ibidio* read *Ibibio*. This is paraphrased from Mrs D. Amaury Talbot, *Woman's Mysteries of a Primitive People* (London, 1915), pp. 205–6, 208, who is more delicate than Williams ('the sacred boughs are drawn over that part of the body regarded as the seat of virile energy...'). '...who have felt the fertility of men in their bodies' is Williams' own phrasing. The passage in inverted commas is taken directly from Mrs Talbot who remarked on '...the striking similarity between this still surviving rite and the strange story of the origin of Horus – that seed of life and love snatched by the widowed Isis from death itself. Indeed, were the account of this Ibibio rite given in full detail it might almost seem as though intended as a re-enactment of the ancient tragedy of the Nile, when the mighty goddess Isis found the body of the slaughtered Osiris, and by her knowledge of the mysteries of birth and death "the Great Mother" wrung a new life from out the very jaws of desolation and despair' (pp. 208–9).

177–   *Two silly women!*
Cf. Edna St Vincent Millay, *Aria da Capo* [1920], Appleton Little Theatre

Plays 9 (N.Y., 1924), where *Thyrsis* and Corydon are male. Williams has combined the pastoral pair with two other characters, 'not essentially different' (p.
47), Pierrot and Columbine, who are 'silly' indeed: Pierrot, who has been
successively painter, pianist, socialist and philanthropist ('I love Humanity; but
I hate people' [p. 10]), offers to teach Columbine to act, and finally becomes a
critic. Columbine says eventually: 'Stop your silly noise' (p. 13). Soon Corydon
and Thyrsis begin to play their 'very silly game' (p. 32), which involves building
a wall between themselves with water on Thyrsis' side; with rocks in a pasture
represented by pillows, and sheep on Corydon's side. The 'game' involves the
shepherd being deprived of water for his sheep by Thyrsis, but finding jewels on
his side and becoming a merchant. He is then unable to make up his mind
'Whether to buy a city, and have a thousand/Beautiful girls to bathe me, and be
happy/Until I die, or build a bridge, and name it/The Bridge of Corydon – and
be remembered/After I'm dead' (pp. 25–6). In the end Thyrsis offers poisoned
water for the sheep, and Corydon strangles him with the necklace of jewels he
has offered in exchange, never having intended to let the jewels go. They both
die.

Miss Millay described her characters as follows: 'Pierrot sees clearly into
existing evils and is rendered gaily cynical by them; he is both too indolent and
too indifferent to do anything about it' (p. 44). Columbine is 'Pretty, but stupid;
she never knows what P is talking about...' (45). There is an interesting reference
to drinking (p. 8):

Columbine: Pierrot, do you know, I think you drink too much.
    Pierrot: Yes, I dare say I do...Or else too little.
            It's hard to tell. You see I am always wanting
            A little more than what I have – or else
            A little less. There's something wrong...

Pierrot is Williams' Corydon, Columbine his Phyllis.

180   *That is the East River*

In December 1946 Williams entered New York Hospital for a second hernia
operation, the first having been unsuccessful: 'One of the finest things about this
room that I have sixteen floors above the city is the view from my bed overlooking the East River and Welfare Island with at night, the lights of the planes
about La Guardia Field in the distance.

But the river is my chief joy, I never tire of looking at it and could wish for
nothing finer the rest of my life than to have a little apartment somewhere in this
part of the city with the view of that river always at hand –' (letter to Kathleen
Hoagland, 18 December 1946 [ViU]).

192, 197   *You've never been to Anticosti...?*

In 1931 Williams took his family on a two-week vacation cruising on S.S.
North Voyageur up the Gulf of St Lawrence to Newfoundland (*Autobiography*, pp.

274-6). A ms., 'The North Shore' (NBuU), shows he had read Napoleon A. Comeau, *Life and Sport on the North Shore of the Lower St. Lawrence and Gulf* (Quebec, 1909), with its several chapters on salmon fishing.

201   *Norman Douglas* (South Wind) *said to me...*
  Cf.: 'In Rome, Norman Douglas had us to tea in his sixth floor rooms overlooking the Roman forum to the north. We talked for two hours – of contemporary writers, their lives, his own life, of his son whom he had not seen virtually since birth. When, the boy having grown to be a man, they met again, each was strongly attracted by the other's qualities, each a man of whom the other thoroughly approved. It was a satisfying experience for them both. It was at that time that Douglas gave me his opinion that the best thing a father can do for his son after he conceives him is to die when he is born. I suppose I had been expressing some doubts as to our wisdom in going off and leaving our own children behind. That was his answer' (*Autobiography*, p. 207).

202   *Curie (the movie queen)...*
  Williams may well have seen *Madame Curie*, the film released by M.G.M. in 1944, starring Greer Garson and Walter Pidgeon and directed by Mervyn Le Roy. It was one of the *Film Daily*'s Ten Best Pictures of the Year.

203   *And Billy Sunday evangel...*
  Cf. John Reed, 'Back of Billy Sunday', *Metropolitan* XLII, 1 (May 1915), 9–12, 66, 68, 69, 70–2. The 'Thank Offering' at Philadelphia had been $100,000, so that handed over at the Hamilton Hotel was modest. In Riverton, N.J., and in Philadelphia Sunday had been called in to preach against drink and women, but his propensity for referring as a good Republican to 'the strike-maddened crowd' endeared him to the mill-owners of Paterson: 'Mr Ackley informed me that a Citizen's Committee, consisting of silk manufacturers and the respectable clergy of Paterson, N.J., were inviting Mr Sunday there. "You see," he said, "Paterson has always had the name of being a turbulent and unchristian city, and they think that Mr Sunday will turn the thoughts of the working population to the salvation of their own souls, and regenerate Paterson"' (p. 12).
  Sunday went directly from Philadelphia to Paterson (April–May 1915), and was back in Paterson in 1934 (see William T. Ellis, *Mr Sunday's Autobiography* (Philadelphia, 1936), pp. 517, 519).
  Williams' baseball analogy has a precedent in Reed's account: 'Sunday flung himself across the platform like a baseball player sliding for second' (p. 70). Sunday had played for Chicago in the National League before becoming a preacher.
  The reference to 'Brighten the Corner Where You Are' is clarified by the knowledge that William Jennings Bryan asked Rodeheaver, Sunday's choirmaster to sing it for him at a lecture, and then gave a secular sermon on it (Homer Rodeheaver, *Twenty Years with Billy Sunday* (Nashville [Tenn.], 1936), pp. 78–9).

Reed gives the following account: 'Then they sang, "Brighten the Corner Where You Are", one of those old revival hymns with an almost negro swing to it. The crowd refused to stop singing "Brighten the Corner" until they had gone through four verses. "Now we'll cross the house with it", shouted Rodeheaver. "You on the left sing the first line..." ' (pp. 68–9).

204–6 *Dear Doctor*:
  A.G. is Allen Ginsberg.

207 *A dissonance | in the valence of Uranium...*

> *Curie*
> *of the laboratory*
> *of vocabulary*
>   *she crushed*
> *the tonnage*
> *of consciousness*
> *congealed to phrases*
>   *to extract*
> *a radium of the word*

(Mina Loy, 'Gertrude Stein', *the transatlantic review* II, 4 [October 1924], 305).

208 *antagonistic cooperation is the key, says Levy...*
  The reference is to H. Levy, *A Philosophy for a Modern Man* (N.Y., 1938), where a law of dialectical change is propounded.

208 *REPORT OF CASES...*
  From Joseph Felsen, Alfred J. Weil, and William Wolarsky, 'Inapparent Salmonella Infections in Hospitals', *Journal of the American Medical Association* CXXXXIII (29 July 1950), 1135–8; *1136*.

209 *On Friday, the twelfth of October...*
  From Columbus' Journals: cf. *In the American Grain*, 'The Discovery of the Indies', pp. 25–6. Williams has substituted 'known' for 'seen'.

211 *...les idées Wilsoniennes nous | gâtent...*
  On 26 February 1934 Williams wrote to Gorham Munson, leader of the American Social Credit Movement, asking him for another copy of an issue of the paper *New Democracy*, 'the one containing a quotation from President Wilson about the "invisible power"' (CtMW). It was *New Democracy* I, 11 (1 February 1934), 4: 'Some of the biggest men in the U.S. are afraid of something. They know there is a power somewhere, so organized, so subtle, so watchful, so interlocked, so pervasive, that they had better not speak above their breath when they speak in condemnation. The control of credit has become dangerously centralized. It is the mere truth to say that financial resources are at command of those who do

not submit to their dictation and domination. The great monopoly in this country is the monopoly of "Big Credits".'

213   *Advertisement...*
    From *Money* XV, 4 (June 1950), 1. The final slogan, 'ENFORCE THE CONSTITUTION ON MONEY', is not August Walters' own, but that of the paper. It is interesting to note that Williams has chosen to omit the headlines to Walters' statement; 'DO YOU FAVOR LENIN OR UNCLE SAM? Our Treasury Officials Support A Legally Protected, Dishonest Finance Plan Which Will Accomplish Lenin's Wish to Bankrupt America. There's Still Time To Wreck Lenin's Wish.' Gorham B. Munson, former General Secretary of the American Social Credit Movement, of which Williams was a paid-up member, in response to an inquiry about Walters' statement replied (26 March 1967): 'Walters proposes producer credits for munitions manufacturers. These are given by the nation and are deposited by munitions manufacturers in private banks. Banks send them to U.S. Treasury and receive U.S. National Credit for them. This is backing for banker's credit now extended to munitions manufacturers, who draws checks against it. All this is debtfree money. U.S. Treasury pays bank a 1% service charge.
    This is fiat money – no basis given for the creation of these producer credits. It would be inflationary. No safeguard against price increases. Unsound. I cannot imagine Wms. approving of it. Contrast with social credit. S.C. is a distribution of purchasing power to everybody – not restricted to a few producers of war goods. S.C. has a basis for the creation of money – namely, the Real Credit (which is precisely defined in S.C. literature) of the United States. Social Credit distributes consumption credits, not producer credits. And Social Credit is counter-inflationary. The Retail Price Discount operates to lower prices. Finally the aim of Social Credit is to bring about economic democracy, not to beat Russia in the arms race. Politically, Social Credit sought to be the Third Force Resolvent of the Right-Left conflict.'

215–16   – *and to Tolson and his ode*
    Melvin B. Tolson, 'From *Libretto for the Republic of Liberia*', *Poetry* LXXVI, 4 (July 1950), 208–15, where '*Selah!*' occurs as musical punctuation. Allen Tate, 'Preface to *Libretto for the Republic of Liberia*', *ibid.* 216–18, claims Tolson to be in the direct succession from [Hart] Crane: 'For the first time, it seems to me, a Negro poet has assimilated completely the full poetic language of his time, and by implication, the language of the Anglo-American tradition' (p. 217). Williams parodies Tolson's multilingual respect for the Anglo-*European* tradition (including the English Pindaric ode) beloved of the South 'generally' with the violence of American slang; 'right in the puss'.

217   *turbine; credit*
    Read 'turbine: credit' (ms. CtY).

218   *INvenshun...renaissance cities...*
Letter from Ezra Pound (CtY).

219   *...all she told me.*
'She' is Emily Dickinson, Williams' paternal grandmother.

221   *– while he was still in the hotel business...*
Ms. (CtY) has: 'That reminds me. Pep West told me once...' Nathanael West ran the Sutton Club Hotel in New York at the time of the second series of *Contact,* which he edited with Williams and Robert McAlmon.

226–32   *In a deep-set valley between hills...*
The local history is derived either verbatim or in paraphrase from Charles Pitman Longwell's *A Little Story of Old Paterson* (see notes to pp. 25–7), in an order of page numbers as follows: 10, 8–9, 11–12, 29, 23, 11, 15, 24, 32–3, 66–7, 21–2, 47, 52–3, 59, 51–2.

227   *A print in colors by Paul Sandby...*
See Plate 9.

227–8   *Dear Doc:...*
From Allen Ginsberg.

231   *Roswell, Colt...*
Read 'Roswell Colt.'

232–3   *...The murder last night of two persons...*
From *The Prospector* II, 26 (25 September 1936), 1, 4. This was the first murder committed in the newly formed Passaic County and drew nation-wide publicity.

233   *Trip a trap o'troontjes*
'Even before he could comprehend the words, the little fellow understood the significance of the motion as he was danced up by fond arms, up and up the Steps to the top of the throne of a loving mother's heart; and he enjoyed the pretended alarm with which he was informed that the pigs were rooting among the beans, and the cows were in the clover, and the horses in the oats, and the ducks splashing in the water puddle, the whole being cleverly acted in pantomime, until he was tossed away up on high to indicate how great – in his mother's estimation – her little Derrick was!' (Nelson and Shriner, *History of Paterson,* vol. I, p. 156).

[240]   On 5 August 1956 Williams wrote to Fred R. Miller: 'Recently read a very moving book on the tragic life of the French painter Toulouse Lautrec,

something about that guy gets me. He knew what it was all about.' The book in question was Lawrence and Elizabeth Hanson, *The Tragic Life of Toulouse-Lautrec* (N.Y., 1956).

244-5   *Dear Bill:...*
    Letter from Josephine Herbst.

247-8   *Dear Dr. Williams...*
    From Allen Ginsberg.

249-50   *The whores grasping for your genitals...*
    From 'Bordertown' by Gilbert Sorrentino, who wrote in reply (29 May 1967) to an inquiry as to how Williams had come upon his story: '"Bordertown" was written while I was on maneuvers in Fort Hood, Texas, in 1952, in the Spring of that year. I was in a medical company at the time, and while I had been attending advanced training school at Fort Sam Houston, Texas, from late 1951 to early 1952, I spent many weekends in various Mexican bordertowns, doing, as is said, what soldiers do. I suppose the bordertown "culture" was what impelled me to write the story, or, actually, sketch. The total lack of American hypocrisy and cant that obtained there. At any rate, I wrote the story in a notebook on my bunk, in, I guess, one sitting. Some years later, I got out of the army, or, I should say, some years later, after *having* got out of the army, I saw Bill's book, *The Desert Music*, and was struck by the vague similarities between his poem and my story...In some crazy moment I sent him the story, saying something about how I thought he might be interested in seeing it and so on – lame. I never thought that he'd answer. But he did, he thought it was strong and fine...'

252   *'n cha cha cha...*
    ''N! cha; cha; cha; destiny needs men, so make up your mind. Here's an oak filling the wind's space. Out with him!
    By carefully prepared stages come down through the vulgarities of a cupiscent girlhood to the barren distinction of this cold six A.M. Her pretty, pinched face is a very simple tune but it carries now a certain quasi-maidenly distinction. It's not at least what you'd have heard six years back when she was really virgin' (*Kora in Hell*, p. 47).

253   *I am no authority on Sappho...*
    A.P. is Arnold Post. Charles Abbott, Librarian at the Lockwood Memorial Library at the State University of New York at Buffalo, was a friend of the editor of the Loeb Classical Library and Emeritus Professor of Greek at Haverford College, Pennsylvania, L.A. Post: 'Abbott urged me to visit the poet and talk about Sappho with him. I avoided a meeting because I was sure that he would be disappointed in my failure to react to his poetry and in my inability to reproduce

the dulcet style of Sappho's verse...Neither WCW nor T.S.Eliot speak to my condition. The latter was in my Sanskrit class at Harvard and I once took a walk with him at Oxford (1915?). Not a word would he say. I told him I was moved by Whitman, whom at that time he detested...W.C.W. insisted that I ought to call myself Arnold Post (hence his A.P.), not L.A.Post (cf. H.G.Wells, A.L. Rowse, etc.). I aped the English in those days...I had nothing to do with Williams' translation of Sappho' (letter to the author from Professor Post, 20 April 1966).

261–2 (*Q. Mr Williams, can you tell me simply, what poetry is?*)...
'Mike Wallace Asks William Carlos Williams Is Poetry A Dead Duck', *New York Post*, 18 October 1957.

267–8 *Dear Bill*...
From Edward Dahlberg.

268 ' . *the unicorn against a millefleurs background*, . '
Williams' attention to the flora of the Unicorn Tapestries at the Cloisters in Fort Tryon Park was almost certainly drawn by a booklet issued by the New York Botanical Garden consisting of a reprinting of two articles from *The Journal of the New York Botanical Garden* (May, June 1941), jointly written by E.J. Alexander and Carol H.Woodward, 'The Flora of the Unicorn Tapestries', and 'Check-List of Plants In The Unicorn Tapestries'. The word 'millefleurs' occurs on the second page of the booklet, of which a second edition was issued in 1947, and reprinted in 1950 and 1965.

274 *A hound lies on his back/eviscerated*...
The fourth tapestry. See James J.Rorimer, *The Unicorn Tapestries at the Cloisters*, The Metropolitan Museum of Art ([N.Y.] 1962), p. 20.

276 – *a fragment of the tapestry.*
Fragment of the fifth tapestry. See Rorimer, *ibid.* [27].

277 ...*Osamu/Dazai and his saintly sister*
See the last chapter of Osamu Dazai, *The Setting Sun* (Norfolk, Conn., 1947). As Williams suggested to Winfield Townley Scott, postcard, 21 January 195? (RPB): 'You will never cease thanking me for steering you to it.' A relevant passage is: 'Even if Mary gives birth to a child who is not her husband's, if she has a shining pride, they become a holy mother and child' (p. 186).

Select Bibliography

WRITINGS BY W.C.WILLIAMS

Manuscripts in Public Collections
'The Attack on Credit Monopoly from a Cultural Viewpoint' (NBuU).
'Author's Introduction to The Wedge' (NBuU).
'Autobiography' (CtY).
'The Baroness Elsa von Freytag-Loringhoven' (CtY).
'A Democratic Party Poem' (NBuU).
'Detail & Parody for the poem PATERSON' (MH).
'The Embodiment of Knowledge: (first writing)' (CtY).
'An Essay for Martians. 1. The Jew' (CtY).
'Health for the People' (CtY).
'Introduction to Book of David Ruth' (NBuU).
'Man Orchid' (CtY).
'The North Shore' (NBuU).
'Note: The American Language and the New Poetry, so called' (MdBE).
'Notes: Miscellaneous and Unidentified' (CtY).
'Paterson' (CtY; NBuU).
'Re. Sidney Hook's article, "Reflections on the Jewish Question"' (NBuU).
'Rome' (NBuU).
'Speech Rhythm' (CtY).
'Vortex – William Carlos Williams' (NBuU).
'What Happens to Money' (CtY; NBuU).

Books
The Autobiography of William Carlos Williams. N.Y., 1951.
The Build-Up. N.Y., 1952.
The Collected Earlier Poems of William Carlos Williams. Norfolk, Conn., 1951.
The Collected Later Poems of William Carlos Williams. Rev. edn, Norfolk, Conn. [1963].
The Great American Novel. Paris, 1923.
In the American Grain. N.Y., 1925.
I Wanted to Write a Poem. Boston, 1958.
Kora in Hell: Improvisations. Boston, 1920; San Francisco, 1957.

Last Nights of Paris by Philippe Soupault, translated by William Carlos Williams. N.Y., 1929.

A Novelette and Other Prose. Toulon, 1932.

Paterson. N.Y., 1963.

Pictures from Brueghel and other poems. Norfolk, Conn., 1962.

Poems. Rutherford, N.J., 1909.

Selected Essays. N.Y., 1954.

The Selected Letters of William Carlos Williams, ed. John C. Thirlwall. N.Y., 1957.

Spring and All. Dijon, 1923.

A Voyage to Pagany. N.Y., 1928.

Yes, Mrs. Williams. N.Y., 1959.

Articles

'Advice to the Young Poet'. *View* II, 3 (October 1942), 23.

'An American Poet'. *New Masses* XXV, 9 (23 November 1937), 17–18.

'The American Spirit in Art'. *Proceedings of the American Academy of Arts and Letters* (Second series) 2 (1952), 51–9.

'Cache Cache'. *View* II, 2 (May 1942) [17–18].

'Cage' by E. C. Fabre, translated by William Carlos Williams. *Blast* I, 1 (September-October 1933), 30–2.

'The Contact Story'. *Contact* (San Francisco) 1 (1958), 75–7.

'Correspondence: The Great Sex Spiral'. *The Egoist* IV, 3 (April 1917), 46; IV, 7 (August 1917), 110–11.

'Emanuel Romano'. *Form* 2 (1 September 1966), 22–5.

'The Five Dollar Guy'. *New Masses* I, 1 (May 1926), 19, 29.

'For A New Magazine'. *Blues* 2 (March 1929), 30–1.

'From My Notes About My Mother'. *The Literary Review* I, 1 (Autumn 1957), 5–12.

'The Genius of France'. *View* VII, 1 (Fall 1946), 43–7.

'A Group of Poems by Marcia Nardi: Introduction by William Carlos Williams who discovered her'. *New Directions* 7 (1942), 413–14.

'L'Illégalité aux Etats-Unis'. *Bifur* 2 (25 juillet 1929), 95–103.

'Jew'. *Hika* VI, 7 (May 1940), 5.

'Letter to the Editor'. *New English Weekly* II, 4 (10 November 1932), 90–1.

'A Man Versus the Law'. *The Freeman* I, 15 (23 June 1920), 348–9.

'Manifesto'. *Pagany* I, 1 (January-March 1930), 1.

'Measure'. *Spectrum* III, 3 (Fall 1959), 131–57; reprinted in *Cambridge Opinion* 41 [October 1965], 4–14 [33].

'Muriel Rukeyser's USI'. *The New Republic* LXXXXIV, 1214 (9 March 1938), 141–2.

'New Direction in the Novel'. *New Democracy* V, 5 (1 November 1935), 81–3.

'Note on the Translation of *El Hombre Que Paresia Un Cavallo*'. *New Directions* 8 (1944), 318–19.

'On First Opening *The Lyric Year*'. *Poetry* II, 3 (June 1913), 114–15.

'Picasso Breaks Faces', *The General Magazine and Historical Chronicle* LIII, I
(Autumn 1950), 40–1.
Review of *An 'Objectivists' Anthology, The Symposium* IV, I (January 1933), 114–17.
Review of H.L.Mencken's *The American Language, New English Weekly* IV, I
(19 October 1933), 9–10.
Review of Parker Tyler's *The Granite Butterfly, Accent* VI, 3 (Spring 1946),
203–6.
'Sample Critical Statement: Comment'. *Contact* 4 [Summer 1921], 19.
'Social Credit as Anti-Communism'. *New Democracy* I, 10 (15 January 1934), 1–2.
'Some Hints Toward the Enjoyment of Modern Verse'. *Quarterly Review of
Literature* VIII, 3 (1954), 171–5.
'Sordid? Good God!' *Contempo* III, 2 (25 July 1933), I, 2.
Statement in notes on contributors, *Poetry* XCIII, 6 (March 1959), 416.
'Surrealism and the Moment'. *View* II, 2 (May 1942), [19].
'Towards the Unknown', *View* I, 11–12 (February-March 1942), 10.
'To Write American Poetry'. *Fantasy* V, I (Summer 1935), 12–14.

SELECT LIST OF BACKGROUND BOOKS

Barber, J.W. and Henry Howe. *Historical Collections of New Jersey.* Newark, N.J.
[1855].
Bergen County Panorama, written by Writers of the Workers' Program of the
Works Projects Administration in the State of New Jersey. Hackensack,
N.J., 1941.
Burke, Kenneth. *A Grammar of Motives.* N.Y., 1945.
Calas, Nicolas. *Confound the Wise.* N.Y., 1942.
Cunningham, John T. *New Jersey: America's Main Road.* Garden City, N.Y.,
1966.
'Flaccus' [Thomas Ward]. *Passaic, a Group of Poems Touching that River: with other
Musings.* N.Y., 1842.
Hartley, Marsden. *Adventures in the Arts.* N.Y., 1921.
Jung, Carl G. *The Integration of the Personality.* London, 1940.
Kandinsky, Wassily. *Concerning the Spiritual in Art,* ed. Robert Motherwell. N.Y.,
1947.
Keyserling, Count Hermann. *America Set Free.* N.Y. and London, 1929.
Lawrence, D.H. *Phoenix* II, London, 1968.
Legman, Gershon. *Love and Death.* N.Y., 1949.
Longwell, Charles Pitman. *A Little Story of Old Paterson.* Paterson, 1901.
Lyons, Eugene. *The Red Decade.* Indianapolis and N.Y., 1941.
McAlmon, Robert. *Post-Adolescence* [Paris, 1923].
    Being Geniuses Together. London, 1938.
Macpherson, C.B. *Democracy in Alberta: Social Credit and the Party System.* 2nd ed.,
Toronto, 1962.
Munson, Gorham B. *Aladdin's Lamp: The Wealth of the American People.* N.Y., 1945.

Nelson, William, and Charles A. Shriner. *History of Paterson and Its Environs.* 3 vols, N.Y. and Chicago, 1920.

New Jersey, A Guide to Its Present and Past, compiled and written by the Federal Writers' Project of the Works Progress Administration. N.Y., 1939.

Newhall, Beaumont. *The History of Photography.* N.Y., 1964.

Paige, D.D. (ed.) *The Letters of Ezra Pound.* N.Y., 1950.

Paine, Levi Leonard. *The Ethnic Trinities,* Boston and N.Y., 1901.

Pound, Ezra. *Antheil and the Treatise on Harmony.* Chicago, 1927.

The Precisionist View in American Art. Catalogue of an exhibition 13 November – 25 December 1960, Walker Art Center, Minneapolis 1960, with an introductory essay by Martin L. Friedman.

Rourke, Constance. *Charles Sheeler: Artist in the American Tradition.* N.Y., 1938.

Schonbach, Morris. *Radicals and Visionaries: A History of Dissent in New Jersey.* Princeton. N.J., 1964.

Seligmann, Kurt. *The History of Magic.* N.Y., 1948.

Steinmetz, Charles Proteus. *Four Lectures on Relativity and Space.* N.Y. and London, 1923.

Taupin, René. *L'Influence du Symbolisme Français sur la Poésie Américaine de 1910 à 1920.* Paris, 1920.

Trumbull, L.R. *A History of Industrial Paterson.* Paterson, N.J., 1882.

Tyler, Parker. *The Divine Comedy of Pavel Tchelitchew.* N.Y., 1967.

Van Valen, J.M. *History of Bergen County.* N.Y., 1900.

Weininger, Otto. *Sex and Character.* London and N.Y., 1906.

Whitehead, Alfred North. *Science and the Modern World.* N.Y., 1948.

Zukofsky, Louis (ed.). *An 'Objectivists' Anthology,* Le Beausset, Var, 1932.

Index

223

INDEX